# Guest Service in the Hospitality Industry

# Guest Service in the Hospitality Industry

Paul Bagdan, Ph.D., C.H.E.

WILEY

Cover Image Credit: Felix Wirth/Corbis

This book is printed on acid-free paper. ∞

Copyright © 2013 by John Wiley & Sons, Inc. All rights reserved.

Published by John Wiley & Sons, Inc., Hoboken, New Jersey.
Published simultaneously in Canada.

For general information on our other products and services, or technical support, please contact our Customer Care Department within the United States at 800-762-2974, outside the United States at 317-572-3993 or fax 317-572-4002.

Wiley also publishes its books in a variety of electronic formats. Some content that appears in print may not be available in electronic books. For more information about Wiley products, visit our Web site at www.wiley.com.

*Library of Congress Cataloging-in-Publication Data:*

Bagdan, Paul J., 1970-
    Guest service in the hospitality industry / Paul J. Bagdan.
      pages  cm.
    Includes index.
    ISBN 978-1-118-07180-9 (hardback)
      1. Hospitality industry—Customer services.   I. Title.
  TX911.3.C8B34   2013
  338.4'791—dc23
                           2012032041

Printed in the United States of America

10  9  8  7  6

# Contents

## Chapter 3:
# Problem Solving for Guest Service  39

## Section II:
# Relating Service to the Sectors of the Hospitality Industry  67

## Chapter 4:
# The Guest Service of Food  69

## Chapter 5:
# The Guest Service of Beverages   95

## Chapter 6:
# The Guest Service of Lodging   115

## Section III:
# Assessments and Planning   179

## Chapter 10:
# Research and Tools   181

## Chapter 13:
# Marketing and Establishing an Image for Service 265

# Preface

## Introduction

Customer service is the heart of hospitality. Students of and professionals in the hospitality industry must understand this in order to be successful. Their futures depend on it. They must understand and anticipate what the customer needs and know how to best meet and exceed those needs. Not only do they need to know how to serve a customer, but also must acquire customer-related problem-solving skills, such as conducting basic surveys and using other tools and techniques to identify and then solve problems. They must be able to plan and deliver quality service because it does not happen on its own. And then, they must be able to manage other people to effectively accomplish all of these things.

*Guest Service in the Hospitality Industry* adopts the premise that there is no one simple solution to managing people who provide customer service. It does not claim one, absolute answer, but, instead, takes a general approach that incorporates various thoughts from different parts of the industry, differing from property to property. By providing several frameworks for instituting approaches, this book opens readers' minds to the idea of customer service. It discusses issues and debunks myths about customer service with concepts that are solid and proven in the industry. The methods of teaching used in this book have been proven in the classroom with the contemporary college student; as a result, these teachings have served those students well.

## About This Book

*Guest Service in the Hospitality Industry* includes all of the major areas of the hospitality industry as they relate to delivering quality customer service. It not only provides a history and an overview of guest service, but it then goes much further to include other essential topics, including problem solving, quality tools and assessments, staffing, marketing, and strategic planning.

The need for this text, *Guest Service in the Hospitality Industry*, came about as a result of my teaching as a professor at Johnson & Wales University, Providence, Rhode Island Campus. I was pioneering a newly designed course in customer-service management. It was a general course, taught to all of our hospitality students in their first or second year. The students' majors encompassed specialization in food, lodging, travel, and events. Furthermore, they each had nearly 30 different concentrations within and among the majors, making their particular interests quite varied. I could not find a textbook that met all of their needs.

The first generation of guest-service books were from the 1980s and 1990s. They featured the guest service/quality movement as seen in its heyday. They were very heavily focused on total quality management (TQM) and continuous quality improvement (CQI). They referenced manufacturing-focused techniques and adapted them to the service industry. Times have changed, and hospitality is now secured in its own sector of the service industry. TQM and CQI principles have since left our common vocabulary, but the ideas of serving the guest and performing well have not left our missions.

Since the guest-service books either made general reference to hospitality or were extremely focused on just one aspect, I wanted a book for hospitality students. My aim was to combine some of the classic material and some of the current material and to focus it all on the areas of hospitality:

- Food
- Beverage
- Lodging
- Sports and events
- Travel and tourism
- Casinos

*Guest Service in the Hospitality Industry* applies guest service to the hospitality discipline as a whole, whereas other texts have either a very general business theme or concentrate on a highly specific component of the industry.

## ❦ TO THE STUDENT

*Guest Service in the Hospitality Industry* is written for hospitality students within any and all of the individual disciplines. It is also relevant to anyone who wants a survey of the past and present findings of customer service as they relate to the hospitality industry.

Written in a straightforward manner intended to introduce the topic of guest service to students of hospitality, the book incorporates a variety of learning features that facilitate various learning styles. Such features include:

- Industry interviews with some of the leading hospitality managers
- Chapter points and concepts with visual diagrams
- Stories and real-life examples
- "Service Insights"—tips incorporated throughout the text that provide extra guest-service–related information to build and support points
- Review questions that reinforce chapter concepts
- Case studies that reinforce learning

*Guest Service in the Hospitality Industry* dedicates a chapter to each of the primary areas of the hospitality industry. All of the examples are related to hospitality, and the case studies and Service Insights relate to the industry as it truly is. It provides a history and overview of guest service, and then goes further by exploring problem-solving

techniques, quality tools and assessments, staffing, marketing, and strategic planning in guest service.

## ❦ ORGANIZATION OF THE BOOK

*Guest Service in the Hospitality Industry* is organized into three sections. The first introduces the concepts; readers become acclimated to the topic of guest service through these chapters. The book then shows guest service in each of the major areas of hospitality: food service, beverage, lodging, events, travel and tourism, and casinos. Students learn about guest service in their focus area and in accompanying areas. A by-product is that they learn more about their discipline as a whole. Learning about other parts of the hospitality industry is great for student internships and their future in the industry, as areas are often blended and many professionals move from one area to another. The last section relates the best of the remaining, related topics within the industry: tools and surveys, strategic planning, staffing, and marketing.

### Section I: Introduction, History, and Basics of Guest Service

This section lays groundwork for the course. An overview of the meaning, the origin, and the progression of guest service is covered. This section includes:
○ Chapter 1: The Basics of Guest Service
○ Chapter 2: Defining Guest Service
○ Chapter 3: Problem-Solving for Guest Service

### Section II: Relating Service to the Sectors of the Hospitality Industry

This section relates guest service to each major area of the hospitality industry. A chapter is dedicated to each of these areas:
○ Chapter 4: The Guest Service of Food
○ Chapter 5: The Guest Service of Beverages
○ Chapter 6: The Guest Service of Lodging
○ Chapter 7: The Guest Service of Events
○ Chapter 8: The Guest Service of Travel and Tourism
○ Chapter 9: The Guest Service of Casinos

### Section III: Assessments and Planning

This last section takes all of the other major aspects of instituting and managing guest service in the hospitality industry. A chapter is dedicated to each of the following topics:
○ Chapter 10: Research and Tools
○ Chapter 11: Strategic Planning for Service
○ Chapter 12: Developing a Staff
○ Chapter 13: Marketing and Establishing an Image for Service

# Supplemental Offerings

A comprehensive online *Instructor's Manual* with *Test Bank* accompanies this book and is available to instructors to help them effectively manage their time and to enhance student learning opportunities.

The *Test Bank* has been specifically formatted for *Respondus*, an easy-to-use software program for creating and managing exams that can be printed to paper or published directly to Blackboard, WebCT, Desire2Learn, eCollege, ANGEL, and other eLearning systems. Instructors who adopt this book can download the test bank for free.

Videos related to hospitality guest services are available on the Instructor Book Companion website (www.wiley.com/college/bagdan), which can be viewed in the classroom. A discussion guide has been created to facilitate discussion around the videos.

A password-protected Wiley Instructor Book Companion website devoted entirely to this book (www.wiley.com/college/bagdan) provides access to the online *Instructor's Manual*. The *Respondus Test Bank* and the *PowerPoint* lecture slides are also available on the website for download.

I sincerely hope that you find this text as valuable and rewarding as I intended it to be.

Best Wishes for Success,
Professor Paul Bagdan, Ph.D. C.H.E.

# Acknowledgments

I would like to thank the following mentors and book reviewers for their significant contributions to the text:

Jane Boyland, Johnson & Wales University
Christine Peraklis, Johnson & Wales University
Jeffrey Hartmann, Mohegan Sun
Daniel Hostettler, Ocean House

I would like to thank the following reviewers for their helpful and insightful comments and suggestions for improvement to the text:

Jane Boyland, Johnson & Wales University
Anne Sandhu, Sullivan University
Denver Severt, University of Central Florida
Jean Hertzman, University of Nevada Las Vegas
Douglas Miller, The Culinary Institute of America
John Womick, L'Ecole Culinaire
Alison Gaylon, Art Institute of Pittsburgh
Greg Quintard, Nash Community College
Heidi Ladika-Cipolla, Palm Beach State College
Christian Raia, West Hills Community College District
David Schweiger, Northampton Community College

I would like to thank the following for helping me put the pieces together to make this project happen:

Mary Cassells
Robb Kok
Jenni Lee
Julie Kerr
Jeffrey Senese

I would like to thank my immediate family for their support through this process:

Florence Bagdan
Luke Bagdan
Samuel Bagdan

Finally, I would like to thank my wife, Kathy, for her unconditional support, advice, and encouragement. It wouldn't have happened without you. Lastly, I thank the readers of this text in advance for their time.

Professor Paul Bagdan, Ph.D. C.H.E.

# The Basics of Guest Service

## Chapter Objectives:

*After reading this chapter, you should be able to:*

Identify and describe the history, ages of change, and current status of guest service in the United States.

Identify the various reasons why guests may not complain outwardly.

Identify and explain the reasoning behind why guests share their poor experiences with others.

Describe the expectations of guests as they relate to hospitality.

Explain and apply the concept of using quality service as a competitive advantage.

Describe details regarding the legends of guest service.

## Terminology:

Age of Communication
Age of Service
Age of Technology
DRIFT
MBWA
Moment of Truth
PDCA
Quality Customer Service

# Introduction

Guest service cannot be studied in a vacuum. The concepts of this book are a unique blend of the materials essential to deliver quality guest service in the hospitality industry. It involves history, terminology, tools and instruments, human resources, problem-solving, strategy, marketing, and technology. Furthermore it, must also be applied to each sector of the hospitality industry.

This book is aimed toward hospitality management students in the first, second, or third year of their college studies. It may also be easily used by practitioners, laypeople, and those in other secondary education areas.

## ❖ A SCIENCE AND AN ART

This book aims to explain the primary aspects in customer service management within the hospitality industry. We all know that you should be nice to people, so why are there so many negative guest experiences in the hospitality industry? This is because good service doesn't just happen by itself. It requires a special blend of procedure, technique, and skill combined with the human element. It is, essentially, both a science and an art.

## ❖ INTEGRATION OF CUSTOMER SERVICE

Providing service is a concerted effort. There is much more to providing good service than simply being nice to people. In order for customer service to be successful, it must be integrated into the overall business model. Customer service must be part of the company's identity, or brand. It must be tailored to the individual operation and customized, planned, and executed with systems that support it. Employees must be knowledgeable about the brand, the products, and the operations. Also, the customer must be properly gauged or assessed to ensure proper alignment with the brand image.

So, the brand image, operations, and employees of the business must all align with the target customer whom they are aiming to attract, serve, and retain. In other words, providing quality customer service is more than being friendly. **It is part of the core of the business. It is integrated into nearly every decision. It is calculated and planned. It is evident in all of the operations, the people, and the plan.**

## ❖ MEETING GUESTS' EXPECTATIONS

There are a variety of definitions for customer service. Essentially, anytime patrons, or even prospective patrons, interact with a facet of the organization, customer service is rendered. **Quality customer service** is meeting and exceeding the individual customer's expectations. If service meets or surpasses customer's expectations, in any situation, it is said to be quality customer service.

Meeting or exceeding the expectations of customers, or quality customer service, can occur anywhere and at any level of establishment. Good service can occur at a concession stand, at a fine-dining establishment, at a show, or on a tour.

**Quality Customer Service**
Meeting and exceeding the individual expectations of the customer.

## ❧ OVERVIEW OF HOSPITALITY– HOW IT RELATES TO CUSTOMER SERVICE

The hospitality industry is a service industry. The guest is served through many different means. The industry has many segments. Food, lodging, and travel have traditionally been the primary three. Controversy has recently entered the industry. Arguments support that events, sports, gaming, health care, and assisted living are other major segments. Some argue that "almost all of the industry is travel and tourism," or "marketing" or "business management." Despite this controversy, most would agree that all of these disciplines fall within the service sector of the economy.

**Being a service industry means that customers determine the success of the operation and business. The customer can make a business the most popular business in town. The customer can also shut down a giant operation by choosing not to patronize it.**

This text dedicates specific chapters to the food, beverage, hotel, casino, travel, and events sectors of the industry, recognizing the individual nature of each.

## ❧ EXAMPLES OF BAD SERVICE

Why does bad service exist? There are many reasons for bad service. The reasons are endless and often appear to be out of direct control. Some appear acceptable to the staff, the manager, or even the guests. Following is a list of common excuses. While many may appear legitimate, none is truly acceptable.

*I'm in Training*

A name tag states, "I'M IN TRAINING." Employee turnover, cross-training, system changes, and employee development means that there will always be someone in training. How should this best be handled? Does it always have to be simulated behind the scenes? Or, can it be assisted training in front of the guest? Surveys suggest that customers are generally more patient and have lower expectations of service when they see that an employee is in training. Others, though, are immediately intolerant because they feel that the business has provided them with less-than-adequate attention and that errors are likely.

Suggestions: Do as much training as possible behind the scenes. Don't release employees to the public who aren't ready. Use role plays and simulations until trainees are competent. The customer service setting is not a training ground. Always give direct supervision when training in front of a guest. Make it obvious they are training and that support is immediately available. This will show the customer that the business cares about providing them with service.

## ❖ EXCUSES FOR BAD SERVICE

### Staffing

They are understaffed.
They aren't paid enough.
They aren't properly trained.
They are just having a bad day.
No person or system is present to monitor.
They are in training.
They are overworked and tired.
It isn't their responsibility.
The boss isn't present or doesn't care.

### Systems

The computer is slow.
The kitchen is slow.
The _____ is broken.
We just got a new _____.

### Capacity/Customers

There are too many customers.
They didn't expect this many customers.
The customer is rude.
The customers are too demanding.
The customers don't know what they want.
The customers don't pay attention.
The customer doesn't seem to mind. No one has complained to corporate.
The party next to us or in the other room is too loud.

### Setting

Everything in this neighborhood stinks.
This place is all about low cost.
We are renovating.

There are numerous reasons why poor service is delivered. Most of these reasons are common to all customer service settings. They are used regularly. **It is important to have a mindset that none of them is truly acceptable.**

*Renovations*

Renovations are inevitable. Some upgrades can be made with little or no disturbance to the customers. Sometimes, however, this is not possible. How should a business communicate to the customer that it is performing renovations?

Some businesses announce: "Please pardon our appearance." Others decide to say nothing and simply conduct business as usual. If it is mentioned before customers arrive, some customers will avoid coming altogether. If it is noticed at the time of service, some will forgive and others will be very disappointed. Their expectations will not have been met.

There are advantages and disadvantages to informing guests about construction, which must be carefully weighed. There is no one best way to approach a renovation. Keeping the inconveniences and loss of expectations to a minimum is key. Customers will be inconvenienced, and allowances must be made, so it is important to have a good service-recovery program in place. Also, a good contractor and project manager will greatly add to your success. Make sure they are aware of your expected level of service during the construction period.

## ❦ REASONS WHY CUSTOMERS DO NOT COMPLAIN

Most customers do not and will not complain. They will not give the business a chance to know what is wrong. Instead, they simply will not return. They may not tell you because they think you do not care or that you don't deserve to know. They may think that you should figure it out for yourself or that it would be too difficult for them to complain and actually be heard. Or they tried to complain and their concerns fell on deaf ears. Perhaps no system was in place to receive or correct the issue.

Lack of complaints doesn't always imply that service is great. Even the best-run companies struggle with issues. Also, it has often been said that *if you think that you have no problems, then you aren't listening hard enough.* Below is a list of reasons describing what might be going through the minds of guests.

- I don't think it's worth it.
- I tried before and no one listened.
- I am in a hurry.
- I don't want to make a scene.
- I feel bad for the staff.
- It isn't the staff's fault.
- I don't want to get anyone in trouble.
- There seems to be no solution in sight.
- I'm afraid that they'll mess with the food.
- I don't think that it will make a difference.
- I don't think anyone cares.
- I just hate this place and I want to leave.

You may not always know the reason why a customer doesn't complain. While they won't tell you, they will be sure to tell many of their friends.

## ❦ GOOD SERVICE CAN MAKE UP FOR BAD FOOD

Service may just be one reason why an experience is poor. What do you remember most about a poor hospitality experience? Was it the service? Was it the decor? Was it the event, the room, or the food? Or was it a combination of these things? A common phrase is:

*"Good service can make up for a bad food, but good food cannot make up for poor service."*

With this in mind, consider the following two scenarios.

## SCENARIO A

You are at a nice restaurant with a date. Your evening plans are for dinner and an evening show. You mention to the server that you have show tickets. The server says, "OK." You are unsure what that means, but continue to order a medium-rare steak. Your date orders the pasta special. Within a reasonable amount of time, the dinners arrive at the table. You cut into your steak and discover that it is overcooked to the point of almost being well done. You look around and cannot find your server. After a few minutes, you catch a glimpse of your server walking back into the kitchen. You spend the next few minutes trying to get the server's attention as he runs around tending to other guests. You are finally successful and able to explain the situation. The steak is returned to the kitchen and you are left with nothing in front of you while your date sits uncomfortably waiting for your new steak to arrive. Despite your requests for your date to begin eating, he or she feels awkward eating while you have no food. Your new steak eventually arrives. By that time, nearly 20 additional minutes have passed and you have to eat quickly, with no time to enjoy your food. You are nervous that you will be late for your show. You try to get the check as soon as you can, but spend the rest of the time anxious that you will be late for the show.

## SCENARIO B

You are at a nice restaurant with a date before an evening show. You mention to the server that you have tickets. The server inquires whether the show is at the nearby theatre and confirms the time. The server then smiles, nods, and says "Very well. We will do our very best to ensure that you have a great experience and make the show in plenty of time." You order a medium-rare steak. Your date orders the pasta special. Within a reasonable amount of time, the dinners arrive at your table. You cut into your steak and discover that it is overcooked to the point of being well done. You look up and realize the server has remained at the table to address any issues. He immediately apologizes and rushes the steak back to the kitchen to correct the issue. He promptly returns with a complimentary appetizer so that you and your date can begin eating together. Before you know it, your new steak is delivered to the table. Again, the server stays to ensure that it is cooked to your liking. This time it is. You are delighted that it was solved so effortlessly. You are asked if there is anything he can get for you. Your response is no. At that point, your check is placed on the table and you are told that there is no rush but that it can be settled at any time that you would prefer. You finish your dinner pleasantly and arrive at your show in plenty of time.

Shortcomings will occasionally occur. When they do, good service can help to make them much more bearable. Remember that good service can make up for other problems, but those other items cannot make up for bad service. Even if the steak was prepared perfectly, the guest would have worried about making the show on time. No matter how great things are, good service must be present.

## ❖ COMPETITIVE ADVANTAGE OF SERVICE

While each business is slightly different, most hospitality businesses offer a generic product. Nearly every:

- hotel offers a bed in a private room with a bath.
- restaurant delivers a meal with seating.
- theatre has seats and a stage with performances.
- airline flies you from a gate at one city to the next.

Of course there are different styles, settings, shapes, and colors, but what really makes the difference is the specific service of the business or establishment. This idea can generally be applied to all businesses that offer guest individual service. The tangibles and logistics can be copyrighted but are quickly replicated. Employees and managers transfer among brands, and companies benchmark each others' ideas. What competitors have the most difficulty with is replicating the individual service experience.

**The Interview**

All businesses realize that they need to be nice to the guest and deliver quality guest service, but a few rise above the rest and actually consistently meet or exceed guests' expectations. Some boast of this as part of their brand marketing and use it as a competitive advantage. One such example is the Ritz Carlton Hotel chain. This company has based its strategy on providing exceptional customer service. As a result, it has twice won a prestigious Malcolm Baldrige Award for quality excellence. Much planning, training, and preparation resulted in standards that are copied throughout many industries. Most notable is their motto stating: "We are Ladies and Gentleman serving Ladies and Gentleman." This statement gives the employees a high status, leading them to take pride in their positions while treating the guests with the expected high standards.

They also have a credo telling the employees to "fulfill even the unexpressed wishes of our guests." The customers are referred to as "guests." The services provided

are "wishes" that are fulfilled, and the employees should anticipate the needs above and beyond those verbalized.

Ritz Carlton also implements empowerment to a high degree. Their service values include statements such as: "I own and immediately solve guest problems." It does not matter who caused the issue or what department it is in, the employee owns the problem and will see to it that it is solved immediately.

The Ritz Carlton goes on to train their employees to think about the big picture. Another service value tells employees to, "build strong relationships and create Ritz Carlton guests for life."

The Ritz Carlton also trains its employees on the basics of service with the "Three Steps of Service," including:

1. *A warm and sincere greeting. Use the guest's name.*
2. *Anticipation and fulfillment of the guest's needs.*
3. *Fond farewell. Give a warm good-bye and use the guest's name (The Ritz-Carlton).*

## ❦  BAD NEWS TRAVELS FAST

Advertisements show happy customers and boast about award-winning service, but how convincing is that compared with the testimony of a friend sharing his or her personal experience? These experiences have an especially great impact when they are about bad service. When a customer goes away unhappy, they are far more likely to tell another about their experience.

> *A woman and her friend were finishing their meal at a small café when she asked the waitress if they had decaffeinated tea. The woman informed the waitress that, because of health reasons, she could not have caffeine. The waitress replied that she wasn't sure but would check to see. The waitress quickly returned to the table and informed the customer that they only had regular, caffeinated tea. The customer, prepared for this situation because she enjoys tea and cannot have caffeine, requested a cup of hot water and took a decaffeinated teabag out of her purse. A few minutes later the bill came and she saw a miscellaneous charge of $2.00 on her bill. The woman inquired about the miscellaneous charge to the waitress who replied that the manager assesses a $2.00 charge for hot water. This was verified after the manager came to the table. Despite the reasoning, the manager simply ignored her feelings regarding the matter. Granted, it was only a small charge, but it wasn't about the money. As it turns out, the customer was a group session counselor at the local Weight Watchers Center. She told everyone in her classes about the situation. She vented and they became worked up for her cause. Those people went home and told others, who told others, and so on. This small café was dependent on the population from the small community. They will likely see the result of this seemingly insignificant incident amounting to much more damage than $2.00.*

"Bad news travels quickly" is a common expression. A customer will tell people, and those people may tell other people, who may tell more people, and so on. By some accounts, *customers will share a bad experience with 8 to 10 people.* The actual number varies, but a commonly accepted notion is that a guest who has a poor experience will tell several others and the word will continue to spread Occasionally, someone

receiving poor service has a large audience, as in the story above. Online ratings are especially important because of the potential audience size or "reach" of the postings.

There are reasons why bad news travels so quickly. Perhaps these customers weren't heard or they want revenge; other reasons come to mind. Below is a list of reasons why bad news travels quickly to help explain the reasoning behind this phenomenon:

1. *The customer still needed to vent.* Customers need to be afforded the chance to express themselves. Venting is a normal part of the customer service process. Customers will need to share if they believe they weren't given the opportunity to be heard or understood. As a result, they recount their experiences to anyone and everyone who will listen.

2. *Customers may seek revenge.* If customers believe they have been wronged, they want to get even. When people feel as though they haven't received what they had expected and paid for, they feel the need to level the playing field. They tell friends and write poor reviews or anything else that justifies their pain and loss.

3. *Customers remember unusual events.* Because we have so many experiences throughout life, we filter the mediocrity from our brains. Customers continually take in information and filter all but the most unusual, emotional, or important of information. They tend to forget usual, typical, or mediocre experiences. If the guest experience was just OK or even good, people are not as likely to share the experience because it is deemed insignificant by their memories and is quickly forgotten.

4. *People love to repeat extreme events.* Really great and really bad events are more interesting and therefore more worthy of sharing with others.

5. *People can relate to these incidences.* Everyone has been wronged at some time. Bad news is particularly worth sharing because it has a sense of wronging that others can easily connect to.

6. *Service organizations and employees appear impersonal.* Talking about people may be seen as gossip, and criticizing others may be seen as unforgiving and impolite. However, talking about businesses is fair game. Businesses appear as large, non-human entities. Employees can easily be lumped into this same, disconnected state. Since they have no human connection, they can be easily blamed and criticized. While humans may make mistakes, businesses are faceless. Hotels, casinos, restaurants, and their employees are not seen as real people with feelings.

Each service encounter is important. Every time a customer is wronged is an opportunity for bad news to travel quickly. Management and staff should keep this in mind in their daily operations by imparting this knowledge upon their employees through training, and then monitoring their performance to ensure the point is remembered.

## ❧ THE VALUE OF A RETURNING CUSTOMER

Imagine running a small restaurant, with a loyal customer base of 800 who eat at your establishment once a week. Out of a small town and surrounding area totaling 100,000 people, you have successfully captured just under 1% of them. You don't need to market, because you already have all the customers you need. You and your staff quickly learn all of their names because they are all repeat customers and you don't need to attract anyone new. You know the likes and dislikes of these regulars, and can tailor

the experience to precisely meet their needs. You know how many to staff for and how much food to prepare. You run at maximum efficiency and reap the rewards.

While this would be an ideal situation, the truth is, it is never that easy. Loyal, return customers are highly sought-after prizes. **Businesses spend infinite amounts of money attracting customers and then undervalue them as they arrive and experience the product.** They are often treated as if it is the first and last time they will ever be seen. A return customer costs far less to keep than obtaining a new one. Businesses should spend less money attracting customers and more effort retaining the ones that they have.

## ❦ HISTORY OF SERVICE IN THE UNITED STATES

**Age of Service**
The current age in the United States. As the United States lost its manufacturing jobs, they were replaced with service-related jobs.

The history of customer service is not very old, at least from a scientific management point of view. References discuss innkeepers being hospitable and tavern owners keeping people happy, but the application of scientific methods to the art of customer service has expanded into what it is now only within the past 100 years.

Within that time, the United States has seen ages of change advance relatively quickly. We have transitioned from an agrarian society to a service society in just about the past 100 years. It is unlikely that either agriculture or industry will ever return as it once was, so the **age of service** should be present for quite some time.

**FIGURE 1.1   Ages of Change in the United States.**

**Age of Technology**
Another recent age in the U.S. The increase and dominance of technology in U.S. culture and business operations.

**Age of Communication**
The service economy combined with proliferation technology created an age in which services can be communicated instantly, information can be accessed cheaply, and ratings can be found easily.

**Age of manufacturing**: Originally, the United States was largely an agricultural nation. It evolved into a thriving manufacturing nation but then quickly lost its dominance to other nations. A large portion of the management techniques used in the service industries have been adopted from manufacturing, which dominated the literature before the late 1900s.

**Age of service**: At present, the U.S. economy is comprised largely of service organizations. As the United States lost many of its manufacturing jobs to other countries, it began replacing them with service-related jobs.

**Age of technology**: Coupled with service, the United States also saw a boom in analog, then digital technology in the 1980s and 1990s. This heavily influenced the way that businesses operate. Business functions were expedited by computerization. Customers enjoyed the many new conveniences associated with technology.

**Age of communication:** While service continues to dominate the economy and employment of the United States, the advances and proliferation of technology spurred a new phenomenon of communication. Never before could so much information be so readily available so cheaply and easily. This spread of communication has forever changed the way that customer service operates in the United States and the world. Suppliers, businesses, and customers can now all communicate in real time and have the ability to access each other's records. A bad-service situation, such as an airline attendant berating fliers, a foodborne outbreak at a restaurant, or bedbugs in a hotel can now be seen around the world instantly. Customers' opinions can now be accessed by other potential customers, for better or worse.

## Most Popular Sharing Websites

- Communicative
  - Facebook
  - Twitter
  - Blogs
  - YouTube
  - Wikis
  - Digital Pictures (Flickr, Picasa)

- Customer Engagement
  - Company websites
  - Fodor's
  - Google Alerts
  - Trip Advisor
  - Urbanspoon
  - Yelp
  - Google places
  - Four Square
  - QR Codes

Sporting events could poll their fans on their cell phones. Conference attendees could tweet by use of a hash tag. New hotel guests could be recognized and their preferences known before they utter a single word.

## ❧ BACKGROUND OF SERVICE

Until recently, a majority of people lived in relatively small neighborhoods where everyone knew each other. Traditionally, workers had a craft or trade. They took pride in their craft, so quality and service was natural. As a few businesses became larger, the smaller businesses could not compete with lower prices of the bigger businesses. The small craftsman went out of business. As more and more people began working for an hourly wage for big-businesses, craftsmen began to lose their sense of neighborhood and craft. **More and more, a job was simply a job, and only a means to earn money. The idea of a proud, neighborhood craftsman was lost**.

This forever changed the idea and tradition of service. Management also changed to reflect the progression. Rewards, motivations, standard operating procedures, and punishments reduced craftsman to a subhuman standards. Trust in employees dwindled and customer service suffered. Good economic times, coupled with an increase in disposable income, only made the situation worse. It wasn't until the 1950s and 1960s that management began to change and treat humans as a resource, spawning the now common phrase, "human resource."

Since the end of World War II in the late 1940s, Americans developed a "need for speed." The world began to want and need all things fast. This cultural phenomenon also changed the way that the hospitality service industry operated. This shift gave way to an explosion of fast food, fast travel, fast service, and fast communication. Customers could be impulsive, and expectations increased. Suddenly, speed was added to the list of quality, comfort, personalization, and price.

The past two decades have also spawned the recent increase in self-service. Has the replacement of computers in customer service really made things better, or are they worse? At present, we have self-service at many places that we now take for granted, including:

- check-ins, check-outs
- banks
- ticketing

- streaming entertainment
- toll booths
- coin redemption

Over time, customers have adapted and the playing field has changed. Consider the following service examples of just 20 years:

- Most all banking was done through bank tellers.
- Only a few ATMs existed, and many customers did not trust them.
- No Internet banking existed.
- Self check-outs did not exist, and bar-code technology was not yet standardized.
- Shopping was done in stores or through mail-order catalogs.
- Reviews were read in newspapers, magazines, and travel booklets.
- No smart phones or "apps" existed.
- People went to the movie theatre to see a new release.
- Air travel was booked only through airlines or a travel agent.
- Hotel reservations were booked through reservations agents or travel agents.

Things have certainly changed. The idea of self-service is now ubiquitous. It has provided the industry with both advantages and disadvantages. Below is a list of each.

### Advantages
- Decreased labor
- Increased speed of service
- Increased processing
- Shorter lines
- Increased access

### Disadvantages
- Loss of human interaction
- Subject to input error
- Difficulty fixing errors
- Unfamiliar with technology
- Unfamiliar with process
- Uncertainty of transaction

Despite the loss of the craftsman, the need for speed, and the increase in self-service, quality customer service remains the cornerstone of the hospitality industry. We seldom refer to total quality management or customer quality initiatives in recent times, but the techniques are still used to this day. Guest service has evolved but still continues to be an underlying assumption of the hospitality industry. It continues to set businesses apart from one another. Most businesses claim to have a passion for service, but only a few do it exceptionally well. When a business masters customer service, that service truly becomes a strategic advantage.

## ❧ LEGENDS IN SERVICE MANAGEMENT

Photo courtesy of
Dr. W. Edwards Deming

### W. Edwards Deming: Total Quality Management

Dr. W. Edwards Deming, a talented statistician and management consultant, is considered to be a leader in the customer service movement because of his work with the total quality management (TQM) movement. While most of his earlier work was attributed to manufacturing, his efforts have been transferred to non-manufacturing, including the hospitality industry. TQM management is an effort geared toward promoting quality products through many methods, including suppliers, employees, and management working together.

Dr. Deming tried to lend his talents to the U.S. manufacturing industries but his advice went unheeded. After World War II, Deming approached the Japanese with his ideas of applying statistics to automotive manufacturing. They accepted and embraced his ideas. He helped the Japanese automakers implement "continuous process improvement." As a result, the 1980s saw Japanese cars dominate the U.S. market, while domestic cars were left suffering. Deming was very direct at involving the employees in the process. He showed them that management cared and that they should also care about the product. He later involved the customers in the process. As a result, the Japanese automotive industry went from last to first.

The TQM movement advanced and was re-popularized throughout the 1990s, but then lost steam as the economy improved and customer service had less of an impact because businesses did well regardless.

Dr. Deming was also popular for his Deming Cycle, most commonly referred to as the **Plan–Do–Check–Act (PDCA) Cycle**. This is a four-step process for implementing change, or, continuous improvement. It is useful for incremental or breakthrough improvement. It promotes the idea that a business can always improve.

**PDCA**

Plan–do–check–act cycle. A four-step process for instituting continuous improvement.

**FIGURE 1.2   Plan–Do–Check–Act (PDCA) Cycle.**

**Instructions:** Apply your change process to the following four-step process:

1. Plan
   - Determine the appropriate strategy.
   - Organize to conduct the change.
   - Form teams.
     - Define problem.
     - Collect and review data.
2. Do
   - Test the change.
     - Pilot test.
     - Observe.
     - Change as needed.
   - Implement the change.
3. Check
   - Measure the effects of the change.
4. Act
   - Take action according to the results.
     - Document.
     - Standardize and formalize.
     - Promote the change throughout.
5. Start back at step 1, making it a continuous process.

## Joseph Juran

Joseph Juran was credited as being the Father of Quality Service. A friend and colleague of W. Edwards Deming, Dr. Juran also helped to introduce quality to the Japanese. He first spoke to Japanese managers in a series of 1954 lectures promoting quality. He was a lecturer and business consultant in over 40 different countries. He published the *Quality Control Handbook,* among other texts. He established the Juran Institute to help develop and test new quality assessment tools. Steve Jobs, founder of Apple Computers, credited Dr. Juran's "deep, deep contribution" to the advance of quality.

## Philip Crosby

**DRIFT**
Doing it right the first time. A quest to reduce errors and inefficiencies so that you won't have to fix as many things and pay the price for producing a poor product.

Later in the Quality movement, Philip Cosby was originally a quality manager for International Telephone and Telegraph (ITT) before leaving and setting up his own consulting firm in 1979. He published a well-known book, *Quality is Free*. He was able to show that quality programs would save much more money than they cost. He is popularized for **DRIFT** (do it right the first time) and Zero Defects. DRIFT was originally derived from manufacturing. It is an idea that promoted processes and procedures that ran smoothly and efficiently, thus, doing it right the first time. This reduced wasted, repeats, comps, and the need for service recovery efforts. This followed with the notion that, "if you don't have time to do it right the first time, how will you ever have time to do it over?"

## Tom Peters: Management by Walking Around (MBWA)

**MBWA**
Management by walking around. Idea that managers should "get in touch" with the employees and customers to learn what is really occurring.

Author of numerous books, including *In Search of Excellence*, and a presenter and business consultant, Dr. Peters was one of the first and most influential gurus of contemporary management. He has advocated for service excellence through practical means. **MBWA** is a simple but highly effective premise that managers should spontaneously walk around and talk to their staff and customers. Paperwork and other tasks prevented managers from walking around the department or property. MBWA promotes listening and qualitative assessment. The management can stay in touch with the staff and customers and identify problems and seek solutions more effectively than sitting in the office and looking at reports.

## Peter Drucker

Commonly known as the Father of Modern Management, Peter Drucker was an author and management guru who advocated for the human side as opposed to the numbers. He was popular for ideas such as "management by objectives" and the "knowledge worker." He was very interested in the concept of permitting workers to think for themselves. He made many predictions, some of which came true. He, too, helped the Japanese and was also involved in helping General Motors.

## PARADIGMS

A paradigm is a belief that is commonly accepted as being the proper way or method that something is to be done. This was popularized by Thomas Kuhn in 1962. This promoted "thinking outside the box," in which a paradigm was considered to be "the box." The idea of a paradigm shift became very popular with the quality movement. The cliché of thinking outside the box is still very popular today. For example, fast-food giant Taco Bell has a mainstream advertising campaign encouraging customers to "think outside the bun," imparting the idea that fast food doesn't have to be burgers.

## MOMENT OF TRUTH

**Moment of Truth**
A point of service at which customer service is either made or lost.

The concept of the moment of truth was first popularized by Jan Carlzon of SAS Airlines. Jan theorized that a service experience is comprised of many different moments of truth at which customer service is either made or lost. Different situations have varying amounts of **moments of truth**. For example, a quick-service restaurant may have three to five, but a resort hotel may have several hundred. In breaking down the experience into moments of truth, management and employees can better analyze, realize, and monitor the crucial points in the process.

---

### Service Insight

**Paradigm Shift**

In 1967, technology for the quartz watch was presented to the world at a watch trade show. The Swiss, who had led fine watch-making for decades, dismissed the idea as being insignificant because they believed that it wasn't how watches were supposed to be made. Despite being cheaper and having fewer mechanical parts, it went against the watch-making belief, or paradigm. The Japanese saw the quartz technology as a new way to make watches; they saw the potential. They saw it as a new way of making watches, or a paradigm shift, and embraced it. Two years later, in 1969, Seiko introduced the first commercially available quartz watch. It caught on so well that the Swiss forever lost their hold on the traditional watch market.

---

*The public—the most important people in our business. They are not dependent on us—we are dependent on them. They are not an interruption of our work. They are the purpose of it. We are not doing them a favor by serving them—they are doing us a favor by giving us an opportunity to serve them. They are not outsiders in our business—they are our business! They are not a cold statistic—they are flesh and blood, human beings with feelings and emotions, likes and dislikes. They are not there to argue with or match wits with, or try to outsmart. No one ever wins an argument with the public. The public—people who bring us their wants. It is our job to handle their requirements so pleasantly and so helpfully that they return again and again.*

—Gold, C. 1983. *SOLID GOLD CUSTOMER RELATIONS.*
New York: Prentice Hall.

# CHAPTER REVIEW QUESTIONS

1. What is the definition of *quality guest service*?
2. Why do some customers choose not to complain?
3. What "Age of Change" are we currently in?
4. List five examples of self-service that you have used in the past week.
5. How did Deming help the Japanese?
6. Why do we tend to forget certain events while remembering others?
7. When did the need for speed become popular in the United States?
8. Why does bad service still exist?
9. Who is the Father of Quality Service?
10. Who is the Father of Modern Management?

# CASE STUDIES

### A Loyal Following

A loyal following is very important. Giving customers what they want, when they want it, and how they want it can produce a great following. This has been extremely evident in the following performances. DJs, niche bands, and other events have struck a chord with the public to produce overwhelming results.

An example of this was the band the Grateful Dead. Led by Jerry Garcia, the Grateful Dead formed in 1965 and played over 2300 concerts until Garcia's death in 1995. The legend of their music was much more than a performance. It gave society what it needed at a crucial time in California. They were part of the hippie movement of peace and performed more free concerts than any other band in history. It struck such a chord in society that few bands are even close to having the same impact on their fan base. Loyal followers, or Dead Heads, as they were called, would follow the band anywhere they performed. They were easily spotted by their tie-dyed shirts and famous dead art, including dancing bears, Uncle Sam skeletons, and a Red, White, and Blue "Stealie Skull" with a lightning bolt going through it. People would camp out for days before a concert and follow the band for lengthy periods. Networks were established. Fans traded and exchanged information regarding performances and band news like no other band at that time. All of this happened before Twitter, texting, and Facebook. There were crowds of tens of thousands at nearly every performance. Tickets were difficult to obtain, no matter what the going rate. People weren't just entertained by the Grateful Dead; they knew and loved the band, its members, and its music. For most of the fans, it was a lifestyle.

1. List the customer traits of a Dead Head.
2. How did the band differentiate itself from the competition?
3. What did the band do to produce such a loyal following before the age of communication?

## Club Me

Club Me is a new dance club in a downtown area, in close proximity to a three colleges. It is located in an old factory building. It has a loft, balcony, and many cool private areas around the sides of the dance floor. Its main target market is the students attending the three local colleges. Dance clubs are a very competitive market in this area. Loyalty does not exist. The students can decide to go to one club or another within an instant and the whole scene changes.

Club Me was off to a great start. It was new and fresh and fun and had a mass of people waiting to get in, which only made more people want to get in. They had a great line-up of DJs and regularly held contests with giveaways. It was packed every night of the week, and Club Me became more and more crowded. At first, it was a fun, packed atmosphere. As time passed and crowds continued to grow, it became apparent that Club Me couldn't adequately handle the crowd. This became apparent when a fight broke out in one of the private areas, when one woman attacked another. Security was stationed at the door, the dance floor, and the bar, but had little notice of the secluded areas, which were largely ignored. When a security guard was told there was a fight between two women, he smirked and said, "Cool, a chick fight." He did not call for back up, thinking it was just an argument. By the time he responded, a woman was beaten to the point of unconsciousness while others just watched. She had to be taken out in an ambulance and remained in critical condition. The club had failed to react to the incident to the point of neglect.

Club Me quickly hired more trained security, but the crowds stopped coming. This news had spread throughout the club scene. Females didn't feel safe. When the females stopped coming, so did the males. They felt unprotected against attacks and they stopped going to Club Me.

1. Why did large crowds go to Club Me?
2. How had Club Me met customer expectations?
3. How had Club Me failed to meet customer expectations?
4. How can Club Me change the attitudes of their target market?

## Chivo's Banquet Hall

Chivo's Banquet Hall is a landmark. It is a family-owned establishment that boasts the offerings of the Chivo family. Nearly everyone in the immediate and extended family can be found there during an event. The Chivos are very proud of their establishment. Mama Chivo, as she is called, can be found running the front-of-the-house operations. It is not uncommon to find her giving orders to her staff, hugging and kissing repeat guests, and even offering advice to attendees. She is a true old-style Mama.

Mr. Chivo runs the food. He is a proud chef. He is very passionate about his work. Occasionally he and Mama will have an argument over the best way to serve an event. Mama usually wins and Chef Chivo retreats into the kitchen.

Chef Chivo's way of ensuring customer satisfaction is by walking around the room in his chef's attire. After the food has been served, Chef Chivo works the room and stops by every table. He asks everyone at each table if they liked the event and the food. Everyone always says that everything is great. He looks at everyone's plates. If it is empty, he directly asks them if they would like more. If it has food on it he asks them what was wrong with it. He puts people directly on the spot. People almost always tell him there is no problem at all. He looks at them suspiciously and shakes his head letting them know that he is offended. Sometimes he will tell them that they need to eat more and that they look thin, even if they are not.

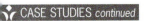

CASE STUDIES continued

1. Describe the tone of guest service at Chivo's Banquet Hall.
2. Critique Chef Chivo's unique style of customer service.
3. What are some likely reasons why the Chivos seldom hear complaints?
4. If you could give the Chivos advice regarding customer service, what would it be?

## Mount Will

Mount Will is a small, steep mountain. It features skiing and snowboarding in the winter and offers other extreme opportunities throughout the rest of the year. It is known for having the most extreme offerings to make up for its small size. Its motto is "Little mountain, big adrenaline." Mount Will attracts many visitors who want a special challenge in a mountain experience. Luckily, it's located beside a major highway and is highly visible to people traveling through the area. The managers try to change the options every year to keep it fresh. This year, they have arranged for a company to bring in a large crane to allow bungee jumping right next to the highway. Everyone passing by could watch the falls, and it would be great for publicity. They negotiated a great price with the subcontractor and are pleased to offer this attraction.

Unfortunately, Mount Will has not been very successful this year. Very few people have dared to brave the bungee jump, and their overall attendance is down for the season. Feeling the pressure in the loss of revenue, Scott, the Mountain Manager, decides to set up a small booth at a local grocery store to promote the event and hand out coupons. People are typically polite but he doesn't count it a success.

He decides to go out front to the crane by the road to discuss this matter with them. What he sees amazes him. There is a different view from the highway. The front of the contractor's crane looks dingy and dull. The cables appear rusty. The staff are unshaven and dressed poorly. Upon mentioning it, he is told that the cables are more than adequate and that it is only surface rust. The crane was inspected by the state and it passed the quality tests. Still, Scott is concerned with the image. He now realizes the issue.

1. As a customer, list your expectations of a bungee-jumping crew and equipment.
2. What are the thoughts of potential customers passing by on the highway?
3. How could the expectations of the potential customers best be met?

# Defining Quality Guest Service

There are many definitions for **quality guest service** available. When summarized, most can be condensed to this one simple definition: exceeding guests' expectations.

While seemingly simple, this is often easier said than done. A challenge with this definition is that much work goes into consistently pleasing the guest. There are many variables that must be accounted for. Below are many of the aspects that go into the coordination and execution of guest services.

**Quality Guest Service**
Exceeding guests' expectations.

## ❧ ASPECTS OF GUEST SERVICE

There are many aspects that comprise guest service. Despite the initial definition, it demands much explanation. The following is a list of common ideologies that define customer service:

*Focusing on serving the guest*: The guest is the primary focus. The guest can fire everyone by deciding not to patronize an establishment. Everything that you do should result in pleasing the guest.

*Consistency in service*: Every guest experience is unique and important and cannot rest on its laurels. Dan Kaplan (Hertz Equipment Rental Corp.) makes a good analogy when he calls it "hitting 1000 singles." Failing to provide quality service even 2% of the time can result in nearly 150 customers a week who may never return and may tell others about their poor experience.

*Efficiency in service*: People have a sense of efficiency on an unconscious level. They can detect inefficiencies, which often manifest themselves through irritability and impatience with a situation. Good service is often quick service with little wasted time or energy. Customers love to be a part of a well-run machine!

*Guests defining quality and value*: Everything is subject to the guest's perception. The guest brings many ideas of what is acceptable and what is unacceptable. Every guest is different. It is important to be able to recognize the guests' individual expectations and accommodate them as much as the system allows.

*Knowledgeable employees*: The knowledge of your employees is often derived through proper hiring, on-going training and motivation, and proficient shift management. This also brings a competence in your staff that feeds into the guest experience and helps to eliminate potential problems before they escalate.

*Commitment from the top of the organization*: Customer service must be supported by the top management of the organization. This will ensure that systems and resources are allocated and in place to effectively handle the demands of service.

*Processes that allow service to continually improve*: All good processes have a system of checks and balances built into them. You can learn a lot from your mistakes. Process improvement is done through a series of feedback evaluations from which learning points can be derived and used to repair the system so that you are constantly getting better.

## ✔ PERISHABILITY OF SERVICE

You cannot inventory service. It is not a commodity. It needs to be ready as dictated by the customer. Most of what we do in the hospitality industry is perishable because service is produced and consumed simultaneously. Furthermore, the human element is interjected. It is subject to interpretation by the staff and the customer. This makes service very difficult to control.

## ✔ MEDIA REPORTS OF CUSTOMER SERVICE

Each year, there is an MSN Money-IBOPE Zogby report that produces a ranking of customer service companies. Respondents are asked to rate companies as being excellent, good, fair, or poor. Those with the most "Excellent" ratings are listed on their Hall of Fame and those with the most "Poor" ratings are Hall of Shame Companies.

Recent Hall of Fame winners with the highest scores are:

- Netflix
- Nordstrom
- Southwest
- Publix
- Apple
- FedEx
- Costco
- UPS
- Marriott
- Whole Foods

Recent Hall of Shame Winners are:

- Bank of America
- AOL
- Capital One
- Sprint Nextel
- Time Warner
- Comcast
- Citibank
- Progressive
- JPMorgan Chase
- Farmers

According to MSN Money, the top three most important attributes are:

- Knowledge of staff
- Friendliness of staff
- Readily available staff

To contrast, *Businessweek* assembles a Customer Service Elite poll assembled from J.D. Power and Associates data. It uses criteria such as "People," "Processes," and "Would recommend." The report produces a letter grade. Recent top 10 A+ companies are:

1. USAA
2. L.L.Bean
3. Fairmont Hotels and Resorts
4. Lexus
5. Trader Joe's
6. Starbucks
7. JetBlue
8. Edward Jones
9. Lands' End
10. Ace Hardware

Also on the *Businessweek*'s Elite List are:

- Marriott
- Ritz Carlton
- Whole Foods
- Apple

In J.D. Power's own travel section of their top-rated customer service companies, the following continue to rank highly on their lists:

- Four Seasons
- Southwest
- Enterprise

It is not surprising that these same companies continue to rank high on the lists. This type of publicity cannot be bought. These are companies that have taken service to new levels.

## ❧ TYPES OF SERVICE

Another way to define service is by categorizing it by type. Service can be generally categorized into three different types: assistance, repair, and value-added. The first two types of service are typically expected. The third type can almost always involve exceeding the guests' expectations.

*Assistance Service*: This involves basic service. It is meeting the expectations of the customer. Providing this type of assistance to others is crucial to any business.

    *Example*: I need help choosing a good seat for the show.

    *Example*: I need help choosing an appropriate wine.

*Repair Service*: Fixing a problem for a customer. It may have been a fault of the business. It is reactive, instead of proactive. It involves "putting out fires." Unfortunately, some people in the hospitality industry are better at putting out fires than avoiding them in the first place.

    *Example*: Repairing a leaky faucet in a guestroom.

    *Example*: Helping a traveler find an alternative flight in bad weather.

*Value-Added Service*: This involves exceeding the customers' expectations. This has a positive impact on the customer experience. It involves going a step past basic job requirements. It raises average service to the level of exceptional service.

    *Example*: Remembering a guests' favorite drink.

    *Example*: Offering a free upgrade.

## ✿ TANGIBLES AND INTANGIBLES

What are we really selling? Is it just a steak? Is it just a glass of wine? Is it just the rental of a room? Is it just a seat at an event? No, of course it is not. There is so much more in addition to the tangible items. In hospitality, we sell an entire experience. Thus, a great portion of your product is the experience. This experience turns into a memory of a pleasant event, exchange, or service offering.

To further understand what the customer experiences, it is important to break everything down into parts or components. Two of the most common components are tangibles and intangibles. By breaking down each of the components, they can be monitored and evaluated and improved upon.

To do this, it is important to observe the entire customer service experience through the eyes of the customer. In doing so, you will find that most customers experience both tangible and intangible products. Tangibles are anything the customer can touch, consume, or take away from the experience such as a comfortable bed or a delicious meal. Intangibles are anything that cannot be touched or easily quantified, such as an appropriate referral or a warm smile. (See Table 2.1.)

**Table 2.1 Tangibles and Intangibles of the Hospitality Industry.**

| Tangibles | Intangibles |
| --- | --- |
| Comfortable bed | Suggestion for a nice restaurant |
| Delicious meal | Warm, welcoming smile |
| Hot coffee | Willingness to serve |
| Chocolate truffles in the room | Accurate reservation |
| Luxurious bedspread | "Thank you" and "Good night" upon exit |

# Meeting Guests' Expectations

Receiving truly great service is receiving more than you expected. It is something that a guest would want to tell others about. They want to tell others about their favorite restaurant or a fantastic hotel that they just visited or a wonderful show that they attended, or a wonderful trip that they just took. You are selling, in a sense, bragging rights. Most people enjoy hearing these stories, as they can see in their friends' eyes how much they enjoyed it. Is it the great product they received or did they receive exactly or even more than they expected? It was likely both. And the first step in meeting expectations is understanding them.

Expectations can be as complex as people themselves. Most customers do not ask for anything unreasonable. Only a few want the world on a platter. Most customers simply want their expectations met. In fact, they even have tolerance if a few things are lacking but they are treated well. Meeting those expectations can be best accomplished through first understanding them. Expectations can also be categorized a few ways.

## Service Insight

### The Customer Ultimately Decides

Who pays the salaries of the management and the employees? Who pays the rent, the utilities, and the taxes? Who can fire the entire establishment? Who can bring the business to a screeching halt? Customers can. Customer satisfaction is the reason that all of this is possible. The customer can fire everyone and bring the whole place down by voting with their patronage. They return as infrequently or as often as they wish. They may be easily swayed, but are difficult to convince. They should be treated as the ultimate critic, because ultimately they are.

The first to evaluate are the type of signals you are putting out as a business. These signals begin to establish or set the level of expectations. They can be explicit or implicit. They all make up the brand or image that you portray. This idea is commonly referred to as **brand management**. All decisions, both implicit and explicit, would be related to this central theme, from the wallpaper and décor to service style.

- **Explicit expectations**: Those expectations that are fully expressed. They are set by promises made by staff, contracts, menus, signage, advertisements, and service promise.
- **Implicit expectations**: Those expectations that are not fully expressed. They are set by prices, décor, location, and service style.

## ⋎ LEVELS OF EXPECTATIONS

You can also define expectations by level. In the perfect world, you would want to achieve ideal expectations. Reasonable levels, however, are still quite meritorious, particularly if accomplished on a consistent level.

- *Ideal Expectations*: The best possible outcomes, those that exceed the typical expectations. These experiences wow the guests. They create memorable experiences.
- *Reasonable Expectations*: These are typically met by following the standard protocol. They are the expected outcome and still very worthy and held in regard.
- *Minimal Expectations*: The least the guest will tolerate. Not ideal for most guests. This level is advantageous for competitors. Some guests will complain, but many will endure, leaving the management and staff wondering what went wrong. Others will move on, particularly if lured by the competition.

## ⋎ ORDER OF EXPECTATIONS

Expectations are also defined by order: primary and secondary. The primary expectations are assumed, while the secondary expectations are initially less important.

- **Primary expectations** are generalizable to most hospitality settings. They are the main wants and needs of the service experience.
  - ○ Prepared and ready for the guest
  - ○ Attentive, professional service
  - ○ Efficiency
  - ○ Comprehension of the process
  - ○ Knowledge of the times
  - ○ Wants are heard and understood
  - ○ Follow-through of a product that is what it claims

---

**Brand Management**
The idea of organizing and controlling a theme that is consistent throughout the entirety of a company.

**Explicit Expectations**
Expectations of service that are clearly provided or given by the business.

**Service Promise**
Often stated internally and externally, a guarantee of goods or services that the customer will be satisfied. In the event that this is not achieved, the business promises to correct the error. Common in organizations.

**Implicit Expectations**
Expectations of service not fully expressed or stated, but certainly implied by a business.

**Primary Expectations**
Essential expectations, crucial to the quality guest service experience.

■ **Secondary expectations** are less important to basic, essential service and may be omitted with a certain level of tolerance by the customer. They are the things that take away from the guest service. Guests don't usually mind until they become a larger issue, although it would certainly be best to provide all of these expectations in a desirable situation.

  ○ Knowledgeable, pleasant staff
  ○ Options made known
  ○ No transferring
  ○ Competence
  ○ Acknowledgment—know the customer. Or, respect their anonymity.

##   INPUTS THAT SET EXPECTATIONS

Every customer is different. There are many inputs that determine the individual customer's expectations. Some come from the business while others come from the guests. As a result, the expectations may be low, high, or even undecided. To understand what the guest expects, let's look at examples of the different inputs that define their expectations.

Table 2.2 begins to explain how guest expectations are formed.

**Table 2.2   Guest Expectation Inputs from Businesses and Guests.**

| Inputs from Business | Examples | Guest Expectations |
|---|---|---|
| **Marketing** | | |
| Advertisements | Nobody beats us . . . | ↑ High |
| Reviews | 4 Stars | ↑ High |
| | Critics dislike | ↔ Undecided |
| **Operations** | | |
| Name | Is it vague? | ↔ Undecided |
| | Complex or sophisticated? | ↑ High |
| | Cheesy? Cliché? | ↓ Low |
| Menu prices | High prices | ↑ High |
| | Low prices | ↓ Low |
| Menu offerings | High-quality items, tableside preparation | ↑ High |
| Service Type | Full | ↑ High |
| | Limited | ↓ Low |
| Décor | Food service: tablecloths, high-back chairs | ↑ High |
| | Hotel: valet, concierge, many amenities | ↑ High |

(*continued*)

| Inputs from Business | Examples | Guest Expectations |
|---|---|---|
| **Guests** | | |
| Personal knowledge | They took a course in wine appreciation. | ↑ High |
| Standards | They do not mind seating themselves. | ↓ Low |
| Personal view of quality | They are accustomed to all meals being fine dining. | ↑ High |
| **Others** | | |
| Influence of others in party | Trying to make a good impression on others in the party. | ↑ High |
| Competition | Competitors are weak. | ↓ Low |
| Word of mouth | Word-on-the-street says that you are awesome. | ↑ High |
| **Occasion** | | |
| To relax | Laid back | ↓ Low |
| To entertain | Business clients | ↑ High |
| To impress | First date | ↑ High |
| Professional | Business meeting | ↑ High |

As you can see, there are many factors that go into assessing the expectations of customers. Some can be managed, like menu offerings, prices, décor, and image, while other factors can only be responded to. The individual customer's personal combination can range from low to high and can change depending on circumstances. It is important to identify and accommodate as best as possible.

## ❦ SCENARIO A: FAST-FOOD RESTAURANT

You can have great customer service at a quick-service restaurant. Consider the following scenario:

As you approach a fast-food restaurant, you have certain expectations. This is your first point of service. As you enter and move to the front counter, you have a certain set of expectations. This continues as you order, wait for the food, receive the food, and consume the food. You expect a moderately clean building, a relatively short and fast-moving line, and a correct order. You would like to be able to place your order reasonably quickly without encountering a rude order-taker. Lastly, you would like to receive the items ordered.

| Point of Service | Expectations | Actual | Customer Reaction |
|---|---|---|---|
| Building | Safe, minimal litter, not too crowded | Average cleanliness, Some straw papers on the floor, some trays stacked around trash can, semicrowded | OK, because minimal litter and some crowd was expected |
| Line | Less than 3 minutes to order | Waited 3 to 4 minutes | OK, because it was close to the expected time |
| Cashier | Cashier mood: average, not disgruntled | Indifferent | OK, because cashier wasn't disgruntled |
| Order | Order accuracy: accurate as described, with minimal issues | Customer had to restate order, cashier was mostly familiar with menu (had to search for buttons) | OK, because the menu/order issue was minimal |
| Wait for food | Less than 3 minutes | 3 minutes | OK, because it took 3 minutes |
| Quality | Food quality: average | Average, fries were hot but not straight out of fryer; one onion ring mixed in | OK, because food was average; one onion ring mixed in didn't bother customer |
| Table | Available with minimal effort, all members in party can sit together | You find an adequate table, you clear off a few crumbs from previous customer | OK, because everyone can sit together; small mess seemed reasonable |
| Was it a good experience? | | | Yes, because they received what they expected |

## ❦ SCENARIO B: FINE-DINING RESTAURANT

| Point of Service | Expectations | Actual | Result |
|---|---|---|---|
| Building | Safe, spotless, not too crowded | Average cleanliness, a few drinks discarded outside entrance, semicrowded | Not pleased, but able to overlook these small issues at first |
| Entrance | Maître d' greets customer within 20 seconds of arrival | Waited 3 to 4 minutes to be noticed | Mildly upset, 3 to 4 minutes seemed like a long time for such a nice place |
| Maître d' | Is pleased to see guests | Indifferent, somewhat hurried, no special recognition | Feel unimportant; paying a great deal of money and want to feel welcomed |

(continued)

| Point of Service | Expectations | Actual | Result |
|---|---|---|---|
| Reservation | Reservation correct as requested and table ready | Correct with mispronunciation of last name | Perturbed; they have the reservation, but the mispronunciation is mildly frustrating, causing customer to roll their eyes |
| Table | Open and set | Open, but busman setting it | Inconvenienced; dislikes having to stand in dining room, feels in the way of passing servers, patrons stare; wonder why they were walked to table if it wasn't fully ready; smell of cleaning solution emanates |
| Server | Attentive, friendly, professional | Indifferent, rushed | Feels like a burden to the server; wonders what is going on with management and operations |
| Order | All accurate, memorized, server had a superior command of menu knowledge | Accurate, used a pad, customer had to restate order, average menu knowledge | OK, but frazzled from previous feelings |
| Wait for food | Only reasonable timing is acceptable | Reasonable timing | OK, but frazzled from previous feelings; beginning to feel better |
| Food | Perfection | Perfect except for a smear of sauce and two green beans hanging off side of a plate | Preposterous! Wonders if the kitchen cares at all |
| Was it a good experience? | | | No! Expectations not met; food and service not acceptable |

Was either scenario truly horrible? Probably not, but according to the guest in the fine dining restaurant, it was preposterous! The guests believe that they were not provided with the level of service they expected. A customer might make comments such as, "What's the matter with this place?" and "The service was absolutely hideous!" Meeting expectations of service can make all the difference.

Neither scenario was great, but although it wasn't an exceptional experience for either example, the customer at the fast-food restaurant left pleased and would likely return. The party at the fine-dining restaurant will probably tell many of their acquaintances about the disappointing experience they had.

Also notice that some small issues are permitted in both cases. As the customer service encounter progresses and service points are not meeting expectations, Customer B becomes quite upset. Meeting expectations is important as is the collection of several smaller points.

**High Expectation Guest**                    **Low Expectation Guest**

---

### Service Insight

***Providing Guest Service Basics:***

To help meet or exceed the guests' expectations, consider the following:

- Become familiar with your customers, survey them.
- Demonstrate your dedication to your customers.
- Tell your customers what they can expect, then keep your word.
- Develop your expertise and maintain consistency.
- Treat all your customers and workers with the same high level of respect.
- Apologize if you are wrong, and remember that credibility is much harder to regain than it is to attain in the first place.

---

## ❖ ISSUES WITH EXCEEDING EXPECTATIONS

Is it possible to always exceed customer expectations? Perhaps you should just meet them. Consider this:

If you are always "delighting" customers, logic might lead to the conclusion that you are consistently underselling and overdelivering. If this were the case, wouldn't the customers come to expect more than you say? And wouldn't they be disappointed when they did not receive more than promised?

Wouldn't your competition be able to make greater claims if you are underselling? What happens if you can promise only a 45-minute show (that is typically 55 minutes) and the competition is able to promise a 55-minute show? They look better than you do.

Aren't you going to lose money by giving everyone a free meal, a free room, a free show, and a free plane ticket? Of course you are. You cannot upgrade everyone to first class, and eventually someone has to pay for all of the items that you comp. After all, businesses are in business to earn a profit.

Consider this, the other part of the definition of quality guest service is "consistently meeting expectations." You can still exceed expectations, but it must be done with grace, tact, finesse, and logic that all properly trained hospitality professionals have. To give something extra doesn't mean giving away your business, it could mean personalizing a service, giving extra attention, recognizing a familiar face, or giving extra help with bags or the elevator. Using the human touch is what makes hospitality what it is!

Hospitality companies are quickly adopting an approach to getting to know the customer and adding a human touch by what they call, "developing lifetime relationships with the customers." They have developed a large database with all of their customers' information that is shared among properties. This database keeps records of the guests' profiles, which stores items such as:

- Name and title preferences
- Likes and dislikes
- Pictures of pets
- Food and beverage preferences
- Past issues
- Lifetime usage and frequency

They review these in advance of the stay and include these in the meetings. They can do things like set the lights and temperature as the guests prefer and print a picture of the customer's pet, place it in a frame, and set it next to the bed. Now, that's a special touch!

# CHAPTER REVIEW QUESTIONS

1. Give an example of empowerment in a counter-service setting.
2. What is the difference between implicit and explicit expectations?
3. Explain how the definition for the term *quality service* can be generalized to facets of the hospitality industry.
4. Define basic expectations of guest service and explain why they may be met but quality guest service may not be perceived in the eyes of the customer.
5. Provide three recent examples of a service experience during which your expectations were exceeded.
6. List five tips for delivering quality service.
7. Explain why expectations differ between customers and establishments.
8. List and briefly describe three types of service.
9. Explain the difference between tangibles and intangibles in a service setting.
10. What does the term *perishability of service* mean in relation to the hospitality industry?

# CASE STUDIES

### Ghost Tours

Ghost Tours is a small tour company that specializes in walking tours through the town of Salem, Massachusetts. A small New England town, Salem is known for its famous witch trials. People come to Salem from all over the world to experience the history and lure of the town. Ghost Tours provides them with an opportunity to experience this firsthand.

Ghost Tours is a low-budget tour company. It was started a few months ago by Dana Robinson. She saw other companies doing this and thought that she could do an even better job with just a small investment, some creativity, and a lot of hard work. She was right. Ghost Tours quickly gained a reputation of being the best in town. It won as award from a local magazine and was featured on the Best Small Businesses of the Year.

She operates her business using a website and a cellular phone out of her home. Ghost Tours began in the spring with 4 tour guides and is now up to 10 employees since the late summer going into the busy Halloween season. The tours meet people at predetermined locations to begin the tours. A popular starting point is her friend's coffee shop, which enjoys the extra business before and after the tours. Dana's creativity has produced a great website that offers reduced payment if patrons pay online, in advance. Business is growing and, in general, it has worked quite well.

Many of the tours have gone quite well. Guests have returned to the coffee shop excited. However, Dana's friend at the coffee shop is noticing a trend. Guests are arriving unprepared for the early darkness and the cold, inclement weather. Dana figures that people should realize what they are in for when they sign up for a walking tour. As she begins to send out e-mail surveys to her customers, she realizes that she is wrong. She is struggling with how to remedy this problem.

Dana looks at her website to see what could be done. She writes, "You will be scared, on this walking tour. Be prepared, and dress accordingly."

Despite what it says on their website, guests are not always dressed accordingly. The temperatures drop quickly and the wind blows, adding wind chill, which causes complaints.

1. Why was Ghost Tours successful?
2. Why did the customers begin to become dissatisfied with Ghost Tours?
3. What could Dana do to satisfy her customers?

### RodeoSpectacular

"Rodeo Spectacular—good ol' fashion family fun!" was the motto of Rodeo Spectacular. It was in an awesome spot on the open range just outside of town. It overlooked the Grand Teton Mountains. The sky was big, and it felt like the West. It also had a regular flow of tourists passing through the area.

The proprietor was Sam Revo. He was a cowboy and a showman through and through. He was a fourth-generation cowboy who loved all things Western. Everyone knew Sam. He was everywhere at the rodeo. Sam was very likable. Like all cowboys, Sam was very polite to everyone he met. He would say howdy to all of the guests as they entered the rodeo. Some would ask to take his picture, as they had never seen such a true image of a cowboy. He always obliged.

As great as Sam was, Rodeo Spectacular was hardly a spectacular experience for many of the tourists. Sam, being a simple man, wanted to provide his guests with an authentic rodeo experience. Guests sat on rustic bleachers made of rough planks. They were exposed to the elements, often making it difficult to stay for the entire show. Children had a play area with a small petting zoo. This generally went well, but the chickens, ducks, and geese left droppings, causing obvious health issues to unknowing children. Tourists were permitted to explore most of the ranch before the show. This came to as a surprise to many because they were not accustomed to the realities of a working ranch.

Sam had a philosophy for Rodeo Spectacular. He would advertise, advertise, advertise. Sam believed that locals already knew about his business, so he targeted tourists. Billboards were spread out on highways for over a hundred miles each every direction. There were brochures in every hotel and restaurant lobby in the area. Posters advertised Rodeo Spectacular at the local airport and on cabs and shuttle vans in the area. All of this advertising was beginning to become a burden in costs. Sam cut back on advertising and saw a sharp drop in business. Consequently, he resumed his heavy advertising campaign because he felt that he couldn't stop.

1. Why did Sam always have to advertise?
2. Why was Rodeo Spectacular less than spectacular?
3. What did the guests expect?

## Bar 229 Main

Bar 229 Main is a trendy new bar. The owners had a vision to make it the coolest, trendiest place in town. As many places do, they used a common method of naming by using the type of establishment as its address. This trendy name was accompanied by a trendy setting and décor. Being downtown, they were located in the middle of the nightlife and the pulse of the metropolitan neighborhood. They had a small window in front and an open door. Eclectic music spilled out into the street. The inside was dim and inviting, with small, color-changing LCD lights that illuminated the clear tables, chairs, and bar. The place was exotic. People walked in and thought, "Wow, that's cool." It was the place to be.

As trendy as the Bar 229 Main was, the owners also had a unique hiring technique. They hired the most attractive people who applied. The owners cared little about background or qualifications. Instead, they thought, anyone can wait tables, and we could train a monkey to tend bar. If they don't know how, we can train them, or they can shadow another person who does.

Initially, this worked. A few of the applicants had previous experience and worked with the others. This did not last, and soon service suffered greatly. The skilled workers became agitated covering for the unskilled workers, and customer complaints began to increase greatly. To make things worse, the owners scheduled workers without taking skill into account. At first, the unskilled workers used charm to overcome their lack of ability, but it was not long before customers grew intolerant.

1. Describe the brand management of Bar 229 Main.
2. What was Bar 229 Main selling?
3. How could Bar 229 Main overcome the customer complaints?

## Beachside Hotel

Beachside Hotel was a typical, small hotel by the water. It had 32 rooms. All but 2 of the rooms had a view of the beach and the water. Beachside was once a branded hotel, but the owners didn't feel it was worth paying for the name, the standards, and the hassle of the inspections. In fact, it was questioned whether they gave up the name or lost it.

Eda and Surge were the owners of the Beachside Hotel. They were minimalists, placing all of their efforts into the hotel. They were frugal and strict with every aspect of their personal lives and business, and lived in a small apartment in the back of the hotel. They had acquired the hotel as a rundown property many years ago. Having scraped together all of their money to repair the property and pay the mortgage, they closely monitored all of the expenses.

Surge would often tell employees: "You just check them in and clean the rooms. They don't need anything extra. It just costs me extra money and they don't need it. They have the beach and water. What more could they want? You give them good, basic service. You take their money and give them a key to their room and that is it. What do you think that we are running the Taj Mahal here?" In fact, Beachside did provide the basics. The rooms were clean. They were basic, but did provide access to the beach and the water.

1. List the tangibles and intangibles of the Beachside Hotel.
2. Did the Beachside Hotel meet the expectations of the customers?
3. What suggestions would you make to Surge and Eda regarding customer service?

## 6-Star Restaurant

6-Star Restaurant had an ideal location in downtown Chicago, surrounded by other restaurants, hotels, and major businesses. Several of the restaurants in this area were considered world-class. The owners and design staff had an idea to make 6-Star Restaurant stand out from those. They envisioned a restaurant that was better than the rest. They decided upon a name that would help it to stand out, "6-Star Restaurant." They based this name on the rating system of 1 to 5 stars, placing their establishment off-the-scales. Although it was never formally rated, the owners believed they deserved an extra star above the rest because of their ability. They believed they would have a restaurant like no other.

Much work went into substantiating their claim. They trained their staff to deliver outstanding service. They chose some of the nicest place settings available. They recruited the best chef and kitchen staff available. They were off to a great start. They were delivering outstanding food and service.

Despite this, customers left feeling slighted. Many of the competitors in that area were also delivering outstanding food and service. 6-Star Restaurant was good, but not overly impressive. It was not the entire step above the competitors that would have warranted their claims. Because of these claims, the customers' expectations were not met.

1. Describe the concept of 6-Star Restaurant.
2. Describe the expectations of the customers.
3. In your opinion, is it possible to deliver 6-star service?

# Problem Solving for Guest Service

## Chapter Objectives:

*After reading this chapter, you should be able to:*

Contrast the expectations of guests and staff.

Explain and apply the concept of red flags.

Identify and assess the contradictions behind the premise that "the guest is always right."

Identify and apply the five steps to resolve guest issues using the G.U.E.S.T. method.

Identify the different types of problem guests and outline strategies for handling these.

Explain the science of anger and apply specific strategies for dealing with angry guests.

Provide an overview of psychological theories and relate them to customer communications.

## Terminology:

Duty of Loyalty

Emotional Intelligence (EI)

Emotional Labor

Empathy

G.U.E.S.T.

Intent to Return

Keep Important Stuff Simple (K.I.S.S.)

Keirsey Temperament Sorter

Lateral Service Principle

Lifetime Customer Value

MBTI

New Customer Cost

Rate of Dissatisfaction

Red Flags

Service Recovery

Transactional Analysis

"Customers don't expect you to be perfect.

They do expect you to fix things when they go wrong."

—*Donald Porter, British Airways*

# Considering Different Points of View

## ❧ WHAT DO PEOPLE REALLY WANT?

At the root of it all, people need to be heard, understood, and appreciated. This is applicable to nearly every relationship and interaction.

**People need**

- to be listened to.
- to be made to feel special.

**People expect their host to**

- have their best interest at heart.
- be confident and competent.
- be believable in their statements and promises.
- give them what they ask for.
- surprise them, or at least the customers appreciate being surprised.

# Dealing with Guest Issues

**Popular Advice**

- Don't punish employees with negative feedback from the customers.
- Eliminate the complaint department because complaints should be part of everyone's job. Everyone should be able to, and be responsible for, handling customer complaints. There should be a system in place to train employees on how to deal with customer issues.
- **Keep Important Stuff Simple (K.I.S.S.),** also known as "Keep it simple, stupid." This is the idea that processes don't always need to be complicated. There is great merit to sticking to the basics. This term is widely used among many industries. It refers to keeping processes as simple as possible, thus reducing the chance for error.

**Keep Important Stuff Simple (K.I.S.S.),** also known as "Keep it simple, stupid" the idea that processes don't always need to be complicated. Instead, keep processes as simple as possible, thus reducing the chance for error.

## ❧ HOW TO HANDLE COMPLAINTS

A woman ordered a cheeseburger at a quick-service restaurant. At her table, the woman immediately realized the cheeseburger was assembled with two bun-tops on it. One bun top was on the top and another bun top was on the bottom. She went up to the manager at the counter to just explain the situation. Before she could get a single word

---

### Service Insight

*Good Service Often Goes Unremembered*

It is an exceptional experience that is remembered: exceptionally good or exceptionally bad. Our lives are filled with so much information and stimuli that we filter out unexceptional experiences. We forget mediocrity. We remember the "wows" in life. The same holds true with customer experiences. Customers remember great experiences and horrible experiences, and forget the in-betweens. When they remember, they want to share with others. Review sites are filled with "love its" and "hate its" with little in between. Most don't take time to right a review, a letter, or even share a mediocre experience. This leaves us with two options:

1. Wow the guest.
2. Seize the opportunity to fix it, to make it right and allow the customer to leave feeling special.

Certainly option 2 isn't preferred, but it is an option that reinforces service recovery. A problem is an opportunity to not only correct, but also to have a guest leave with something great to remember and share. They can leave with a great "wow" memory, no memory, or a great (fixed) memory.

---

**Service Recovery**
Popularized by Ron Zemke, a system for acknowledging, apologizing for, and fixing customer complaints. Other authors have devised their own variations of rectifying mistakes, each version being slightly different.

out of her mouth, the manager immediately handed her another cheeseburger. She didn't want another cheeseburger. Instead, she only wanted to explain what happened. As she tried to explain again, the manager quickly held his hand up stopping her and said, "It's okay, just take a new one." She only wanted to tell him what happened, and he only wanted to give her a replacement cheeseburger.

This is an example of a lose–lose situation. The restaurant lost a cheeseburger, and the customer felt unheard and disrespected. Problem resolution is often more complex than people think. The solution isn't always what you would first believe, and it isn't always about a quick replacement.

The term **service recovery** was originally popularized by Ron Zemke when he made a science out of fixing customer mistakes. He came up with a system for acknowledging, apologizing for, and fixing customer complaints. Other authors have devised their own variations of rectifying mistakes, each version being slightly different. For example, Marriott International uses LEARN (listen, empathize, acknowledge, record, and notify).

Whatever method is used, it is important that each business have one that fits their level of service and is adaptable to its customers. This provides a means to train and provide consistency throughout the organization. Below is an example of **G.U.E.S.T.**, which can be easily adapted to resolving customer issues. It is straightforward, but detailed enough to serve as a foundation for others to follow.

## ✿ G.U.E.S.T.

G.U.E.S.T. is an acronym used to remember how to handle customer complaints or issues. It is an easy-to-remember, easily adaptable problem-solving model.

### G—Greet

- Stop what you're doing when you see a customer.
- Turn toward the customer; make eye contact.
- Say your name and ask how you can help them. Customers are the reason you have a job. Let them know that you will respect their time and situation.
  - ○ *"Hello, I'm Julie. I see that you aren't doing well. I am here to help. Can you help me to understand?"*
- If you are with another customer, acknowledge the presence of the new customer and let him or her know that you will help just as soon as you're done. Call for backup if needed.
  - ○ *"I'm sorry. I'll be with you in just a moment."*

### U—Understand; Listen, Repeat

- A complaint offers you an opportunity to learn about a problem.
- Listen to the guest.
- Try to identify all of the needs and wants.
- Nod your head.
- Don't speak until the customer finishes (even if you know what is being said).
- Lean in slightly toward the customer.
- Don't interject your own beliefs (yet).
- Project a sincere face (practice in the mirror).
- Repeat by summarizing what the customer says to ensure that you heard correctly and ensure that you have all the facts. This will help you to determine the problem.
- Take notes if needed.
- Be sure not to complain about other departments and how it's their fault.
- Don't challenge the customer or trade wits.
- Don't argue with the customer because no employee has ever actually won an argument with a customer.
  - ○ *"So your luggage was lost on your flight over, and the air conditioning wasn't working in the shuttle? Your children are upset from the flight and now your room isn't available early?"*

### E—Empathize; apologize

- Respect the customer. Let the customer know you care. Customers typically like to be recognized. Human beings crave attention and recognition.
- Do everything you can to keep from embarrassing your customers.
- Thank the guest for bringing the issue to your attention (don't always wait until the problem has been resolved).
- Empathize. Acknowledge the customer's feelings. Use phrases like "I understand" and "I know how you feel." Consider illustrating your empathy by briefly relating to a similar incident that happened to you. **Empathy** is crucial to customer service

---

**G.U.E.S.T.**
Greet–Understand–Empathize–Solve–Track. A system of resolving guest conflicts using an acronym to remember how to handle customer complaints or issues. An easily adaptable problem-solving model.

**Empathy**
Understanding and compassion for someone else's emotion. When expressed, it often creates a connection between the staff member and the customer.

resolutions. Different than sympathy, which expresses regret, empathy is a much more personalized emotion; this means that you feel and can relate to the other person's hurt, sharing the emotion.

Apologize for what happened to the customer and for how he or she feels. Even if it wasn't your fault or it was beyond your control, it does not matter. Briefly restate what happened to the customer and then say "I apologize." If you are face to face with the customer, be sure to look him or her in the eyes with sincerity, and continue to look for 2 to 3 seconds after you finish speaking.

Don't get caught up in details of assigning blame. You aren't admitting blame. Instead, you are apologizing to the customer because it happened to him or her. Even when it's not your fault, don't make it look like it's a big hassle. Don't bring up problems from the past. Don't let your anger get hold of you.

Also, remember that each customer is a new experience. You may have heard it 10 times today, but it's probably the first time for the guest today. Be careful not to relate to other customer experiences because it may not be viewed as professional.

- ○ *"I apologize for that happening to you. Thank you for letting me know. That makes for a difficult beginning to your trip."*

## S—Suggest/Solve

- ■ Suggest—If you can, offer some type of suggestion. Be careful to be tactful and to not force your own agenda by strongly interjecting your own opinion.
- ■ Solve—If you can, solve the problem right then and there. Improve whatever service you can. Try to solve a customer's problem immediately using all the resources at your disposal. Anticipate the customer's needs, but be careful not to provide much more than she or he wants or will expect. Look for a win–win, not a win–lose, solution. Consider the wins and losses of both sides. Envision what the customer may lose versus what the business may lose.
- ■ Observe the impact of the resolution. Did it work? Was it effective? What are the implications?
- ■ Assure the customer that the situation will be resolved. Explain what is happening. Let the customer know that you are working on the problem instead of just getting back to the customer with the resolution sometime afterward. The customer may not know that you are working on the problem or that you're going to act on it right away.
- ■ Ask for an opportunity to continue to resolve the situation and to continue to do future business. This reinforces intent to return. Let the customer know that you're going to make things right and that you want to satisfy and keep him or her as a customer and that you care.
  - ○ *"Let me see if the concierge floor is available so that you can get some refreshments in the air conditioning. There are couches up there and a television for the children. I will call up there right now and make George, our Lead Concierge, aware of the situation."*

**Intent to Return**
The belief of a customer that he or she will patronize the establishment or services in the future.

### T—Track; record/document/write up

- It is important to let the organization know by documenting the issue. Most businesses have a manager's log or an incident report and/or a reason for a void or comp (short for compensate or compensation). Note the likelihood of future business or the customer's **intent to return**. This information can be troubling to report and is easily overlooked. Be sure to look for patterns.
- Tracking is important to identify weaknesses in the processes and be proactive in preventing problems before they occur.
- Be professional about the situation; avoid complaining to others.
- Envision scenarios of alternative positive resolutions. Store those in your memory for future instances.
- Take care of yourself. Realize your feelings. Are you stressed?
- There is much reward and personal satisfaction to be derived from being able to please others.

# Types of Customers

It is important to realize that while all customers are unique, they can often be categorized. It is important to understand different customer categories. Each customer is a bit different and you will need to adjust to each, but you should have tactics for dealing with each type of customer.

Some refer to it as "games" while others merely categorize them. Either view works, providing that it is handled professionally and effectively.

1. One of the first things to do is to identify which type of customer you are dealing with. This may be done by recognizing familiar catchphrases.
2. Use this to understand the premise or motivation behind their type.
3. Use your strategy to find a resolution.

You will quickly learn to recognize popular customer tactics. Occasionally, you will encounter a new version of or twist on them that will require a blending of strategies. Place all of these in your memory for your "mental toolkit of skills."

## ❖ LEVEL I–REQUIRE LEAST WORK

Level I customers require some work, but are generally easy to deal with. The tactics are relatively harmless traits of humanity, but can detract from the customer service experience. Be ready because these softballs can turn into strikes if you aren't prepared.

| Type | Catchphrase | Premise | Solution Strategy |
|---|---|---|---|
| Advice giver | You know what you should do? | I know more than you. I can improve any situation. | Welcome ideas. Let customers know that they are valued, but you have to keep moving. Agree to pass the ideas on, but keep transaction moving. Show that you are noting the advice. |
| Anxious | Is this going to take long? | They have constraints that concern them greatly (travel, bedbugs, phobias) | Show confidence. Give specific praises. Instill confidence in them. Assist them in taking actions. |
| Arrested youth | Lighten up | They are an adolescent in an adult's body. | Be friendly, but guard your boundaries. Let them know that they are accepted, but must follow basic rules. |
| Bliss | Isn't this awesome! | This person is thrilled. | Keep it friendly. Ensure they focus on the transaction at hand. They may forget essential pieces. Ensure their needs are met. |
| Compliments | That's a pretty name. | They want you to like them. They may be afraid of bad service. | Acknowledge and accept the compliments when appropriate. Don't lose sight of the transaction. Let them know what you are doing to serve them. |
| Friendly | Let me show you a picture of my grandson | They love to share. They desire attention at any cost. | Be polite, but be sure not to allow too much time and attention. After the transaction, tell them it was a pleasure meeting them and that you now have to tend to another task. |
| Gossiper | Is there something going on in the ballroom? Was that guest ok? | They like to talk and are hoping for gossip. | Some knowledge can be shared, while some is highly confidential. Learn what is permitted to share. Respond empathetically by stating you don't know or cannot say in a curious way. |
| Hot mess | It's in here somewhere . . . | Disorganized. Cannot get things together. | Have patience. Sensing anxiety in you will likely make them worse. Make them feel welcomed, understood, and accepted. Suggest alternative methods and service as appropriate. |
| Jokester | I just flew in, boy are my arms tired. | Desperate for attention. Wants to humor others. | Show good humor and smile at jokes when appropriate, but direct them toward the business transaction. |
| Pleaser | It's okay, really. | Wants to please everyone. Often wants others to be at ease. | Politely let them know that they deserve your best service. Ensure they get everything needed so they aren't secretly unsatisfied. |
| Ponderer | Umm, what was the first choice again? | Fear of making the wrong decision. | Suggest options when appropriate. Assure them about their decision. Let them know the options available if they change their minds. |

*(continued)*

| Type | Catchphrase | Premise | Solution Strategy |
|------|-------------|---------|-------------------|
| Shy | None (and no eye contact) | Some people are shy, afraid of things: looking foolish, making mistakes . . . | Give them an easy out. Respect their shy nature. Reassure them. Sincerely tend to them. Keep service as low-key as possible. Keep transaction discrete so as to minimize their exposure. |
| Too much information | I just lost my job. | They will talk to anyone who will listen. | Handle with compassion, but expeditiously. Note and help if appropriate. Wish them well with their situation. |
| No questions please | Yes. No. | They don't want to interact for some unknown reason (shy, tired, cranky, ill). | Respect that. Use caution in trying to get them to open up. Small talk isn't always essential or welcomed. |
| Questioner | What time is the 3 o'clock parade? | Want to ensure they have the best possible information. Disbelief in information. They believe in the security of redundancy. | Calmly answer each question. Point out where information is available. Repetitively reassure. Be sure to complete necessary transactions. |

## ❖ LEVEL II—REQUIRE MODERATE WORK

Level II customers are more difficult to deal with. Their tactics tend to be more coercive, with a goal of achieving more out of the situation. Boundaries are key to dealing with this group. Realize what you can give and what you cannot.

| Type | Catchphrase | Premise | Solution Strategy |
|------|-------------|---------|-------------------|
| Controlled | The menu does not state that. | These people are very exact. They have precise expectations. | Knowledge of your operation is key. The more you know about your product the better. Let them know how it could be interpreted that way. Apologize for the oversight and assure them that you will mention it to the person in charge of communications. Matter-of-factly let them know what you can and cannot do at this time. |
| Manager request | Let me talk to the manger. | Assuming you have performed your job, they want special privileges. | Offer to solve, but then call the manager if they refuse you. Realize that it is not likely about getting you in trouble. It will happen on occasion. |

(continued)

| Type | Catchphrase | Premise | Solution Strategy |
|------|-------------|---------|-------------------|
| Flirt | I'm much better now, thanks. | Can be from a male or a female. Trying to charm their way into getting something extra. | By the book. Stick to the standard procedures. Don't use emotion. Don't gag or swoon. Be sincere. Stand your ground. Let them know that you are providing great service. |
| Free is good | Got any specials going on? | Either they have a genuine desire to save or they like to play the game of manipulation for self-esteem. | Remind them of the values in your product and service. Let them know of discounts when appropriate. |
| Grumbler | We paid all this money and . . . | Mildly aggravated. The world is against them and owes them. Many complaints, but nonspecific in their demands. | Try to get them to tell you how you can please them. Assure them that their comfort is your number one priority. |
| Space invader | I just have to go backstage because . . . | These people like to go where others are not permitted. He believes he is special and rules do not apply to him. | Be straightforward and direct. Maintain boundaries. Smile, but be firm in your limits. Suggest all permissible options. |
| Partyer | Which way to the bar? Woo! Partay! | Cannot be bothered with formalities. | Let them have fun, but ensure that they do not interfere with others. Politely, be sure transaction or business is still conducted. |
| Royalty | I'll have the usual. | Like to be made to feel special. Feel entitled to be acknowledged as more deserving than others. I'm not just anybody, I am me! | Let them be king. Show respect. Remind them of all of the services being given. |
| Whiner | I have had such a bad day . . . | Want someone to listen. Cannot handle situation alone. Wants others to help. | Listen, then let them know what you can do. It may be nothing this instant. Offer hope as you can. Tell them what they can do. Be optimistic and constructive in your advice. |

## ❦ LEVEL III—REQUIRE SUBSTANTIAL WORK

Level III customers typically require substantial work to resolve their situations. Watch for changing of tactics and escalations of anger. Separate these customers from others if they begin to cause a scene. Many of these tactics are directed at you personally. Stay focused, respond to the tactic, maintaining professionalism, and successfully complete the transaction at hand. Your goal is for it to end well.

| Type | Catchphrase | Premise | Solution Strategy |
|---|---|---|---|
| Bully | I pay good money . . . | Want special attention and will say just about anything to get it. | Give the attention, but realize that you aren't there to knock them down. Don't let them distract you from protocol. Know your limits and the limits of the business and stick to them. |
| Embarrasser | Well if you knew how to . . . | Pent-up issues. | Similar to a bully. Don't allow yourself to digress. Direct them to stick to the business transaction. Be specific to obtain their needs. Keep professional and don't let it get personal. Direct them to the "professional discussion." Finish as quickly as possible. |
| Excuse | The menu board was confusing. | Fear of something and looking to blame. | Apologize. Reassure. Don't be critical. Know the boundaries. Present solutions. |
| Inappropriate | %^\$#@#\$% | Another tactic to gain the upper hand in the situation. May be intoxicated. | Similar to embarrassers. Don't lose momentum by being offended. Know the limits and professionally, but directly, let them know when the line has been crossed by making statements such as, "I am sorry, but this is a family-friendly establishment and that language is frowned upon." Call security and remove if intoxicated. |
| Narcissist | Do you know who I am? | These are self-centered people who care only about themselves. | It should be about them. Let it be about them. But you must also balance to make sure that they don't compromise service to others and that everyone is provided appropriate service. |
| Nasty | Are you stupid? | Place others on the defense without concern. | Similar to embarrassers and inappropriate tactics. Focus on the task and don't take it personally. Let them know that you don't wish for them to feel as though they receiving inadequate service. Put on your most professional face. They have issues that you cannot resolve. Realize that this is a tactic to get the upper hand. Know the boundaries and stick to them. Complete the transaction as soon as possible. Call for back up if necessary. |
| Promised | I was promised . . . | Perhaps they were promised; or perhaps they are manipulating and controlling. | Be straightforward: "I am really sorry. This is what we can do: I can promise you that. . . . Does this seem reasonable?" Or, "what would you suggest as an alternative?" |
| Campaigners | I'm going to start an Internet boycott! | They see themselves as leaders who speak up. | If possible, immediately separate them from other customers and present options. Enlist their help by asking what they can do to resolve situation. Realize that others are not as likely to follow as these customers may believe. |
| Seeker | Oh, you must help me to . . . | Enlist the help of others to get things accomplished. | Only help if appropriate. Build their confidence. Let them know what you can do within your limits. |

*(continued)*

| Type | Catchphrase | Premise | Solution Strategy |
|---|---|---|---|
| Slur | Are you [fill in protected class here]? | They are looking for a weakness. They likely have a prejudice. | Answer only if appropriate. Tell them that you would prefer to continue the business conversation. Complete transaction as soon as possible. Note in manager's log. |
| Injured | I have never been more insulted in all my life! | Lives on extremes, using drama to their gain. | Separate from other customers if possible. Acknowledge the purported struggle. Realize that it may take time to recover from the drama before they are rational. Meanwhile, apologize, present options, and maintain boundaries. |
| Unacceptable | This is unacceptable. | Accustomed to getting everything their way. | Reassure them that you are working toward a solution. Act promptly. Show respect. |
| Unchangeable | That's how I am. | Resistant to change, childish. | Inform them of the policies and how much can be accommodated. Expect them to push as far as you will allow. Also expect a shift to another role, such as bully, narcissist or nasty, or demand a manager. |

### Codes and Systems

Hospitals have codes, supermarkets have codes, police and rescue have codes, but hospitality staff have very few. Should they have codes? Having a system of codes is a great way to communicate between management and staff. Guests can be categorized according to sales, importance, and difficulty with terms or numbers. Requests for help can also be coded. It eliminates embarrassing situations, eliminates laborious descriptions, and facilitates immediate communication. It can be a very simple system.

- Tables and seats should all be numbered.
- A bell, a shout-out, and a pager are all old-school techniques.
- A tap on the manager's left shoulder means assistance requested when possible, and a tap on the manager's right shoulder means an emergency situation.
- Customer intoxication can be relayed in a green light, yellow light, red light system.

Realize that you are not going to change many of these people. You can only work with them to make this guest service situation work well for them at this time.

## ❖ HANDLING ANGRY CUSTOMERS

Sometimes even the best systems fail. It would be great if all customers were reasonable and rational and if systems worked, but that is not always the case. When things go wrong, emotions run high, and employees must be ready for the unexpected. This is when anger heats up.

True anger manifests itself within our bodies. The blood is pumping, the stomach may be turning, and the face maybe reddening. People often say things they may not mean and shouldn't say.

When a customer is at this point, it may be very difficult to immediately diffuse and resolve the situation because they are no longer hearing, comprehending, or thinking with great rationality.

Anger often has three phases:

1. Building
2. Exploding
3. Cooling

Realize that it may take some time once they explode. Don't take it personally. Mentally remove yourself from the situation. One way to mentally remove yourself is to understand what is behind the anger. It can help you to form a defense, or at the very least, to categorize it. This can also help in the aftermath as you process what happened.

### What Is the Primary Goal behind the Anger?

- Fun: They have power and actually enjoy anger as a hobby.
- Wear you down: They achieve success through repetition.
- Bullies: They desire power and often get their way by getting angry.
- Unexplained: Something else happened in their life.
- Blame: They don't care who's to blame. They are venting and want to blame someone and you are in front of them. Remember, they may not always be logical.

It is natural to want to respond in the same manner as the customer. If someone picks a fight, your natural reaction might be to get defensive or fight back. No one should ever be subjected to physical or verbal abuse; occasionally you will encounter an angry customer and abuse may occur.

Call security or the police. Call for the assistance of other staff and managers. Be direct. Get them away from others. Record facts as soon as you can and note witnesses.

### When Dealing with Angry People, Consider These Tips:

- Try to keep your voice low and quiet.
- Deal with the emotions first. Otherwise, logic won't be appreciated.
- Get them out of view if possible.
- Realize that they need to vent. When people are angry, it often takes a few minutes or more for their body and emotions to adjust and logic to prevail. During this time, don't be overly pleasant, because it won't be appreciated. Instead, slow your speed and be factual. Speaking quickly will only elevate their mood.
- Use phrases like: What can I do to help you?
- Think of ways to neutralize the situation.
- Increase continuous eye contact.
- Focus on the options, not the limitations.
- Involve them if appropriate: How can we solve this?
- Don't take negative customer comments personally.
- Mentally remove yourself from the situation.
- Let them know when you are thinking or looking or calling. Don't just leave to "surprise them." Instead, let them know that you are working on the situation.
- Pause to think and pause for emphasis.

### Service Insight

#### Handling Stress

In addition to the physical demands are the psychological demands of customer service. Dealing with customers causes stress on a personal level. This stress can be referred to as **emotional labor**.

Stress can be good. It can be a motivator. It can show that you care. It helps to reinforce your determination, and it is part of life. More typically, though, people are plagued by the inability to effectively moderate their stress.

Below are three categories: pre-stress, occurrence, and post-stress. By breaking stress into these categories, it can be evaluated and monitored more effectively.

#### Pre-Stress

- Are you going into the shift already stressed?
- Realize that stress will likely occur.
- Visualize how you will act when it occurs.
- What motivates you?

#### Occurrence

- Mentally remove yourself from the situation.
- Note your body reacting to the stress.
- Label the stressor, or the reason for the stress.
- Is it your own stress, or are you assuming the stress of others?
- What steps can you take to fix the situation?
- Can you allow time to pass? Realize that it will take time for your body to adjust.
- Do you have to have this argument?

#### Post-Stress

It is important to think about what happened. Change what you can for the next time, then leave it alone.

- What did you do correctly?
- How could you have improved?
- Can it be avoided in the future?
- Can you talk to someone about it?
- Can you change your environment?

Other tips:

- Exercise.
- Give yourself permission to make mistakes.
- Realize what you are currently doing to cope with the effects of stress. Realize whether a vice is taking hold of you.
- Remember your professional and personal goals.

---

**Emotional Labor**
Psychological demands of customer service.

- Don't argue. If you have to disagree, it doesn't have to be personal. Perhaps you can agree to disagree. They don't always have to agree with your side and you don't always have to agree with theirs. In which case, you should reemphasize what can be done. Try to stick to facts.
- Do your best to remain calm. No one ever wins a shouting match with a customer. Try to get them to use logic as the anger subsides.
- Keep your eye on the prize/goal; your aim is to get past the anger and solve the problem. Remember that this is not a contest.
- Keep in mind that your inside/private thoughts may show. If this happens, you will appear to be insincere. Most people are discerning enough to know.

---

### Service Insight

***Dealing with Other Cultures***

Technology and travel are increasing, and the world is becoming a smaller place. A majority of new customers come internationally. Foreign travelers spend about three times as much as domestic travelers, so businesses find them lucrative as customers. It can be difficult to exceed their expectations when you don't know them. Language, customs, and cultures are different. When you do business with foreign guests, it is important to understand them if you want to succeed. First, it is important to make them feel comfortable. Begin with a smile. A smile is welcoming around the world. For most foreign travelers, their top priorities are typically:

1. safety
2. a new experience
3. comprehension of all that is occurring

Then, consider these tips for delivering proper guest service to foreign travelers:

- **Communicate**: This might be difficult, but communication is a key to customer service. Find a translator, learn basic terms, or find other ways to communicate. Signage is also very important. Most international venues have brochures available in many languages. Technology is also a new key in translation.
- **Understand their cultures**: Understand their customs and traditions. Good service is not universal. Expectations vary greatly between countries and cultures. Make it a point to understand the meanings and importance behind their requests and actions.
- **Survey your clients**: Determine what they are thinking and feeling in an effort to better serve them. It is important to know the areas you need to improve.
- **Get educated**: Make it a part of your on-going training to get to know these customers. Learn how to say hello, good-bye, and thank you in 20 different languages. Even just a few phrases or gestures could be very impressive to them. They will understand that you are trying to serve them and they will sincerely appreciate it.

## ✦ STAFF EXPECTATIONS

There are many expectations of a front-line service worker. They don't just represent the company, they *are* the company! There are several qualities management would expect to be present in anyone who works directly with customers. Most of us would think that these are common sense, but to quote Mark Twain, "common sense isn't all that common." Therefore, as a manager, it is important to tell these workers during orientation, at reviews, and whenever else reinforcement is needed.

**Duty of Loyalty**
Regarding employees, it implies they have a responsibility to act in the best interest of the business in all of their actions. This means they should: want to help, be empathetic, give their full and personalized attention, and have a sense of pride regarding their work.

> *Personal Care*: Make it clear that it is the employee's responsibility to stay in proper shape and rest before a shift so that they are comfortable. They should be well-groomed.
>
> *Attitude*: We expect employees to care about the guests, the business, and their co-workers. Let employees know and be able to understand that they have a **duty of loyalty** to the betterment of the business. This means that they should:
> - want to help.
> - be empathetic.
> - give their full and personalized attention.
> - have a sense of pride.

## ✦ IS THE GUEST ALWAYS RIGHT?

Everyone has heard the claim, "The guest is always right." This phrase frustrates both the business and the customer because it simply cannot apply to every situation. It sets up unreasonable expectations on both sides.

Employees disagree that the guest is always right, arguing: How can a guest always be right? How can anyone always be right? That is theoretically impossible. What if they are overly demanding? Or what if it is impossible to fulfill their requests? What if it compromises other customers? Employees feel bullied and caught between the customer and the management. Why should the guest always be right? What if they don't realize or won't listen to the entire situation?

Owners want the employees to please the paying customers, so this statement is made. They also think they have to give away profits. Often, they do. Sometimes, they consider it merely "the cost of doing business." Other times, the customers may be trying to get something for nothing. Owners wonder whether a customer is lying. Occasionally, people lie, especially when it is to their benefit and associated with a business's profits instead of an individual.

In the end, it is a very difficult statement to make. You should serve the customers, but a situation may occur during which a customer is unreasonable. Customers can be very rude, and believe they have more rights than they actually do.

Others say, "While the customer may not always be right, the *perception of the customer should be right*." This does change the notion, but it is still difficult to consistently apply it to real-world scenarios. It continues to set up a difficult situation for all parties involved. In an effort to better explore the notion of the guest always being right, you are essentially implying that your answer should always be yes and that a guest should never be refused.

## ❦ CAN YOU SAY NO?

If the idea is to always please the guest, and the guest is always right:

- Should your answer always be yes?
- Can you say no to a customer?
- Can the guest be wrong?
- Are there limits?

Yes. Yes. Yes. And Yes.

It may seem odd for the answer to be yes to all four of these questions, but consider this. Always saying yes does not have to mean total compromise. The customer does not have carte blanche, the employee doesn't have to be frustrated, and the owner doesn't always have to give away the profits. Your answer should be yes, but in a way in which you can accommodate the customer's needs. In a sense, you are saying no to a customer, but in a way that still accommodates her or his wishes and needs.

Are there limits to what you can do? Of course. There are budget and legal restrictions. You have other customers to serve and a business to run. The point is to not get caught up in the details and to look at the larger picture. Look for alternative win–wins, where you can say yes while remaining within your limits.

Keep your eye on the prize.

***Remember that your goal is problem resolution in everyone's best interest.*** *Also know that:*

- Occasionally the business will take a loss.
- Occasionally you will make a mistake.

Use these instances as learning opportunities so that you can change your system to minimize the likelihood of future occurrences.

Other thoughts that would help your decision to say "Yes" or "No" would be:

### Lifetime Customer Value

**Lifetime Customer Value**
All potential future sales from the customer.

- How much is the customer worth? This would be all potential future sales from the customer. Also consider word-of-mouth.
- The entire amount of worth generated from a patron. A combination of all potential sales revenue and unquantifiable word-of-mouth.

### New Customer Cost

**New Customer Cost**
All of the costs associated with obtaining a new customer.

- All the costs associated with obtaining a new customer.
- How much would it take to replace or obtain another customer? This is a complex estimate of your marketing expenses and time. Estimates claim that it takes between 4 to 20 times the amount of money to obtain a new customer than to retain an existing customer. It really depends how much you spend on marketing and what they are asking for.

**Rate of Dissatisfaction**
Amount or percentage of errors in a system. If calculated through a survey, the amount of low-scoring results.

## Rate of Dissatisfaction

- The amount or percentage of errors in a system. If calculated through a survey, the amount of low-scoring results.
- How often does this happen? If it occurs often, then there is likely a process error that is of most importance.

## ❖ IT'S ALL THE LITTLE THINGS

The customer service experience starts even before customers enter the establishment. It begins with their first contact with the business. It could be when they make a reservation or buy a ticket. It is a culmination of the little things. It may not be a single issue that influences or bothers a customer. Or it may be a series or combination of seemingly small, insignificant issues. Essentially, those red flags—a squeaky door, an extra minute to wait, dust in the corner, or a few crumbs from a previous customer—may not seem like much individually but can quickly add up to a less-than-stellar encounter.

Jan Carlzon popularized the phrase from his best-selling book, *Moments of Truth*. In it, he wrote about how the service encounter is made up of many individual moments of truth. Within one encounter, there are many points at which quality guest service can be made or lost. It is a nice way to think about all the little things that go into quality guest service.

## ❖ WATCHING FOR RED FLAGS

**Red Flags**
Indicators that go off in customers' minds when they do not receive what they need and expect. Not easily detected by employees. The red flags have a cumulative effect and result in a poor service experience.

You cannot be all things to all people. Even the best businesses have problems. To further complicate things, customers bring in preconceived notions and expectations. Employees need to be able to read the subtle signs of the customer who probably won't tell them exactly what he or she wants. When customers do not receive what they need and expect, issues arise. As this occurs, **red flags** go up in a customer's mind. Some of the obvious signs may be a reddening face, a change of posture, a glance at a watch, or a sigh. Other signals may be difficult to detect. The customer may not even be aware of this, and some may be unable to verbalize all of the issues. The red flags are indicators of gaps or disparities between what the customer needs and expects and what they actually do receive.

When just a few red flags pop up, most customers are tolerant because they are resistant to changing their behavior. They don't typically want to find another place to do business or stop the transaction midstream. They aren't wowed, but they file these red flags away in a mental folder. The red flags are totaled. Too many red flags at once, one that is huge, or too many small ones that have built up may cause a customer to complain, blow up, or never come back. A great question to ask when evaluating service and serving the customer is, "Are they getting what they need and expect?" Look for the signs. Place yourself in their shoes, or try to see it from their perspective.

## ❦ "MISS" VERSUS "MA'AM" TITLES

Women are usually concerned about their appearance and age. Most women, particularly those above 30, prefer to be seen as young. Women feel old when referred to as "Ma'am." It isn't typically anything they will remark on outright, but they will notice, and we want people to feel comfortable. Miss implies a younger age. Make it a point to refer to women as Miss, despite their age. This also has regional variations between the North and the South of the United States, making the rules ambiguous. Nonetheless, be aware of your personal jargon that may unintentionally upset others.

## ❦ REMEMBERING NAMES

Customers like to be recognized and remembered; it makes them feel special. Calling them by name and a title helps to create a special guest experience. Consider using the following tips to remember names:

- *Listen* intently to the pronunciation.
- *Repeat* it immediately and then at least a few more times in the conversation.
- *Memorize* their appearance—anything unique?
- *Relate* it to something or someone that you know. This is sometimes referred to as an *anchor*, or *anchoring the name*. For example, Bob is my uncle's name and he reminds me of my Uncle Bob. Mrs. Supperski is a Polish name and it reminds me of supper—Polish Supper—Supperski. Mr. Ross reminds me of Ross from the television show "Friends," so, Ross from "Friends"—Mr. Ross. Whatever it takes. Sometimes obvious or odd associations commit better to memory better than practical, boring ones. You could also relate or anchor it to their appearance. Also consider rhyming as an anchor, but be careful it doesn't come out embarrassingly incorrect.

### Actions

We expect employees to do things, but don't always state the obvious. Ensure that employees are told they should:

○ always stop what they are doing and acknowledge the guest, smile, and make eye contact.

○ be adaptable and flexible to meet customer needs by using the **lateral service principle** to solve customer problems that they are aware of, even if it's not in their department.

**Lateral Service Principle**
The idea that employees are to stop what they are doing and help to solve customer problems even if it is not in their department.

### Example of a Lateral Service Issue

A guest has an issue. Someone else is sitting in her seat at a concert. She mentions it to the ticket counter. The staff at the ticket counter know that it isn't their specific job and they could simply send her to security, but they stop and help her regardless. They verify the ticket, then ask her to wait just a minute while security is called to the ticket office. Once security arrives, they explain the situation and escort the woman back to her seat to resolve the rest of the issue. Security is also informed of another available, upgraded seat that is available in case it cannot be resolved.

# Psychological Theories

## ❖ TRANSACTIONAL ANALYSIS

Dr. Eric Berne was a psychiatrist who first captured the idea of **transactional analysis** and brought into the mainstream. He released a book in 1964 entitled *Games People Play*. It was originally written for practitioners, but it quickly went mainstream and hit the *New York Times* Best Sellers list. It spawned a field of analyzing all human encounters as transactions during which each player benefits or manipulates. He devised levels of the closeness that encounters can experience: withdrawn, ritual, pastimes, games, activities, and intimacy. Its application to the service industry revolutionized how we deal with customers. Many programs began to see it as more of a method. As a result, the field of customer service adapted many derivations of this science.

Every time two people come together, they are constantly evaluating and making assessments. Some people claim that they do not judge. But consider this situation: You are alone working night audit at a hotel. You look up and see a man walking quickly toward you at the front desk. It is late at night. He is wearing sunglasses, a hat, and an overcoat, and his hands are in the pockets, you must quickly decide whether this person is nervous and walks quickly, has recently had cataract surgery, is a rock star, or is going to rob you. Dr. Berne provided a system for understanding and controlling the behavior of others.

This struck a chord with the general public. He referred to anger as a racket, writing that it may be self-righteous, adversarial, or even fun. Regardless of the reason, he viewed it as a choice within one's control. This influenced how we deal with angry customers. Just because they are mad, doesn't mean that we have to be mad. We choose how we will react to any situation. We are also helped by realizing that they are after a goal and are leveraging their behavior. When identifying the goal and the behavioral tactic, we can react to this in constructive ways to achieve our desired outcome—quality service and customer satisfaction.

There are three types of ego states:

1. *Parent*: People mimic their parents. Some shout, while others nurture.
2. *Adult*: People are rational, informed, and free from overwhelming emotion.
3. *Child*: People think, feel, and behave as they did when they were children.

He theorized that people interact three different ways:

1. *Reciprocal*: Parent to Parent, Adult to Adult, Child to Child
2. *Crossed*: Parent to Child, Child to Adult
3. *Covert*: When messages have Parent and Child responses combined.

To look at it in another light, we can process this as a game, trying to analyze and manipulate, or control their attitude, hopefully before it reaches the blown-up stage. We can let them vent, and we can help them to calmly reach a solution. The options are ours. If it goes wrong, it is likely that we didn't perceive and adjust correctly.

**Meyers–Briggs Type Indicator (MBTI)**

Tool used to outline personality and temperament types.

## ❖ TEMPERAMENTS

The **Meyers–Briggs Type Indicator (MBTI)** was developed by Katharine Cook Briggs and her daughter Isabel Briggs Meyers and based on the theory of psychological types originally outlined by Dr. Jung. MBTI is another tool used to explain personalities and temperaments. It is useful to explain why we do something or may react in a certain way. It is also helpful in understanding and relating to others. You may not agree with them, but at least you can modify your strategy and understand the premise. Modified versions are also helpful to assist in job selection. It includes four dimensions, producing 16 different personality types.

- How they view the outer world: **E**xtroversion versus **I**ntroversion
- How they take in information: **S**ensing versus **IN**tuition
- How they make decisions: **T**hinking versus **F**eeling
- How they structure things: **J**udging versus **P**erceiving

## ❖ KEIRSEY TEMPERAMENT SORTER

**Keirsey Temperament Sorter**

Tool used to outline personality types into four primary categories: Artisan, Guardian, Idealist, and Rational.

Another labeling tool is the **Keirsey Temperament Sorter Instrument (TSI)**. Produced by David Keirsey, the Keirsey TSI correlates with the MBTI. In it, four different temperament types are produced. These categorical names can serve as quick labels for understanding, communicating, and relating to personalities.

- *Artisans*: These are observant troubleshooters who want to make an impact.
- *Guardians*: These are responsible and dutiful organizers.
- *Idealists*: These seek inner meaning, mediate, and use diplomacy.
- *Rationals*: These use self-control and strategy.

## ❖ EMOTIONAL INTELLIGENCE (EI)

**Emotional Intelligence (EI)**

A view of personalities, personal encounters, and success. It consists of four dimensions: Self-awareness—knowing your emotions; Self-management—controlling your emotions; Social awareness—knowing others' emotions; and Relationship management—the ability to manage interactions with others.

It is helpful to know yourself and how you react to situations. It is even more helpful to be able to gauge others and be able to change yourself to produce the desired outcome in service settings. Much of this logic is present in Daniel Goleman's more recently popularized **Emotional Intelligence (EI)**. This most recent take on personalities was developed in the past 20 years. EI claims that IQ does not tell the whole picture in relating to others and being successful. Instead, it uses four dimensions to assess an emotional quotient (EQ).

- *Self-awareness*: knowing your emotions
- *Self-management*: controlling your emotions
- *Social awareness*: knowing others' emotions
- *Relationship management*: the ability to manage interactions with others

Goleman claims that none of these skills is independently best. Instead, a person should be proficient in all to be successful. The theory of EI claims that a blend of ability to read emotions, know your own, and alter accordingly to produce your intended gain is often the best.

**Service Insight**

*Ethics Checklist*

When analyzing a specific action, consider the following:

- Is it legal?
- Is it fair?
- How do I feel about it in my conscience?
- Would the court of public opinion find my behavior incorrect?
- Am I fearful of what those I trust and respect would say about my actions?

# CHAPTER REVIEW QUESTIONS

1. In every service situation, a customer has certain expectations. List and briefly describe these expectations.
2. Is the guest always right? Explain your argument and provide support for your answer.
3. Recall a service encounter in which you became angry. Apply it to the phases of anger and provide five tips for the service provider in dealing with the situation.
4. What is a red flag? How does it relate to a moment of truth?
5. How does G.U.E.S.T. help a business to train for customer service?
6. Customers have reasons for acting the way they do. Recall four of the "types" listed in the chapter that apply to you and your personality.
7. Explain the purpose of an anchor when remembering names.
8. List three reasons why you would have to politely tell a guest, "No."
9. What should you do after a stressful guest-contact situation? List ways to effectively handle the situation.
10. Explain why mediocre service often goes unremembered.

# CASE STUDIES

**Backstage Pass**

Freak-3K, a popular European band, was giving a concert at the Gen-Z Center. Kenson was a friend of the band who was invited to attend the show and discuss other promotional opportunities while touring in the United States. A meeting was scheduled backstage after the show. Kenson was given a VIP Pass and lanyard. This was a big opportunity for him, since he had just begun his own music promotion company.

The night of the concert, Kenson went to the gate at Gen-Z Center and displayed his VIP pass. He was escorted to a VIP box overlooking the arena. He was afforded complimentary snacks, wine, and beer. Kenson enjoyed the show immensely. After the show, Kenson asked for directions to the backstage area. Things seemed to be going well until he approached a security guard standing in front of the entrance to the backstage area.

Kenson smiled and displayed his VIP pass. The security guard told Kenson that no one was permitted backstage without a backstage pass. Kenson began to explain that the VIP pass is what he was given and that he was scheduled to have a very important meeting with the band backstage after the concert. The guard told Kenson the Director of Security told all guards that he would terminate any of his security staff who admitted someone without a backstage pass. He added that because of an enhanced security imperative everyone had to have proper credentialing, and the Director fired other guards who breached orders. It was zero tolerance, no questions asked.

Kenson explained his situation again. The guard politely replied that he had no knowledge of this and reiterated that he could be terminated if he admitted Kenson, who pleaded for the guard to call the band or manager or anyone and verify his story. The guard replied that people say all kinds of things to get backstage and that he wasn't going to call the band every time someone requests it. Meanwhile the band wonders where Kenson is.

1. Was the security guard correct to disallow Kenson to gain backstage access?
2. What could be done to salvage the situation at this point?
3. How could this have been avoided?

### Two Different Groups

Buena View Resort is a 3½-star property located in Tampa, Florida. The beautiful property boasts splendid views of the ocean from the endless pool in a tranquil environment. The artwork and the landscaping are palatial. It typically accommodates business travelers during the week and leisure travel and catered events during the weekends. Mr. and Mrs. Baker traveled to Tampa for an extended weekend getaway to celebrate their 40th wedding anniversary. The rates were relatively high compared to what they were accustomed to, but they decided to splurge because of the occasion and the wonderful property that they would surely enjoy.

The Bakers checked in on Thursday evening and enjoyed a quiet arrival. They noticed a few other couples and business travelers scattered around the pool area quietly enjoying the view. They decided to have dinner and enjoy the tranquility. It was a delight! After dinner, they had a few cocktails and then retired to their room for the evening. They were off to a great start in celebrating their anniversary. They rose early the next morning and had breakfast by the pool. It was so beautiful.

Just after breakfast, a number of vans of young girls began arriving. The girls immediately ran out to the pool area with their luggage and lounged in groups. They were laughing and joking and performing small, theatrical dance routines throughout the pool area. Others groups arrived and began congregating in the other public areas of the resort.

The Bakers questioned a few of the girls near them and soon realized that they were the early arrivals of what would be a cheerleading competition at the resort. From that point forward, the resort was filled with groups of texting tween and teen cheerleaders and their chaperones.

The Bakers realized that the cheerleaders had a right to be there, but their tranquil experience was being infringed upon. They couldn't go anywhere around the resort without being inundated by spontaneous chanting and cheer practice of groups.

By the Saturday morning, they were very aggravated. They approached the front desk and described their situation. They explained they had paid a lot of money and that they expected a tranquil experience. The front desk attendant quickly apologized. He admitted that it can be distracting with all of the commotion and that he would speak to the organizers

of the event. He gave them both a free pass to the spa for a massage. He told them that he hoped the massage would help them to regain the tranquility. The Bakers thanked the attendant and took the passes and left to get a massage. However, the cheering and groups continued. They overwhelmed the couple, who left feeling very aggravated.

1. Describe the issue between the two sets of guests.
2. Rate the service recovery effort. How could it have been helped?
3. List ideas for accommodating both groups.

## Let Me Tell You Want You Want

Mr. Garrison is a seasoned business traveler. He travels in excess of 200 nights a year. He typically stays at another popular 3-star hotel because of the brand and the reward points, but tonight decides to try a new, sleek hotel named T.

After a long flight, Mr. Garrison's cab pulls up to the curb at the T. He gets out and looks around. It is a great-looking property, but something is odd. It is very quiet and he sees no one. He grabs his bags and enters through the front doors. He looks around and sees small stations with computer modules arranged around a small lobby. It is oddly small and very quiet, and he sees no one. He walks up to one of the computer stations and begins to look at it. Within a few seconds, Josh, an attendant in a fashionable uniform, comes out of the back office and greets him. Josh asks if Mr. Garrison is checking in. Mr. Garrison looks down at his bags and replies, "Of course." Josh then asks him to step over to another computer station, where he is logged in. Josh is very polite and smiles the entire time. Mr. Garrison is a bit troubled because Josh did not notice that Mr. Garrison is new to the property and the protocol. Josh quickly finds the reservation and notes that there are no preferences. He asks if Mr. Garrison has any allergies. Mr. Garrison, acting troubled, replies, "No." Josh assigns a room and then asks him if he would like help with his bags. Mr. Garrison refuses help, stating that since he has already brought them in it doesn't matter at this point. Mr. Garrison is directed to the elevators. Upon looking at the room number, he realizes that it is on a higher floor than he expected. He prefers lower floors so that he won't have to deal with traffic in the event of an emergency. He says nothing and proceeds. Upon entering the room, he sees that it doesn't have the king-sized bed he is accustomed to. It is also very cold in the room because the thermostat was set to 55 degrees. He tries to change it but realizes that it is controlled through a computer module in the room. He turns and opens the curtains to find that the room also doesn't have much of a view. He tries to connect his computer and realizes that he isn't sure how to connect to the Wifi. A short time after this, Josh calls the room to see how everything is going and to ask whether Mr. Garrison needs anything else. Mr. Garrison begins to take Josh up on his offer. He replies, "Yes. There are many things. No one helped me with my bags. I prefer a low floor, and I received a high floor. I need to use the Internet before I can go to sleep. I prefer a king-sized bed. What kind of view is this? Who lives in temperatures this cold? I need the air conditioning changed now! In fact, I think that I need a new hotel!"

Josh is surprised to hear this. He thought things were going well.

1. Describe the expectations of Mr. Garrison.
2. Describe the gap between Mr. Garrison's expectations and the service provided.
3. How should Josh handle Mr. Garrison at this point?
4. What should the hotel have done differently to avoid this disparity?

 CASE STUDIES *continued*

## Sunset Cruises

Sunset Cruises is a small, family-owned and operated sailing operation located in the quaint port of Grand Island. It provides sightseeing cruises throughout the tourist season. It features music and provides appetizers, wine, and cocktails. It accommodates mostly couples and groups. It provides breath-taking views in a relaxed setting.

Ken and Stan were a middle-aged couple that had been vacationing in the area and decided to attend the evening cruise after noticing it during an evening walk. The price on the sign read:

- sailing nightly
- $45 per person
- reservations encouraged
- sorry, no refunds

The pier was busy. They did not have a reservation, so they approached the counter. Ken asked if there were openings on this evening's cruise, to which the attendant responded, "Sure. We sail in just a couple of minutes. Two?" They were pleased, because the boat appeared to be filling. He replied, "Yes. Two please." Ken then asked, "Do you have any discounts?" The attendant replied, "No, I'm sorry there are no discounts available at this time." It was Sunset Cruises' policy not to offer discounts or negotiate at the counter. Only previously negotiated discounts would be honored. Ken was reluctant to pay the full price of $90.00 for two tickets, but agreed and paid, then he and Stan moved over to the side near the boat to wait for the cruise to begin.

Next in line was a young couple. The attendant asked if they have a reservation, to which they smilingly reply, "Yes, Mr. and Mrs. Drew." They had reservations that were made through their Inn, a preferred vendor who had discount coupons for 50% off a cruise for two. The couple had received it as part of a midweek promotional package. Ken and Stan overheard the attendant ask the couple for $45. Concerned, Ken waits until their transaction is complete and then immediately approaches the counter, pushing in front of the next person in line. He begins to raise his voice and state to all that could hear the previous couple only paid $45 for two tickets. He then accuses the attendant of lying to them because she "does not like their type" because she didn't tell them about the deals. Ken demands that they receive an apology and a half-price discount or a refund immediately.

1. Describe the issues. Was the attendant at fault?
2. Should the same discounts be made available to every guest?
3. What should the attendant do to remedy the situation?

## Bakery Pricing

Main Street Bakery is an upscale, trendy bakery that recently opened in a renovated filling station. It resides in a transitional, mixed neighborhood that is being rejuvenated by a local artisan crowd. The area still has a traditional class of blue-collar locals, but has recently seen an influx of a younger class of professionals and lovers of art, literature, and all things socially conscious that has spilled out from the nearby city. Main Street Bakery features

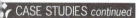

socially responsible prepared breads and pastries baked on the premises in an open kitchen. It also roasts its own coffee on the premises.

One day, two customers enter the bakery and begin to complain loudly about the size of the coffee for the money. One of the customers walks up to the counter and abruptly asks how they justify charging that much for coffee. The customer loudly states that the chain down the street is way cheaper.

The owner-manager of the Main Street Bakery hears this and walks over to introduce herself. She smiles and welcomes them to her bakery. She thanks them for entering her establishment to check it out. She explains that it is premium coffee, fair trade certified, and roasted in-house. She assures them it is a much better cup of coffee than the competitor down the street and offers to give them both a free sample. The two customers are hesitant but begin to cautiously let down their guard.

1.  Describe the idea behind Main Street Bakery.
2.  Describe the difference in the types of clientele they are likely to serve.
3.  Rate the response of the owner-manager.

# EXERCISES

### Exercise 1: Answering a Customer Complaint Letter

**Directions:** Below is a complaint letter. Consider the type of customer, the service experience, and the impact of the situation.

1.  In this letter, list all of the red flags.
2.  As the owner, compose a letter of apology. Take any actions you deem most appropriate.

October 1, 2011
Mary and James Swanson
The Jan House on John's Pond
Covington, New Hampshire

Dear Mr. and Mrs. Swanson:

This is the first time that I have ever written a letter like this. We are so upset that we felt compelled to let you know of our recent experience. We had dinner reservations at the Jan House for a party of six under my wife's name, Dr. Harrigan, for Saturday evening, October 1, 2011. We were hosting my wife's sister and her husband visiting from New York.

We were promptly seated according to our reservations at 6:00 pm in the dining room. The dining room was nearly empty with at least three-quarters of the tables unseated. We were given menus, a wine list, water, rolls, and butter. We then sat for nearly 20 minutes until the cocktail waitress asked us for our drink orders. I think that she was out back smoking, because she smelled of cigarettes. My sister-in-law said, after being asked "What else would you like," "I'll have a Grey Goose martini straight up with an olive"—a relatively standard

drink. The cocktail waitress immediately responded, "I'm not a stenographer." My sister-in-law politely repeated her drink order. There was no apology for the lateness.

The dining room was quiet so we could hear the kitchen and bar area. We sat there for the next 10 minutes listening to our cocktail waitress tell the bartender about her broken-down car and her boyfriend troubles. By the end, we felt as if we knew her life story. It was troubling to listen to, and she should have been tending to our drinks! Finally, our waiter arrived, informing us of the specials for the evening. I do not remember his name, but he had blonde hair, wore glasses, and had his sleeves rolled up, displaying tattooed arms. Our drinks still had not arrived, so I asked about them and he said that he would check into it. He immediately left to check on the drinks. It was so quiet that we heard him ask about the drink order, and a small argument erupted between the cocktail waitress and our waiter. We could hear the whole thing! He returned promptly with our drinks. He acted concerned but was unaware that we heard the entire dispute.

We then requested appetizers so that we could get started with the meal. He politely informed us that he could not order appetizers without ordering our entrees and dessert at the same time since it was a prix-fixe meal. We felt placed on the spot, so we decided to order everything. When the waiter asked my wife for her order, he addressed her as "Dear." When he served her the meal, he also called her sister "Dear." They did not appreciate this term.

At of 7:00, we requested that our salads be brought to us as soon as possible. I then asked an assistant to bring us more rolls as each of us had been served one when we were seated. His response was "Who wants a roll?" Caught off guard, we went around the table saying yes or no so that he would know exactly how many "extra" rolls to bring to our table. It seems as if rolls should automatically be refilled at an establishment such as yours.

Our salads were finally served at 7:15. At 7:45, we asked about our entrees. They were served at 8:00. This was 2 hours after we were seated in a restaurant that was three quarters empty. I must also add that we had to make constant requests for water refills and a butter replacement.

The food was excellent and the property is delightful. Despite all of this, our dinner was a complete disaster. We were extremely upset and insulted with our experience at the Jan House. Your staff is not well trained and very unprofessional. We will not likely return to the Jan House. Also know that we will share our experiences with friends and business associates.

Sincerely,
Dr. E. Harrigan
10 Main Street
Boston, MA

### Exercise 2: Handling Difficult Guests

**Directions:** Below is a chart with customer catchphrases. Fill in the chart with the most appropriate customer type, premise, and solution strategy.

| Customer Type (fill in) | Customer Catchphrase | Premise (fill in) | Solution Strategy (fill in) |
|---|---|---|---|
| | You people are so uptight in your suits. Why don't you wear flip-flops? | | |
| | This whole process is so confusing that you need an MBA to figure it out. | | |
| | I think my 15-year-old son is having a party at home and my husband is about to leave me. | | |
| | I would like to know all of your specials and the lowest price available. | | |
| | I've had better days. | | |
| | I am doing so much better now that you are waiting on me. | | |
| | Don't they train you people? | | |
| | I'm going to call my friend, the CEO of the company! | | |

*(Continued)*

| Customer Type (fill in) | Customer Catchphrase | Premise (fill in) | Solution Strategy (fill in) |
|---|---|---|---|
| | I have never been treated this way in all of my years! | | |
| | Why did the chicken cross the ice skating rink? | | |

# Section II

# Relating Service to the Sectors of the Hospitality Industry

# The Guest Service of Food

## Chapter Objectives:

*After reading this chapter, you should be able to:*

Identify and describe all the major food-service styles.

Identify and define FOH and BOH positions as they relate to service.

Identify and explain the uses of various service wares.

Compare and contrast the differences between classical dining, American fine dining, and casual dining services.

Explain and apply the procedures of greeting and seating customers in a full-service restaurant.

## Terminology:

BOH
Chit
Classical Brigade
Cover
Crumbing
FOH
Frontline Worker
Mise en Place
Turnover

# Introduction: About the Service of Food

There is much more to the service of food than meets the eye. To the customer, the service of food represents many things sacred. They may not initially come to mind, but they are certainly noticed when they are absent. Food service may represent:

- *Offering*: A gift, although you pay, is offered.
- *History*: The ideas, rules, and rituals associated with the serving of food dates back to the beginning of civilization.
- *Artisanship*: The pride and skill of mastering a craft.
- *Community*: Of time with family, friends, or even others at the counter or in the dining room.
- *Function*: A meeting or a business transaction.
- *Occasion*: An appreciation, a date, or a celebration.
- *Retreat*: To a memory, an adventure, or an escape.
- *Indulgence*: A deserved reward or a welcomed treat.
- *Promise*: A trust that food is wholesome and safe.
- *Statement*: Of status or religion, belief, or consciousness.
- *Rest*: A signal to stop work briefly and relax.
- *Nourishment*: It may be basic calories, as provided in a quick lunch, or very formal, but everyone needs nourishment for life. It is at the base of Maslow's Hierarchy of Needs.

Photo Courtesy of Darden Concepts, Inc.

Food service is much more than the serving of food. Consider this, when something goes wrong, it may represent far more than a simple breach of a rule. To the customer, it may represent:

- An insult to someone's religion.
- An important celebration or business transaction.
- The only rest time of their day.
- Something they were looking forward to for a long time.

Treat these things as sacred and you will be on the way to successful service of food with quality guest service.

# Positions

Most food-service operation positions are divided into two separate areas:

- **Front of the House (FOH).**
- **Back of the House (BOH).**

**Front of the House (FOH)**
The service area in view of the customers.

**Back of the House (BOH)**
All areas that are not seen by the typical customer.

**Frontline Workers**
The employees who directly serve the customers.

The FOH is in plain view of the customers. The staff in FOH positions are under close watch of the public eye. The **frontline workers** are the employees who work directly with the customer. Their presentation and professionalism are of utmost importance. The BOH is all of the area where the customers typically cannot go. Most of the actions of the BOH are behind the scenes and out of view of the general public. Despite being out of the general view of the customer, their role in supporting the customer should not go unmentioned. They are essential to supporting customer service and the industry. The terms *FOH, BOH,* and *frontline worker* are used throughout the hospitality industry. Walt Disney World uses the terms *on stage* and *off stage* to impart the idea of a performance whenever an employee is within view of the public.

## ❦ FRONT OF THE HOUSE

In a small restaurant, there may just be a handful of employees in the FOH. In a large operation there may be as many as 50 or even 100 or more. The positions that make up the FOH may be combined, but when separate, they are as follows:

- *Greeter or Host/Hostess:* This is often the first person guests see. They are the first point of contact and set the tone of the establishment. This may be on the telephone, at the door, or at the host station. Their primary duties involve welcoming, receiving, guest concerns, safeguards for concerns (bottlenecks, notifies kitchen, servers . . .). They give wait times, assign tables, seat guests, provide menus, and provide general information. This position is not needed in quick-service or operations in which the customers seat themselves.

- *Bartender*: This position may prepare drinks or "tend" the main bar or a service bar, which is designed for the dining room orders. This position is covered more in the beverage chapter.
- *Bar Back*: This position is the assistant to the bartender and performs lesser tasks.
- *Servers*: This is often the primary point of contact for the guests. They oversee the service of the table. Depending on the amount of support staff and level of service, they may make suggestions, take beverage and food orders, deliver food and beverage, present bills, and provide general care for the table.
- *Busser*: This position is an assistant to the server. They clear and set tables, provide bread and water, and provide general assistance to the servers.

## Service Insight

### FOH versus BOH

Like cats and dogs, like brothers and sisters, like night shift and day shift, the front of the house and the back of the house fight. They also tease, flirt, and harass. This common discontinuity will break down even the best of operations. A key to helping this is to break down the barriers. Allow employees to experience the other positions. Cross-train employees, rotating them through departments. This can be done in orientation, or to break up the routine of a stagnant worker. Much respect can be gained as a result of walking in the shoes of another.

## ❦ BACK OF HOUSE

The BOH is very different from the FOH. You can feel the entire climate change as you pass through the kitchen doors and proceed "off stage." The carpeted floor stops, air conditioning stops, and the fine décor is replaced with functional, militaristic décor. It is all about getting the job done in the BOH to support everything that occurs seamlessly in the FOH.

**Back of house kitchen setting.** Photo Courtesy of S. Markham.

Part of the origins of the BOH as we know it comes from Augustus Escoffier. He was known as the Father of Modern Cuisine. He was the first credited with creating a system of organization for large hotels and kitchens commonly referred to as the **Classical Kitchen Brigade**. He was also credited with creating one of the first versions of the modern-day menu. Escoffier ran his kitchen like a military post. Everyone had a specific position, or station, with specific tasks. There was little or no duplication of these tasks. It was simple, effective, and efficient. Scaled-down versions of the stations and the militarist demeanor are carried over into today's Americanized versions of the classical brigade. French terminology is also still common, especially in upscale food-service operations. Below are some of the stations of the classical brigade:

**Classical Kitchen Brigade**
A system of stations in the kitchen where everyone has a specific purpose.

- *Chef du Cuisine*: the Head Chef; in charge of the kitchen
- *Sous Chef*: second in charge of the kitchen
- *Saucier*: in charge of sautéed items and soups, sauces
- *Poissonier*: in charge of seafood dishes
- *Grillardin*: in charge of grilled dishes
- *Friturier*: in charge of fried
- *Rotisseur*: in charge of roasted items, mostly meats
- *Entremetier*: in charge of warm vegetables
- *Garde-Manger*: in charge of cold food and salads
- *Patissier*: in charge of pastries

As kitchens progressed and less food was prepared from scratch, the positions were combined. Below is a table comparing the relationship among positions of classical European dining, American fine dining, and American casual dining. Note, many of the positions have been combined.

## ❖ BOH STAFF COMPARISON

| Classical European Dining | American Fine Dining | American Casual Dining |
|---|---|---|
| Chef du Cuisine | Executive Chef | Kitchen Manager |
| Sous Chef | Sous Chef | Combined |
| Saucier | Saute Station | Saute Cook |
| Poissonier | Poissonier | Combined |
| Grillardin | Grill Station | Grill Cook |
| Friturier | Combined | Fry Cook |
| Rotisseur | Combined | Combined |
| Entremetier | Combined | Combined |
| Garde-Manger | Pantry Chef | Cold station |
| Patissier | Pastry Chef | Combined |

The front of the house has also scaled down staff from the classical hierarchies. A few classical French terms such as maître d' and sommelier remain in several settings. Recently French terms have begun to emerge as part of an organizational culture, bringing an elevated level of sophistication to the establishment. Whatever the names, the jobs still get done. The higher the level of service of the establishment, the more positions are required. Below are some of the typical positions present in fine-dining FOH:

- *Sommelier (chef de vin)*: Professional dedicated to wine and beverage service and all aspects from menus to sales to inventory. There are certification and levels. This position is becoming more common in today's culture and renewed interest in wines.
- *Dining Room Manager (maître d'hotel or maître d')*: Supervises all dining room operations. More commonly, greets and seats the guests.
- *Head Waiter (chef de sale)*: In charge of all waitstaff and oversees the table.
- *Captain (chef d'étage)*: Has the most guest contact once they are seated. Explains the menu, answers questions, takes orders, and performs any tableside cooking.
- *Front Waiter (chef de rang)*: Sets the table for each course, delivers food, assists the captain.
- *Back Waiter (demi-chef de rang or commis de rang or busser)*: The least experienced; fills water, clears the table, assists with lower-end tasks.

The positions are reduced and combined with levels of service and the American influence. The table below shows how the FOH service staff changed from classical European style to American fine dining to casual dining.

## ❖ FOH SERVICE STAFF

| Classical European Dining | American Fine Dining | American Casual Dining |
|---|---|---|
| Receptionniste | Host/Hostess | Host/Hostess/Greeter |
| Maître d'Hotel | Dining Room Supervisor | Combined |
| Chef de Salle | Head Server | Server |
| Sommelier | Wine Steward/ Sommelier | Combined |
| Chef d' étage | Server | Food Runner |
| Chef de Rang | Combined | Combined |
| Demi-Chef de Rang | Busperson | Busser |

# Wares and Settings

##  PLACE SETTINGS

Every establishment has its own variation, each claiming to be the correct interpretation and the absolute standard. Variations come from a blend of etiquette books, regions, time periods, necessity, and practicality. With all of the different rules, even the staff and guests are left wondering.

Despite the differences of opinion, there are general rules common to the industry. Below are three levels of service with general rules and variations accompanying each of them.

Photo Courtesy of Cardinal International.

### Casual Place Setting

- Use: casual dining to upscale casual dining
- Courses included: bread and water, salad, main meal, coffee
- Left of plate: salad fork, dinner fork
- Right of plate: dinner spoon, dinner knife
- Top left: bread and butter plate (B&B)
- Top right: water glass
- Optional: salad fork, B&B, butter knife on B&B, table covering, which may be glass over cloth, paper, linen, or matted
- Variations: All flatware may be wrapped in napkin or ring. Fork(s) can be on top of napkin and/or higher-quality disposable napkins may be used. More casual service omits all but a napkin, fork, knife, spoon, placemat, and water.
- Rules: Salad fork is placed on the outside, knife facing inward toward plate.

### Formal Place Setting

- Use: upscale dining establishments, 3 Stars/Diamonds
- Courses included: bread and water, soup, salad, appetizer, entree, dessert
- Left of plate: appetizer fork, salad fork, dinner fork, dessert fork
- Right of plate: dinner knife, salad knife, dinner spoon, soup spoon, teaspoon
- Top left of plate: B&B
- Top right of plate: water glass, red wine glass, white wine glass
- Optional: Plate may not be present. Contemporary interpretations may disregard many rules. Symmetry and space allowance may also take precedence in arrangement.

**Formal setting for individual course with base plate.** Photo Courtesy of Cardinal International.

- Variations: Flatware may be set with each course.
- Rules: Linen tablecloths, no disposable cloths, flatware set in order of use from the outside working inward, knives turned inward toward plate.

### Ultra-Formal Dining

- Use: classical, 4 to 5 Star/Diamond dining
- Courses may include: bread and water, multiple wines, soup, salad, appetizers, intermezzos, seafood, vegetable, meat, aperitif, fruit and cheese, dessert
- Left of plate: appetizer fork, seafood fork, salad fork, meat fork, dessert fork
- Right of plate: salad knife, fish knife, meat knife, dinner spoon, soup spoon, tea spoon, oyster fork, coffee cup
- Top left of plate: B&B
- Top right of plate: champagne flute, red wine glass, white wine glass, sherry glass, water goblet
- Optional: top plate as a base or show plate, removed upon seating
- Variations: There may be as many aspects of the settings as there are courses. The napkin to the left of forks, in a wrap around flatware, or folded anywhere else on table. Flatware and accompaniments may be reset with each course. The dessert spoon and cake fork may be at 12 o'clock above the plate, the oyster fork may be slanted inward. Coffee may be served butler style (as requested). Symmetry of arrangement may not prevail.
- Rules: Fine linen napkins and multiple-layer tablecloths are essential. Napkins are placed on guests' laps by staff upon seating. All flatware should be placed in the order of use, beginning on the outside and working inward. The flatware should be 1 inch from the edge of the table or placed on an invisible median line parallel with the table. Glasses should be an inch above the knives and in order of use, typically champagne, white, red, dessert, and water.

**Formal setting for individual course with base plate.** Photo Courtesy of Cardinal International.

## ❧ MISE EN PLACE

**Mise en place** is a very common term in the hospitality industry. It loosely translates to, "everything in its place." It is the assembling of everything that you will need to perform the job at task prior to beginning it. It requires thinking ahead about precisely how you will execute the task. It requires you to think about the steps and the materials you will need. It eliminates unnecessary running around during the task, builds confidence, and demonstrates competence. Everything will be set up, making the task much easier and more efficiently performed.

Photo Courtesy of Cardinal International.

*Service Ware*: Term for all wares used by the guests
*China*: Plates, dishes, cups, saucers
*Flatware*: Knives, forks, spoons
*Glassware*: All glasses; also carafes, pitchers, decanters
*Hollowware*: Larger ware items such as platters, coffee pots, trays
*Gueridon*: A cart for tableside service
*Recheud*: A heating source
*Side Items*: Bread baskets, crumbing plate, doilies, flatware, napkins, sweeteners, wine bucket, ketchup, mustard, vinegar, birthday setup

**Mise en Place**
Loosely translates to "everything in its place." Having all materials assembled prior to starting a task. For example, a waiter obtains his mise en place prior to beginning his shift. He would ensure that he has his uniform in order, checks his reservations, checks the specials, and makes sure he has his notepad, corkscrew, crumber, pens, and so on.

**Formal setting for individual course with base plate.** Photo Courtesy of Cardinal International.

5 ⅝-inch cocktail fork     5 ⅞-inch escargot fork     7-inch U.S. salad fork

7 ⅛-inch fish fork     7 ¼-inch dessert fork     8½-inch dinner fork

10 ⅛-inch serving fork

Photos Courtesy of Cardinal International.

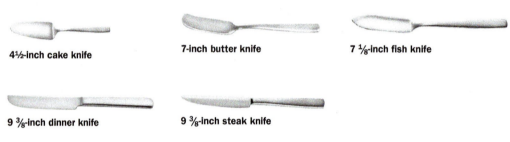

4½-inch cake knife     7-inch butter knife     7 ⅛-inch fish knife

9 ⅜-inch dinner knife     9 ⅜-inch steak knife

Photos Courtesy of Cardinal International.

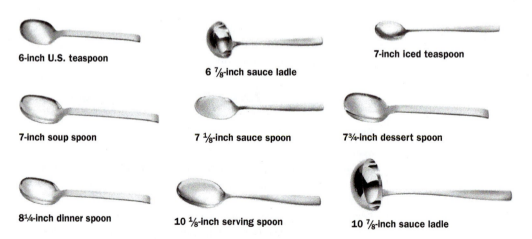

6-inch U.S. teaspoon     6 ⅞-inch sauce ladle     7-inch iced teaspoon

7-inch soup spoon     7 ⅛-inch sauce spoon     7¾-inch dessert spoon

8¼-inch dinner spoon     10 ⅛-inch serving spoon     10 ⅞-inch sauce ladle

Photos Courtesy of Cardinal International.

# Service Styles

## ❧ AMERICAN DINNER SERVICE

The term used to describe service of food is dinner service. It is appropriate for meals throughout the day, with the evening meal being the most formal. Full-service restaurants are also known as American Service or Sit-Down Service in the United States. They are everywhere, and everyone has been to them. Consequently, guests have developed opinions and preferences regarding their expectations. The typical pattern of a sit-down dinner service is:

1. Greet the guests
2. Seat the guests
3. Take the drink orders
4. Serve the drinks
5. Take the dinner orders
6. Serve the dinner orders
7. Clear the dinners
8. Wrap any leftovers
9. Present the bill

Of course, there are variations. Some guests will seat themselves, and other courses are added for appetizers and desserts, but the idea is generally the same: drink, food, and bill. It would be great if it were only that simple to please the guests. Why do so many places get it wrong? In the following, we break it down and provide some tips.

1. *Greet the guests*: Immediately acknowledge their presence.
   - Smile. When you smile, it typically is returned with a smile.
   - Open and hold the door, if possible.

### Service Insight

**Special Occasions**

Many people celebrate special occasions at restaurants. Sometimes the host is told that it is a birthday, and other times the host needs to inquire. Every place has a unique way of handling birthdays. Many casual restaurants have a parade of servers, each dragged away from their table, often singing a version of "Happy Birthday" for the 28th time that evening, before quickly running into the kitchen to tend to their other duties. A complimentary desert is common. Other restaurants have special drinks, sparklers, hats, and even rose petals. However the establishment decides to celebrate special occasions, a few considerations should be kept in mind:

- Make it fitting to the level of service you provide.
- Make it easy to tolerate for the others in the restaurant.
- Make it appropriate for the level of attention that the patron desires.

- Give them a warm welcome. Use their names, if possible.
- Greet them appropriately accordingly.
- Don't label. Don't assume anything. A "daughter" might actually be a "wife" or a "date".
- Ask if they have a reservation.
- Ask for the number in the party and their intentions (for dinner?).
- Ask whether they have a seating preference.

2. *Seat the guests*: Assess their needs and accommodate them. Seat with a server as appropriately as possible. Walk them to the table or inform them of the wait time or options.
   - Pull out the chair for women, if possible.
   - Hand out menus.
   - Inform them of the next step, such as "André will be with you shortly."
   - Inform the server.
   - Also, everyone should know that it is their responsibility to greet guests, not just that of the host/hostess.

   Tables are numbered in a system or pattern. Server stations are generally two to five tables, with three being very common. This will also depend on the level of service dictated. Food orders are typically taken in order of where the patrons are seated at the table.

3. *Take the drink orders*: This step begins the tangible aspects of hospitality. Although the customers are paying, they still perceive it as a hospitable gesture.

---

## Service Insight

### Menu Knowledge

While a menu may be the *silent salesperson*, the server is the *talking salesperson*. The server should know more about the menu than the customer does. They should be well-versed in nutritional information, allergens, tastes, favorites, portion sizes, substitutes, what is 86'd (out), and what is ideal for customers in a hurry.

---

4. *Serve the drinks*: Quickly and accurately assess their needs. Do they want to order? Explain the menu, present specials, and answer questions.

5. *Take the dinner orders*: Begin with a woman and continue counterclockwise. If possible, memorization is great, but it is more reliable if you write it down. In a full-service restaurant orders are taken at the table and entered into a computer system. This system routes the orders to the proper kitchen station. The order tickets, or chits, are printed and then prepared. A **chit** is a slang term for an order ticket. Some kitchen have eliminated paper tickets and gone to a screen in the kitchen.

6. *Serve the dinner orders*: A food runner may deliver the dinner orders; the server or the food runner should stay and ask if anyone needs anything else, or check back within two to three minutes.

**Chit**
Slang for order ticket. Often printed for line-cooks to prepare. Sometimes referred to as a dupe (short for duplicate from the old carbon-copy checks).

---

**Service Insight**

**Approaching the Table**

Table approaches are as unique as restaurants. A few commonly used greetings are:

Hello my name is . . .

I'll be your server this evening.

I'll be your server tonight.

I'll be taking care of you tonight.

I'll be taking care of you guys tonight.

How are you tonight?

Welcome to the _____! Is this your first time with us?

Or, simply, "Drink order?"

What is the best way to approach a table? Most chains have standardized greetings that *most* servers follow. Private restaurants tend to have less standard approaches and are subject to the server's discretion, which can lead to a number of issues. Almost all greetings are pleasant, but also, most are insincere and forgettable. What is the most appropriate way to greet a table? It depends on the setting, the guests, and the expectations. A formal setting will dictate formality in a greeting, while casual operations are open to subjectivity. Some guests prefer a casual approach while others prefer formality and won't tolerate anything less. Gauging this incorrectly can really hurt the experience. It is always better to begin more formally. Lately, the trend has been to begin with formality and then adapt to allow the level of service to be tailored to the individual guest. However, always remain professional.

---

There are strong differences of opinion. Different rules and cultures have blurred the map, each claiming to be an absolute authority. Some of the more contemporary operations instruct their wait staff to follow the general guidelines, while paying close attention to the guest, being reasonable, and remaining flexible in an effort to keep the guest feeling comfortable. Generally, the more formal the setting, the stricter the rules. The most appropriate for American style service is:

- Use a right hand to serve from the left side, and a left hand to serve from the right side.
- Appetizers and salads: Served from the right with your right hand. Flatware preset.
- Soups: Doily, bowl on plate, spoon on right. Preset. Served from right with right hand.
- Entrée: From the right with right hand. Logo or main item facing the guest. Flatware preset or reset between courses. Side dishes to the left.
- Dessert: Preset or reset between courses. Flatware to the left. From the right with right hand.
- Beverages from the right, served or poured from the right.
- Clearing: From the left with left hand.
- Envision a line between the face of the guest and the plate. Never cross over this line.

**Desserts should be served with flatware to the left, and served from the right with the right hand.**
Photo Courtesy of Darden Concepts, Inc.

- Always serve in a counterclockwise fashion.
- Always begin serving with a woman, usually to the left of the host.

**Crumbing**
Use of a tool to scrape bread crumbs from the table between courses in fine-dining restaurants.

7. *Clear the dinners*: Clear after each course unless directed by the customer to leave. Always confirm before removing items. Look for signs: napkin on plate, plate pushed out of way, fork upside down across top of plate, both knife and fork together across plate, no food left, or a lot of time has passed. Crumb scrapers are an essential tool in fine dining. **Crumbing** is the process of scraping breadcrumbs, and the like, off the table between courses. Crumbs are usually scraped onto a napkin held by the waiter on the edge of the table.

8. *Wrap the leftovers*: How are leftovers handled? Everyone has a different idea. Some people consider it rude to take home leftover food. Others place it in a "doggie bag," although most pet owners wouldn't feed it to their pets for fear of making them sick. Others want to enjoy the rest of the meal at another time. For those guests, leftovers can be made special. Some are boxed at the table, while many are boxed out of sight. Leftovers made classy can be a great chance for the guests to have fond memories of the meal, associating the restaurant with class. It can also be a form of advertising. Consider this the next time a meal is thrown into a Styrofoam container in which it congealed on the side of the container.

9. *Present the bill*: Discreetly present the bill to the head of the table or to whoever requests it. Place the bill in the middle of the table when unsure. Thank the host and the rest of the table. People may be ready to leave, so settle payment as promptly as needed according to their terms.

---

**Service Insight**

### Lingering Customers

Customers are wonderful for business. You want them to patronize your business. You want them to enjoy themselves. You also want them to leave in a reasonably timely manner so that you can "turn the table". Many tactics exist to expedite the process without seeming to rush the guests. The courses are kept moving along. The plates are cleared. A check is offered. Lights levels are changed. Despite this, some guests set up camp and linger for hours. What can you do? At a finer restaurant, there is little that you can do. It is considered rude and disrespectful to rush or push customers. In diners, there is an expectation of leaving once finished if other customers are waiting, so it might be acceptable to rush them if the table is desperately needed. If the level of service is between a diner and a fine-dining restaurant, you could offer them a drink or dessert at the bar. If that doesn't work and you ask them to leave, you will likely lose the customer. Before you rush anyone, think about how badly you really need the table.

---

## ❦ SERVICE STYLE OVERVIEW

American service is common, but it is not the only style available. Below are lists of the most common service styles with descriptions of each.

**Outdoor buffet setting.** Photo Courtesy of S. Markham.

### American Service

- Alias: Full-service, sit-down service, plated service
- Formality: Medium to high
- Dynamics: Food is plated in the kitchen and brought out to the customers
- Skill: Medium
- Labor: Low
- Personalization: Low to medium
- Portion control: High
- Space required: Low
- Speed of service: Medium

### Buffet

- Alias: Smorgasbord
- Formality: Low to medium
- Dynamics: Food is displayed on long tables. Guests pick up their own plate and choose their food. Can be assisted or unassisted.
- Skill: Low
- Labor: Low
- Personalization: Low

**Indoor breakfast buffet setting.** Photo Courtesy of Cardinal International.

- Portion control: Low
- Space required: Low to medium
- Speed of service: High

## Butler Service

- Alias: Passed
- Formality: High
- Dynamics: The same as Russian service (see below), except that guests help themselves from the platter. They use the platter utensils. The guests may be standing, as in a reception, or seated at a table.
- Skill: Medium
- Labor: High
- Personalization: Low
- Portion control: Medium
- Space required: Low
- Speed of service: Low
- Advantages: Guests choose food
- Disadvantages: More space needed; possibility of clumsy guests, cold food, spilling . . .

**Butler service for a group a champagne party.** Photo courtesy of Darden Concepts, Inc.

### Counter Service

- Alias: Limited service
- Formality: High
- Dynamics: Typical in fast-food settings, ordered, prepared in the kitchen, served at the counter. Other variations involve customers making choices as their orders are made in an assembly line, such as at Subway or Chipotle. Also, some will finish in the kitchen and bring it to your table.
- Skill: Low/medium
- Labor: Low
- Personalization: Low/medium
- Portion control: High
- Space required: Low
- Speed of service: High

### Cafeteria Service

- Formality: Low
- Dynamics: Guests choose particular items from a display or buffet and then are charged accordingly at the register. May also be one set price, as in college dining halls.
- Skill: Low

- Labor: Low
- Personalization: Low
- Portion control: Low
- Space required: High
- Speed of service: High

### Dim Sum Service

- Formality: Medium
- Dynamics: Many different carts are wheeled to your table periodically or platters are brought to your table; you choose what you would like. There is typically a system of stamping a card or the like for billing purposes.
- Skill: Low to medium
- Labor: Medium
- Personalization: Low to medium
- Portion control: High
- Space required: Low
- Speed of Service: Medium

### English Service

- Other names: Family style (similar)
- Formality: High
- Dynamics: Resembles gathering of families. All fully-cooked in the kitchen. Mimics home-style cooking. Platters from the kitchen are brought to the head of the table or the host for inspection then set on table or passed. Typically in a private room instead of a main dining room. Variations—leaving salad in middle of table. Guests pass it around the table, or the captain serves around the table.
- Skill: Low to medium
- Labor: Low
- Personalization: Medium
- Portion control: Low
- Space required: Low
- Speed of service: Medium

### French Service

- Other names: Tableside service
- Formality: High
- Dynamics: Tableside preparation of food in front of customer. Crepes, or bananas Foster is common in Americanized versions.
- Skill: High
- Labor: High
- Personalization: High
- Portion control: High
- Space required: High

- Speed of service: Low
- Advantages: Showcases food, entertains, warrants a higher price.
- Disadvantages: Servers must be highly skilled, timely, costly, lowers seating capacity, lengthens seating time, therefore reducing table turnover. May bring unwanted attention to customer.
- Tip: Consider a blend such as ladling a soup tableside.

The classical French multi-course menu may involve upward of 20 courses. Meals were times to savor the experience. America has reduced this to fewer courses. Some of the French terms are still present in today's restaurants.

Wine may be treated as a separate course. Sorbets, or water crackers, may also be used to cleanse the pallet. See Table 4.1 for a comparison of courses among French and American menus.

**Table 4.1   Comparison of Courses among Menus.**

| Classical French Multi-Course Menu (Translation) | American Tasting Menu | American Multi-Course Menu (typical) |
|---|---|---|
| Hors d'oeuvre (Appetizer) | Cold appetizer | Appetizer |
| Potage (Soup) | Soup | Salad |
| Oeuf (Egg) | Fish | Main course |
| Farineux (Starch) | Meat | Dessert, coffee |
| Poisson (Fish) | Salad | |
| Entrée | Dessert, coffee | |
| Sorbet | | |
| Legume (Vegetable) | | |
| Salats (Salad) | | |
| Entrements (Dessert) | | |
| Fromage (Cheese) | | |
| Fruit | | |
| Digestif (Alcohol) | | |

**Russian Service**

- Other names: Platter service
- Formality: High
- Dynamics: Food is prepared in the kitchen and served on platters instead of plates. Plates are set and desired portions are served from the platters with fork-over-spoon manipulation. Platter held in left and spoon/fork with right.
- Skill: Medium, fork-over-spoon technique, easy to spill
- Labor: Medium
- Personalization: Medium to high
- Portion control: Low
- Space required: Medium
- Speed of service: Medium

These service styles can be found in many types of restaurants and event settings. Table 4.2 details the types of restaurants most common to these styles.

Table 4.2 Relating Service Styles to Types of Restaurants.

| Types of Restaurants | Fine Dining | Upscale Casual | Casual or Family | Fast Casual | Quick Service | Banquet or Private Events |
|---|---|---|---|---|---|---|
| **Style of Service** | | | | | | |
| American | X | X | X | | | X |
| Buffet | | X | X | X | | X |
| Butler | X | | | | | X |
| Cafeteria | | | X | | X | |
| Counter | | | | X | X | |
| Dim Sum | X | X | | | | |
| English | X | | X | | | X |
| French | X | X | | | | |
| Russian | | | | | | X |

# Related Points

## ❧ VOLUME

The amount of business that a restaurant achieves can be described different ways. Sales, guest-count, **covers**, and **turnovers**. Sales are measured by the dollar per period, time segment, or shift. Covers are synonymous with meals served, and turnover is the number of times a seat is used and re-seated with another guest.

## ❧ TECHNOLOGY

Computers are now in nearly every food-service setting. Potential customers can check out the menu or view the restaurant on a map or in Google Street view. They can look at other customers' ratings. Customer profiles are created and reservations can be made online. Once they arrive, orders may be taken on a wireless system or input into a computer at a server station. Orders are routed to the appropriate stations in the kitchen. Secure payments are accepted using the newest technologies. Redundancy and reliability are built into the system. Uninterrupted power supplies, printouts, backup systems, and the like are all configured and promise to ensure smooth service.

However, even the most robust system will occasionally fail. What happens when the systems is not available? You can call for help from a technician, but meanwhile you must continue service. You should have everyone trained on a backup system. Have that system ready to go in the event of an emergency. This is typically a low-tech pencil-and-paper system with much verbal interaction. Everything but essentials are delayed, and business is reduced to a minimum until systems are restored.

**Covers**
A dinner or meal for one person. Taken from the classical style of covering each dish when leaving the kitchen.

**Turnover**
Also known as seat turnover, customer turnover, dining room turnover, and churn in a full-service restaurant. Typically expressed for a shift, meal period, or day. The number of times that a seat or table has been seated with a new customer.

---

### Service Insight

#### *Special Requests*

Special requests can be a difficult task for servers. They want to please the customer, but the kitchen staff may not always be as accommodating. Some establishments refuse special requests, while others do anything in their power to make it happen. Most fall somewhere in the middle. Server should never promise until they are sure they can deliver. The kitchen staff must realize that it isn't the server's fault. Also, as competition increases, the customers realize that other businesses will accommodate their requests, and they will simply go there.

---

### Service Insight

#### *Serving Children*

Children can be difficult in a restaurant. Some children are well behaved with conscientious parents; others can bother fellow customers and create havoc. Consider the following tips when dealing with children:

- Let the parents serve the children. Give plates and water to the parents first, and allow them to pass it on to the child.
- Give the parents an out, offering food to go or an area where they can walk with the child until the child is calm.
- Remember that you are a stranger. The child does not know you. Don't expect the child to answer your questions or easily welcome your presence.
- Follow the lead of the parents. They are the caretakers. They will often direct you.
- Don't place the children in high chairs. Set the high chair out for the parents and allow them to seat the child.
- Place lids on cups when possible, and do not add ice.
- Remove knives, flames, and anything else from the reach of the child.
- Check the floor when you present the check. Children are notorious for dropping their belongings, and the parents will appreciate your finding dropped items for them.

---

# CHAPTER REVIEW QUESTIONS

1. List and briefly describe three reasons why BOH and FOH employees might argue.
2. Outline the primary differences between French and Russian service.
3. How many more courses might a classical European fine-dining meal have than an Americanized version?
4. What are some of the most popular service styles at weddings?
5. What is the French equivalent of the term dining room manager?
6. In your opinion, what is the most common service style in the United States?
7. Should food be served from the left or right?
8. Who was Escoffier, and what was his impact on food service?
9. Why do you think that buffets are considered to be less formal?
10. What is the purpose of table numbers?

# CASE STUDIES

## French on the Prairie

Chateau le Petite was a small French restaurant located in the Midwest. It was originally a casual family restaurant that closed after many years. The new owner did much research and determined that the town needed a fine-dining restaurant. He looked at the competitors and found his niche within the fine-dining market. All of his competitors served steaks, barbecue, or Tex-Mex cuisine. He would be an alternative with a sophisticated, authentic, high-end, French restaurant. He decided the locals would appreciate the unique cuisine and use it for a special-occasion dining experience. He went on the Internet and gathered French menus. He combined and refined the items. He included many options for courses and kept the original French names on items whenever possible. He stocked a wall-displayed wine case with reasonably-priced wines from France and all over the world. He spent many hours stripping the walls back to bare concrete. He exposed the old wooden beams wherever he could. He wanted it to look and feel as authentic as possible.

He also offered many tableside items. He hired the best candidates possible for the positions. All of them were fluent in French and were instructed to speak to guests in French whenever possible.

Despite his best efforts and the research that the area could easily accommodate another restaurant, he was busy for only a few weeks in the beginning. After that, customers were not returning to his restaurant. The owner built an awesome restaurant and cannot figure why it won't work.

1. Describe the service style of Chateau le Petite.
2. Rate the level of service of Chateau le Petite
3. Why do you think that guests did not return to Chateau le Petite?

## A Lost Art?

Tableside cuisine is thought to be a lost art. It involves the server being a skilled performer who prepares your food right in front of you, explains the process, and shares the craft. The chef is also another prominent figure whose art is in the cuisine of the restaurant. Many consider themselves fortunate to have the chef come over to visit the table. Lately however, the trade of the elusive and exclusive chef and the art of French tableside service have been replaced with assembly lines of aspiring actors begrudgingly posing as order-takers and food runners. When kitchens are closed to them, guests aren't certain how their food is prepared and they aren't sure that they want to know.

Taco Bell radically changed their system years ago to eliminate the conventional "kitchen," replacing it with an "assembly area." Food is cut, seasoned, and cooked by the distributor and shipped in a tube or a bag all ready to be chilled or heated and assembled. This has reduced training costs significantly. It has increased consistency and the safety of the food. Customers don't seem to mind, as Taco Bell is one of the leading names quick-service restaurants in America. Other kitchens are instituting the same type of changes behind closed doors.

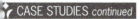

On the other hand, there is a smaller movement for some to open their kitchen doors. Walls are lowered or removed. Guests can and do observe their food being made.

1. Outline the advantages of eliminating the conventional kitchen.
2. Is restaurant service becoming a lost art?
3. What is being done to preserve the artistry?

## Questions During the Day

The Foundry is anything but a foundry. Originally a steel plant, the foundry retained its name as the neighborhood transitioned. Recently, a new restaurant called "The Foundry" has moved into a small storefront of one of the renovated buildings. The Foundry features upscale, American cuisine. It serves dinners only, and is open from 4 to 11 P.M. daily. It has an awesome steel bar with steel bar stools, steel tables, and steel chairs that can be seen from the street through the main window. Many people pass by the storefront and gaze in with curiosity. To help them to decided whether to come in, a telephone number and menu are posted in a steel display case at the front door.

Since it is a small place, a full-time receptionist cannot be afforded during the day. Instead, many calls are fielded when the cleaning and the prep staff are working. They regularly answer questions ranging from simple to difficult. Typical examples of questions might include:

"Are you open?"
"Do you take American Express?"
"Can I bring in a cake?"
"Can I bring my own wine?"
"What is the dress code?"
"Can I reserve for a private party?"

The prep staff is typically busy and ignores the telephone. The cleaning staff usually takes the calls. Most of them speak broken English, but try very hard to always accommodate all requests. They answer what they can, and do the best job possible. They leave notes, but occasionally leave out or miss details.

1. Describe the impression of The Foundry on people walking by during the day.
2. Outline the telephone service at The Foundry.
3. Why is it unrealistic to hire a daytime receptionist?
4. What steps could be taken to ensure appropriate telephone service in line with the expectations of The Foundry?

## Reservations

Fridays and Saturdays, college graduations, Mother's Day, and Valentine's Day can be some of the busiest days for reservations. Some restaurants, like Houston's and Cheesecake Factory do not accept advance reservations. For these restaurants, problems occur. The bar area may be full, the waiting area full, and they end up crowding the entrance. When people have to wait for a long time in these conditions, it takes away from their experience.

For the majority of restaurants who do accept advance reservations, problems also occur. It is not uncommon for guests to make reservations for two, three, four, or even five

restaurants for the same time. They later decide which one to honor and disregard the rest. This causes great turmoil in restaurants that hold tables for parties that do not show. Most restaurants are relatively small and have very limited seating. The host has to stop walk-in seating in advance to ensure there are tables available for reservations. Customers become upset when they are waiting and tables appear open but are being held for late or no-show reservations.

To combat this, most restaurants take a telephone number and a name. Online systems penalize profiles that miss a certain number of reservations. Some restaurants have begun asking for credit card deposits to hold tables. Customers don't like this. Some give a bad card number or will dispute the charge. Despite the best efforts of restaurants, nothing has worked. In cities like Manhattan, some of the most coveted reservations can be found for sale online!

1. Describe the issues with accepting advance reservations in restaurants.
2. In your experience, what have some restaurants done to remedy these problems?
3. In your opinion, is the practice of requiring a credit card for a reservation unacceptable?
4. What do you believe are the best solutions for tackling restaurant reservations?

# The Guest Service of Beverages

## Chapter Objectives:

*After reading this chapter, you should be able to:*

Understand the primary types of beers.

Understand and identify different liquors and their use in cocktail service.

Identify and describe different wines and their service.

Understand the idea and flavor profiles of basic liqueurs.

Identify and describe different types of coffees and waters.

Understand and explain how to serve a bottle of wine or champagne.

Describe the staff positions involved in beverage service.

## Terminology:

| | |
|---|---|
| Aperitif | Premium |
| Call | Proof |
| Cocktail | Speed Rack |
| Cordial | Straight Up |
| Corkage Fee | Tall |
| Decanting | Twist |
| Digestif | Varietal |
| Neat | Well |
| On the Rocks | |

# Wares

Glassware is essential to beverage service. There are many types of glasses available. Each has its specific purpose and holds specific drinks for a specific reason.

- *Stems* are to keep the hands from warming the drink and permit ease of handling and storage. Stems also keep the bowl clean for observation. The staff should never touch above the stem.
  - *Bowls* are often oversized to allow swirling of the beverage. This helps to aerate the beverage after it leaves the bottle. They are usually clear to permit the guest to observe the "legs," "tears," or "curtains" of clear liquid running down the side, which may indicate alcohol content.
  - *Openings* vary greatly. A smaller opening holds in carbonation and fragrance.
  - *Rims* can be thick or thin, open or closed. A tulip-shaped rim closes to maintain delicate fragrances. These qualities also force the mouth to open differently to allow the liquid to hit different parts of the tongue.
  - *Oversizing* is a very popular theme that appears to be here to stay. Average drinks have increased somewhat, but the size of the glasses and garnishes have nearly doubled in recent times. It makes for a spectacular presentation and warrants a higher check average.

Photo Courtesy of Cardinal International.

History, style, use, theme, practicality, preference and expectations all dictate the operation's individual selection and choices of glassware. Hence, there is a great variety in the field. Despite this, there are commonly accepted glasses for most drinks. It is also important to know the common glass types used and to be able to recognize them to identify the drinks.

### Type: Assorted Red Wine Glasses

Qualities: Always stemmed, oversized bowl, clear glass
Sizes: 8 to 20+ oz
Average pour: 5 oz
Uses: Red wines, dessert wines

**11-oz wine glass**

**11-oz tall red wine glass**

**8-oz red wine glass**

Photos Courtesy of Cardinal International.

### Type: Assorted White Wine Glasses

Qualities: Always stemmed, oversized bowl, clear glass
Sizes: 6 to 16+ oz
Average pour: 5 oz
Uses: White wines, nonsparkling wines

**15-oz white burgundy wine glass**　　**4-oz white wine glass**　　**6-oz white wine glass**

Photos Courtesy of Cardinal International.

**Cordial glass**
Photo Courtesy
of Cardinal International.

### Type: Cordial Glass

Qualities: Stemmed, smaller, usually clear
Sizes: 2 to 6 oz
Average pour: 3 oz
Uses: Sweeter dessert wines, such as port, sherry

**Martini/cocktail glass**
Photo Courtesy
of Cardinal International.

### Type: Martini Glass, Cocktail Glass

Qualities: Usually stemmed, classic triangular bowl
Sizes: 6 to 12 oz
Average pour: 4 to 5 oz
Uses: Martinis made of gin or vodka; also manhattans, metropolitans, and gimlets and desserts

**Poco glass**
Photo Courtesy
of Cardinal International.

### Type: Poco Glass

Qualities: Stemmed, simulates hurricane-style lamp
Sizes: 15 to 18 oz
Average pour: 14 oz
Uses: Exotic, tropical drinks such as hurricane, sex on the beach, piña colada, mudslide, and desserts

**Footed beer glass**
Photo Courtesy
of Cardinal International.

### Type: Footed Beer Glass

Qualities: Tapered, larger at top or straight sides with no lip
Sizes: 10 to 20+ oz
Average pour: 8 to 12+ oz
Uses: Pilsner and other beers
*Note*: Beer may also be served in many other items, with the mug being the most common

**High-ball glass**
Photo Courtesy
of Cardinal International.

### Type: High-Ball Glass

Qualities: Stemmed, typically straight or slightly tapered sides
Sizes: 8 to 12 oz
Average pour: 7 to 11 oz
Uses: Elegant mixed drinks, gin and tonics
*Note*: Collins glasses are similar but taller and are used for soft drinks and exotic mixed drinks such as mai tais

**9-oz brandy glass**　**Brandy glass filled**
Photos Courtesy
of Cardinal International.

### Type: Assorted Brandy Snifters

Qualities: Short stem to permit the hand to warm the drink, round bowl to permit swirling
Sizes: 4 to 10 oz
Average pour: 2 oz
Uses: Brandy, cognac, armagnac

**Water glass**　**Water goblet**
Photos Courtesy
of Cardinal International.

### Type: Assorted Water Glasses/Goblets

Qualities: Typically stemmed, heavier to avoid breakage, usually clear
Sizes: 10 to 19 oz
Average pour: Filled and refilled to ½ inch from rim
Uses: Ice water, soft drinks, occasional beer or mixed drink at less-formal venues

**Footed rocks glass**
Photo Courtesy
of Cardinal International.

### Type: Footed Rocks Glasses

Qualities: Sturdy, typically straighter edges, solid base if not stemmed
Sizes: 8 to 12 oz
Average pour: 7 to 11 oz
Uses: Liquors served "on the rocks" or with a "splash"
*Note*: Also known as an old-fashioned glass

**4-oz fluted champagne glass**   **4.5-oz champagne glass (flatter-type)**

Photos Courtesy of Cardinal International.

**Type: Assorted Champagne Glasses**

Qualities: The tall flute holds carbonation the best and has replaced the classic, flatter version in recent times.

Sizes: 4 to 8 oz

Average pour: 5 oz

Uses: Champagne, sparkling wine, desserts

### Monitoring Glassware

- If a glass is half full or less, ask the customer whether he or she wants a refill or another drink.
- Replace the glass each time or as needed.
- Ask before removing a glass.

# Beverages and Their Service

## ❖ KNOWING WINES

Wine is typically made from fermented grapes. Winemakers occasionally use other fruit to make wine, or blend in other ingredients, but the fundamentals of winemaking have not changed over the past several hundred years.

Wines may be classified by color: red, white, and rosé (blush). Most of the color comes from the amount of time wine is kept in contact with the skins of the grapes. Therefore, red wine gets its color from being left in contact with its red skins after crushing. White wines are separated from the skins soon after crushing, and rose or blush wines are left in contact with the skins, but for a shorter period of time than for red.

Wine may be also classified by the type of grape. This is referred to as a **varietal** wine. Common white wine grape varieties are:

**Varietal**
A wine referred to by the type or variety of grape used to make it.

- Chardonnay
- Chenin blanc
- Pinot blanc
- Riesling
- Sauvignon blanc

Common grape varieties that make red wines are:

- Cabernet sauvignon
- Gama (makes Beaujolais)
- Merlot
- Pinot noir
- Syrah/shiraz
- Zinfandel

**A server decanting the wine in front of guests with the proper etiquette.** Photo Courtesy of Darden Concepts, Inc.

sediments from the wine by slowly pouring it into a glass vessel referred to as a decanter. This allows the wine to "breathe" or allow air to come into contact with it. Most of the sediments stay in the bottle, and the rest settle to the bottom of the decanter. A candle is held up to the side of the glass decanter as it is poured to ensure that it is not poured to the point at which the sediments also pour out.

## CHAMPAGNE AND SPARKLING WINE SERVICE

- Present bottle
- Remove cage (be careful where you point the bottle after removal)
- Cover cork with napkin
- Thumb on top, slowly twist the bottle, not the cork
- Pop cork on the edge, slowly permitting the pressure to release, to keep from flying across the room or spilling wine
- Wipe bottle opening
- Pour, wrap napkin around it, and place in the bucket

## ❡ KNOWING COCKTAILS

**Cocktail**
Any combination of alcohols; also known as a mixed drink.

Liquors are the basis of mixed drinks. A **cocktail** is a combination of liquors and/or other sodas, juices, or ingredients. There are seven main liquors used as a basis for most cocktails:

**The bartender's view.** Photo Courtesy of S. Markham.

## Vodka

- Most popular
- Main ingredient: Grain
- Process: Distillation, not aged
- Appearance: Clear
- Taste: No distinct flavor itself, but may be flavored with other ingredients
- Popular brands: Absolut, Stolichnaya, Smirnoff, Grey Goose, Chopin, Skyy, Ciroc

## Gin

- Main ingredient: Grain
- Process: Distillation, not aged
- Appearance: Clear
- Taste: No distinct flavor itself, flavored with juniper berries
- Popular brands: Beefeater, Bombay, Gilbey's, Gordon's, Seagram's, Tanqueray

## Rum

- Main ingredient: Sugarcane, also beets or molasses
- Process: Distillation
- Appearance: Light to dark in color,
- Taste: Rounded, the darker the sweeter
- Popular brands: Bacardi, Captain Morgan, Mount Gay
- Other: Produced everywhere, but originated in the Caribbean

## Tequila

- Main ingredient: Agave plant
- Process: Distillation
- Appearance: Clear
- Taste: Typically biting
- Popular brands: Jose Cuervo, Sauza, Patron, Herradura

## Whiskey

- Main ingredient: Grain mash
- Process: Fermented and distilled, aged in oak barrels, blended or unblended (single-malt)
- Appearance: Medium golden-brown
- Taste: Aromatic, oaky, bold
- Bourbon—American whiskey from Bourbon County, Kentucky (Wild Turkey, Jim Bean, Maker's Mark, Knob Creek)
- Canadian Whiskey (Black Velvet, Canadian Club, Seagram's 7, VO, Crown Royal)
- Irish Whiskey (Bushmill's, Jameson's, Tullamore)
- Scotch Whiskey—Single malts (Dewar's, Johnnie Walker, Chivas Regal, Cutty Sark, J&B)

**Well**
The lowest-quality alcohol of a type on the premises. Usually in the speed rack. Also known as a "pour."

**Speed Rack**
An assortment of the bottles of alcohol most commonly poured. The rack is strategically placed in the most accessible area within easy reach of the bartender. Typically in a certain order, of light to dark, but varies: vodka, gin, rum, tequila, triple sec, whiskey.

**Call**
A high-quality alcohol referred to by its specific brand name instead of type.

**Premium**
The highest and most expensive brands of alcohol, above "call." Also known as "top shelf."

**Cordial**
Any flavored, sweetened alcohol. Also known as "liqueur."

**Digestif**
Alcohol served after a meal.

### Brandy

- Main ingredient: Distilled grapes or other fruit
- The saying goes, all Cognac is brandy but all brandy is not cognac. This is because Cognac must come from the Cognac region of France. Similar definitions occur with Champagne and Bourbon.
- *Cognac* is brandy from the Cognac Region of France.
- *Armagnac* is brandy from the Armagnac Region of France.
- *Calvados* is apple brandy from Normandy.
- *Grappa* is Italian brandy.

### Cordials

Also known as liqueurs, cordials are flavored or sweetened alcohols. They typically have a lower proof than spirits. They are served alone or mixed. Familiarize yourself with the major brands and their flavors:

- Almond: Amaretto
- Anise: Sambuca
- Cherry: Kirsch
- Citrus: Cointreau
- Coffee: Kahlua
- Hazelnut: Frangelico
- Herbal: Galliano
- Honey: Irish Mist
- Melon: Midori

Liquors are typically sorted and priced according to quality. Three main categories are well, call, and premium (they are also called other names) and are ranked from low to high, respectively. Full bars stock all levels and types. Party or banquet bars may stock only a limited selection of the most popular brands.

**Well**: The lowest-quality alcohol of a type on the premises. Usually in the **speed rack**. Also known as a "pour."
**Call**: A high-quality alcohol referred to by its specific brand name instead of type.
**Premium**: The highest and most expensive brands of alcohol, above "call." Also known as "top shelf."
**Cordial**: Any flavored, sweetened alcohol. Also known as "liqueur."
**Digestif**: Alcohol served after a meal.

##  COCKTAIL-ORDERING TERMINOLOGY

Cocktails are ordered in many different styles. Most are chilled with ice. If so, it may be ordered as "on the rocks," or just assumed. If chilled with ice and strained, it is ordered as, "straight up." If preferred at room temperature, it is ordered, "neat." "With a twist" is a request for a twist of a lemon or lime rind to be added as a garnish.

**Neat**
Alcohol at room temperature, without ice.

**On the Rocks**
A drink with ice.

**Proof**
The amount of alcohol in a beverage. Twice the percentage of alcohol.

**Straight Up**
An alcoholic beverage that is chilled, then strained to remove the ice. Also known as "up."

**Tall**
Served in a highball or Collins glass, usually with a larger amount of mixer.

**Twist**
Served with a twist of a lemon or lime peel and rind.

**Neat**: Alcohol at room temperature, without ice.
**On the rocks**: A drink with ice.
**Proof**: The amount of alcohol in a beverage. Twice the percentage of alcohol.
**Straight Up**: An alcoholic beverage that is chilled, then strained to remove the ice. Also known as "up."
**Tall**: Served in a highball or Collins glass, usually with a larger amount of mixer.
**Twist**: Served with a twist of a lemon or lime peel and rind.

## ⚓ KNOWING BEER

**Assorted beers on tap.** Photo Courtesy of S. Markham.

There are two main groups of beers: lagers and ales. While lagers offer a crisp, clean taste, ales offer a more complex taste.

**Lagers:** Budweiser, Miller, Coors, Pilsners, and Bocks are varieties of lagers.
**Ales:** India Pale Ale, Stout, Porter are varieties of ales; they are served at a slightly higher temperature (55°F).

### Beer Service

Serving: Serve immediately after pouring,
Foam head: Tilt the glass at a 45-degree angle and pour onto the side of the glass to control the head. Slowly turn the glass upright as it fills. If pouring from a bottle, twist slightly as you finish the pour to prevent dripping. Lagers 1 inch; ales, slightly less.

**A typical sports bar.** Photo Courtesy of S. Markham.

##  KNOWING COFFEES, TEAS, AND WATERS

Coffees and teas are an important part of beverage service. While not alcoholic, they are still quite special and essential to nearly every operation.

### Coffee Service

- Coffee is often made to order. If brewed by the pot, it should be made fresh and not held for more than 30 minutes.
- Pods (individual portioned coffee) and capsules should be kept sealed and refrigerated or as directed.
- Coffee is to be served black, but should be accompanied by milk or cream and sweeteners.
- Have napkin in one hand to wipe the lip of the serving pot.
- Pour from the right with your right. Cup handle in the 3:00 position. Pour from 1 to 2 inches above the cup to avoid splashing. Allow room for creamer and sweetener to be mixed in. Place teaspoon to the right of the cup; also OK on the saucer. Place cup on saucer first.
- Usually refilled free of charge.

### SPECIALTY COFFEES

Specialty coffees have been quite popular in the United States and are now considered mainstream. There are three main drinks that you should be familiar with:

- *Espresso*: Dark, deep-roasted, finely ground type of coffee. A slight foam forms on top, served black but offer with sugar and lemon twist.
- *Cappuccino*: One part coffee, one part steamed whole milk, and one part foamed whole milk; other nonfat milk or nondairy milks may be substituted. May be served with cinnamon, cocoa, or chocolate.
- *Latté*: Espresso with steamed milk.

## TEA SERVICE

Fine tea service is an art form. There are many aspects of tea to be considered. Most tea is presented with hot water in a teapot with a choice of assorted tea bags. Then it is essentially up to the guest to prepare the tea to their liking. Tea is occasionally brewed in a pot and served generically. As a general guideline, tea can be divided into types and is available bagged and loose leaf. Tea portions vary and are typically revived with 8 oz of hot water. Adding the hot water to the tea is referred to as "steeping". The water temperature varies between types of teas. The following table is a guideline to show the basic differences. Personal preferences may dictate leaving the tea in contact with the water longer for a stronger tea or less time for a weaker tea.

| Type of Tea | Steeping Time | Water Temperature |
| --- | --- | --- |
| White—flavored | 1 minute | 175°F |
| White—blooming | 5 minutes | 180°F |
| Green | 1 minute | 175°F |
| Oolong | 3 minutes | 195°F |
| Black | 2 minutes | 195°F |
| Herbal | 4 minutes | 208°F |

Creamer and a variety of sweeteners and lemon are served with teas and left to the guests' preference.

## WATER SERVICE

- Still: Nonsparkling noncarbonated, tap or bottled.
- Sparkling: Carbonated, naturally or by adding carbon dioxide.
- Ask first for preferences.
- Pour for customers.
- Delivered on a beverage tray.
- Don't touch inside of glasses with hand or with pitcher.
- Chilled to ice-water temperature.
- Water glasses or goblets placed above guest's knife.

bartender may be undercharging the employees for their second and third drinks. The owners want the employees to feel respected but are considering withdrawing this privilege and banning employees from the premise after shifts.

1. List the pros and cons of giving employees a free drink after the evening shift.
2. What is the typical policy of most establishment regarding employees being on the premises after work?
3. How might the owners best go about banning employees from the bar?

## Refusing Service

John is a regular at Cliff's 179 Pub. He is large in stature and presence, with a bold personality and a frame to accommodate it. He is well over 6 feet tall and weighs more than 350 pounds. He is very generous and has always tipped very well. He regularly brought business clients there for meetings and often buys a round of drinks for the entire bar. He owns his own construction company, which has helped to renovate the bar and fix things for little or no cost over the past several years. He is a really nice guy and the owners feel greatly indebted to him. As a result, it was understood that John receives whatever he wants. Despite their tight controls on special orders and overserving of alcohol, John has continued to push the limit. He orders items that aren't on the menu, he orders when the kitchen is closed, and he occasionally drinks more than he should when driving. No one wants to refuse John. He is their best customer.

Lately, John's home-life has been suffering and he has been spending more and more time drinking at the bar. While this is good for business, it is not good for John's health and the Cliff's 179 Pub's liability if John were to drive while intoxicated.

This one particular evening began like most others. John arrived around 6 P.M. He sat at the bar and consumed a few drinks. He ordered dinner, spoke to the other regulars, and watched a game on the television. He continued to drink until closing time. He was obviously intoxicated. He refused hints and demanded to be served even after the bar closed. He didn't like being told to stop. At that point, John wanted to stay longer.

1. Describe the benefits Cliff's has received from John.
2. What ethical liabilities does Cliff's owe to John?
3. What are the legal liabilities of this situation?
4. How should Cliff's handle the situation?

## Rockwood Country Club

Peggy is a new hire at the Rockwood Country Club (RCC). She is a college student who was hired to work in their full-service restaurant during the summer. She has waited tables previous summers at a local cafe. She decided to apply at the RCC because her roommate works there and she has heard that the tips are great. Peggy is not accustomed to this higher level of service, since she has only waitressed at the cafe, but she was able to bluff her way through the interview and the admission test with the help of her roommate. The RCC trains very little. Essentially, they hire experienced waitstaff who follow others for a few shifts until they are comfortable. They give them smaller stations with fewer tables until the dining room

supervisor feels they can handle more. Peggy has been working there two weeks and has done a fine job in the slower pre-season. Tonight is Peggy's first night on her own. In the beginning things are going quite well. Peggy has a sense of confidence that is quite admirable. About halfway through the night a couple at a table points to the wine list and says, "A bottle of Pinot, please." It suddenly occurs to Peggy that she has never actually served a bottle of wine. Regardless, she appears unruffled, trying to recall witnessing many bottles opened when out to dinner with her parents.

Peggy submits the order to the computer system and it is routed to the bar. The bottle is brought to the service bar for pick up. Peggy places the bottle and two wine glasses on her beverage tray. She then smiles and asks the bartender if he could open the bottle for her. He looks at her oddly and says, "It's not a bottle of beer. You open it at the table." Hearing this, Peggy immediately picks up the tray and brings it out to the table. The bartender is nervous from her reply and alerts the dining room supervisor.

Peggy brings the tray over to the tray stand near the table and successfully opens the bottle. She pours both glasses on the tray and serves them to the couple. Immediately, the couple replies, "We ordered the Pinot. What is this red wine?" Peggy looks down at the bottle as she replies, "It is. It's Pinot Noir." The man says, "I pointed to the Pinot Grigio on the list. And we are having the fish special. Why would we order a red?"

Peggy apologizes and quickly returns with another bottle. This time, the man at the table asks if he could first see the bottle. He looks at it. It is the bottle they ordered. Peggy begins to open it, but the cork breaks. She continues to fumble with it, blaming the cork-screw, hoping to make it work but unsure what to do. At this point the dining room supervisor comes over to the table to see if everything is okay. Peggy replies that everything is fine, but the cheap corkscrew broke the cork. The supervisor interrupts and tells her to bring out another bottle as soon as possible. The supervisor apologizes and assures the customers that it will only be a minute. He then tends to other duties nearby. A few more minutes pass, and Peggy reappears with a new bottle of Pinot Grigio. This time she shows it to them right away. Peggy then opens it as quickly as possible and pours both glasses to save time. As she is walking away from the table, they each take a sip and immediately sense there is something off with the wine. It does not taste right. The supervisor, who has remained close by, is called over and confirms that the bottle has turned. At this point, no food has been ordered, they have been at the table 45 minutes, and everyone involved is frustrated.

1. What are the problems at RCC? List the issues of the case.
2. List the procedures for wine service.
3. What steps in this process did Peggy fail to do?
4. What could not have been avoided?
5. What could have been avoided?
6. How could RCC avoid this occurring in the future?

## A Sommelier or Not?

"LiLi's Wine Bar and Kitchen—All Are Welcome" is a rather long name. This is a name of a chic, upscale restaurant and bar that welcomes everyone. Its premise is to welcome diversity and shun pretentiousness. It is the brainchild of entrepreneur and activist Linsey LiLi. She wants to fuse the elements of sophistication and intimacy with a hint of Asia into the

downtown area, but in an atmosphere that makes everyone feel welcomed. Food will be equally as important as the wine, and there is no dress code. She envisions two entire walls and a ceiling filled with wines, celebrating wines from all over the world. The menu will be equally as eclectic. She wants her servers to be prompt and educated, while being as casual and open as possible. She envisions this as being a great hit. In developing a staffing plan, Linsey cannot determine whether or not to employ a sommelier. She realizes that wine is important, but doesn't want to intimidate the customers by the presence of a sommelier. Other places have separate beverage bills to ensure proper tipping, and she isn't sure that she wants to place such emphasis on this position. She would like her staff to have much food and wine knowledge but realizes this isn't always possible with so many different foods and wines. Chris, her chef, friend, and advisor, tells her that the classic idea of sommeliers has changed. They are no longer the stuffy, intimidating man with reading glasses. They are now younger and knowledgeable and make great efforts to make everyone feel comfortable with their choice of a beverage.

1. Describe the service concept of LiLi's Wine Bar and Kitchen—All Are Welcome.
2. Describe the position of a sommelier as it relates to guest service, in the past and now.
3. List the benefits and disadvantages of employing a sommelier.
4. In your opinion, should Linsey employ a sommelier? If so, under what circumstances? If not, how else could she handle beverage service?

**Note about Responsible Alcohol Service:** Laws and regulations vary between states and localities; certifications for bartenders are encouraged if not mandatory.

# The Guest Service of Lodging

## Chapter Objectives:

*After reading this chapter, you should be able to:*

Recognize and understand terminology common to the guest service experience.

Describe the common procedures for checking in and checking out a guest.

Identify and describe common guest service issues and provide solutions for resolving them.

Identify the primary guest service positions within a typical hotel.

Describe the typical procedures associated with walking a guest.

Explain the different meal plans common to hotels.

## Terminology:

| | |
|---|---|
| AP | EP |
| Authorization | Folio |
| Block | Full House |
| Book | Gratuity |
| Bucket | Guest History File |
| Centralized Reservation System (CRS) | House Count |
| Charge Record | MAP |
| Check In | Night Audit |
| Check Out | Post |
| City Account | Property Management System (PMS) |
| CP | Rate |
| Day Rate | Walking a Guest |
| DNS | |

**Check Out**
A procedure of closing a guest folio upon the guest's departure.

**City Account**
An account for nonguests.

**Day Rate**
A lower rate charged to guests who do not occupy the room overnight. Typically, between 10 A.M. and 4 P.M.

**DNS**
Did not stay; guest who checks in and quickly returns to the desk without having occupied the room.

**Folio**
Guest account.

**Full House**
Hotel in which all rooms are occupied.

**Gratuity**
(also known as tip) Typically, money given or charged for service.

**Guest History File**
Record of guest's previous transactions.

- **Check Out**: A procedure of closing a guest folio upon the guest's departure.
- **City Account**: An account for nonguests.
- **Day Rate**: A lower rate charged to guests who do not occupy the room overnight. Typically, between 10 A.M. and 4 P.M.
- **DNS**: Did not stay; guest who checks in and quickly returns to the desk without having occupied the room.
- **Folio**: Guest account.
- **Full House**: Hotel in which all rooms are occupied.
- **Gratuity**: (also known as tip) Typically, money given or charged for service.
- **Guest History File**: Record of guest's previous transactions.
- **House Count**: Record of the total number of hotel guests at any one time.
- **Night Audit**: Daily reconciliation of all accounts receivables, performed at night.
- **Post**: To make an entry on an account.
- **Property Management System (PMS)**: A computer system that records and integrates many systems throughout the hotel. Useful in tabulating, reporting, and predicting.
- **Rate**: Price charged for a room night. Also combined within best available rate (BAR) and lowest available rate (LAR).

## Service Insight

### Grandma Is Visiting

Consider the following approach to customer service. Imagine that your grandmother is visiting you for a couple of days. What would you do? Would you clean more than usual before she arrived? Would you welcome her with a sincere smile? Would you give her the bedroom instead of the couch? Would you cancel your other appointments to give grandma your full attention? Would you show her out when she leaves? Would you help her to the bus or the train or carry her bags out to her car? Would you even do a follow-up call? Yes, of course you would do all of these things.

In hotels, there is a strong correlation between your grandmother and the guest. You are compelled to do this for both your grandmother and the guest. You do this for your grandmother out of love and you do this for guests out of a sincere desire to serve them. You should give the guest a warm welcome and a sincere smile. You should clean everything to the highest level. You should give them the best accommodations that you have and provide them with your full attention while they stay at your property. When they leave you show them out, wish them well, and even do a follow-up.

*Courtesy of Aziz Bandriss, Rooms Division Manager, Central Park Ritz Carlton, New York City.*

**House Count**
Record of the total number of hotel guests at any one time.

**Night Audit**
Daily reconciliation of all accounts receivables, performed at night.

**Post**
To make an entry on an account.

**Property Management System (PMS)**
A computer system that records and integrates many systems throughout the hotel. Useful in tabulating, reporting, and predicting.

**Rate**
Price charged for a room night. Also combined within best available rate (BAR) and lowest available rate (LAR).

**Walking a Guest**
When the guest has a reservation that the hotel cannot honor because they are over capacity. Usually due to overbooking. The guest is transferred to another hotel.

# ❦ PODIUMS/PODS

Podiums, or pods, are a relatively new way of accommodating guests. They replace a large front desk with small, individual stations. It breaks down the barriers between the guests and the front-desk agents. It is also easier for the handicapped guests. Pods can also be used in addition to the front desk or auxiliary areas.

# ❦ DEALING WITH FRONT-DESK ISSUES

Through the process of customer service, inevitably there will be issues that arise. How well you deal with these issues makes or breaks the level of customer service.

### If Busy

Call for backup help. Most hotels have a system with a buzzer to the back office or a telephone. Be sure to use it. Stay calm, and work quickly and efficiently, but still giving guests their deserved attention. Acknowledge the other guests waiting. Let the other guests know that someone will be with them shortly.

### Declined Credit Cards

This is typically a sensitive issue. When this occurs, be sincere, understanding, and direct. In a soft voice, apologize and inform them of the decline. Ask for another form of payment.

### Missing Reservations

It can be quite bothersome when a guest calls or arrives at the desk and you cannot find the reservation. Ask them again to verify spelling and confirm the dates and search again. Ask for other ways to retrieve information such as their confirmation number, company name, or their telephone number. Ask when they made the reservation, because all systems don't instantly update. Tactfully inquire whether they could have made the reservation at another property. If possible, call the other property to assist them. If you have availability, apologize, and suggest a new reservation and give a quote.

### Walking a Guest

**Walking a guest** means transferring a guest to another hotel because the property has overcommitted by accepting more reservations than they could supply. Perhaps other guests have overstayed, the establishment booked too many reservations, expecting cancellations that haven't occurred, or rooms have been unavailable because of repair. In any case, the guests have made a reservation but the hotel does not have an available room. Consider the following steps:
- ○ Realize that some higher-level guests should not be walked. High-priority members may be entitled to cash bonuses. Other considerations

on who to walk: length of stay, business affiliation and if their room was complimentary.

○ Know what other properties are open for rooms.
○ Try to walk a guest earlier in the evening.
○ Make it as easy on them as you can.
○ Apologize, have the manager apologize, have a letter of apology prepared.
○ Ask/think—What can you do to help them? Calls? . . .
○ See if they care.
○ Provide transportation.
○ Have a car ready.
○ Be as brief as possible.
○ Refund or comp the room if policy dictates.
○ Tell the concierge.
○ Call the hotel where they are walked to ensure things are good.
○ See if you can have them come back if it was to be a multiple-night stay.
○ Send to a nicer place.
○ Send a gift to their room?
○ Record the incident.

**The majestic Waldorf Hall of Mirrors.** Photo Courtesy of S. Markham.

## Service Insight

### Making Magic Happen

The hotel has learned that a couple is checking in and the man is going to propose to the woman. The couple is given a room with a view of the park and a telescope in the window. The man goes to the window and sights in the telescope at a predetermined time. He finds a hotel staff member that is sent out into the park to hold up a sign that reads, "Will you marry me?" If the woman says yes, the door will be opened and employees will rush in and fill the room with champagne and strawberries.

*Courtesy of Aziz Bandriss, Rooms Division Manager, Central Park Ritz Carlton, New York City.*

### Giving Information or Directions

Regarding the property or the local area, try to use the following guidelines:
- Begin from your current location or a closer location they are aware of.
- Stick with the most basic, simplest path.
- Use street names and give landmarks.
- Point with entire hand open.

### Surveying the Stay

Ask guests how their stay was. Empower your staff to also randomly ask guests how their stay is going. It is everyone's job. The *Lateral Service Principle* states that a staff member must assist if they see a guest in need, regardless of whether or not it is within their job description. They must stop whatever else they are doing and help the guest.

## ❦ BACK OFFICE

The back office is a part of the hotel that is typically directly in back of the front desk. It is the support area for guest services. Management also typically has its offices there. Entry and midlevel managers are directly involved with guest service. Upper-level managers periodically greet guests, but primarily concentrate on oversight of the property.

## ❦ CONCIERGE

A concierge is a person who assists guests with both hotel and non–hotel-related matters. This involves everything from making dinner reservations in the local area to directions to a shopping center. Concierges have full knowledge of the hotel services as well as the local area. They assess the needs of the guest and make appropriate suggestions. They "pull strings" and make the guest experience extra special through their advice and services.

## ❦ HOUSEKEEPING

The housekeeping department is the heart of the hotel. While all departments must work together, housekeeping is vital. To the guest, it is an invisible department until something goes wrong. As with other facets of the hotel and hospitality

**A hotel bedroom in need of housekeeping.** Photo Courtesy of S. Markham.

**A well-stocked hotel bathroom.** Photo Courtesy of S. Markham.

industry, the management's job is to ensure this department works well with the other departments.

A popular trend in the area of housekeeping is greening. All but the most formal hotels have instituted green policies for reusing and recycling. Another trend perpetuated by the media is an assurance that a property is not contaminated with bedbugs. Housekeepers are now being required to give extra attention to this matter to reduce this concern.

### Turndown Service

To add a special touch to a guest's stay, a great feature is the turndown service—the process of preparing a room for sleeping by making it warm and inviting for the guests. This is usually done between 6 and 9 P.M. This is popular or mandated in exclusive and 4- to 5-star hotels. Some automatically offer turndown service, while others offer it upon request. It typically involves:

○ Closing of draperies.
○ Turning down the lights.
○ Playing of softer music or other music specified in the guest's profile.

- Folding the top corner of the bedspread away from pillow.
- Placing chocolates or mints on the bed.
- If children are present, teddy bears might be tucked in and books are often set out.

### DND (Do Not Disturb) Issue

A DND sign is hung on the door when a guest prefers privacy. This means they do not want housekeeping to enter the room. When this happens, record the time the guest refused service on your report. (*Note*: Many reports are turning electronic to increase communication between housekeeping and the front desk.)

When you have finished all the other rooms, return to the DND room. If the DND sign is still on, most hotels have a "Privacy Card" that is slid under the door reading, "We respect your privacy. If you would like your room to be made up, please call. . . ."

---

### Service Insight

**Who Might See the Guest?**

The front-desk staff typically see the guest, but who else might come into contact with them? The housekeepers in the hallway. More hotels are training their housekeepers to make contact with the guests by acknowledging them and asking how their stay is. When was the last time that a housekeeper asked what else they could do to make your stay better? It is a powerful guest service technique!

---

## Daniel Hostettler
President and Managing Director, Ocean House, Watch Hill, RI

Photo Courtesy of Daniel Hostettler.

### Property

The Ocean House, Resort.

1868—Originally built as a summer resort.

2002—Closed for complete takedown. Five hundred artifacts from the former hotel were moved to a storage area. The hotel was rebuilt using as much of the original materials as possible.

2010—Reopened. It rotates rugs and décor throughout to now be open for all four seasons.

**The Ocean House.** Photo Courtesy of Bluff Avenue, LLC.

(continued)

Because of the rebuild, they were able to expand and integrate many features of a new property while maintaining the grandeur of an old, independent, New England coastal hotel. They have been able to install Vocera technology into 260 points of contact throughout the hotel. All of the managers can instantly communicate using a voice-activated lapel device. Their locations are tracked, and telephone calls are seamlessly routed. Also, video cameras are placed in guest areas throughout the hotel. They were originally installed for security, but are found to be most helpful in monitoring guest traffic. They can easily track bottlenecks, and managers are able to be in the right places at the right times.

The average room rate is $800 to $900 night, and there is an expectation that the rate will rise because of increases in fees.

The hotel is also very sustainable. It was built to near–*Leadership in Energy and Environmental Design* (LEED) standards. Smaller things resulting from 5-star standards, like the use of gray water and visible recycling receptacles prevent them from pursuing official LEED certifications. They are petitioning the standards to allow a blend of the two.

### Background Highlights

Mr. Hostettler is a graduate of the University of Denver School of Hotel and Restaurant Management and the Cornell University General Managers Program and has worked in Beverly Hills, Napa Valley, Santa Fe, and Great Britain in 4- and 5-star hotels for over 25 years. His hotel training was provided by old-school hoteliers and chefs from Europe who were very demanding.

2001—Employed as Managing Director of Ocean House to oversee renovation, strategic positioning, and opening.

2011—Named Hotelier of the Year by the Rhode Island Hospitality and Tourism Association; hotel achieved AAA Five Diamond Award in its first year of operations; as of the time of this writing, the hotel is awaiting the results of a Forbes Five Star inspection.

### Mission

To be the premier luxury hotel on the Eastern Seaboard of the United States.

Service level: 5 Stars

### Developing the Brand

Mr. Hostettler's mantra for success is that, "Everything revolves around supporting the brand." The brand is the mission and the service level. Everything goes into that. When speaking with his chef, we were told that his choice of hot dog to serve for the casual beach grill is just as important as his decision about china and wine glasses because every decision is in support of the brand positioning of the property.

Mr. Hostettler asks the question, "What are you selling?" and answers it by stating that he is selling uniforms, smiling people, service, experience, and local food fresh from the farm to table within 150 miles. All of these things must be considered. Be careful of things that detract from the brand. Monitor every touchpoint, from the shade of paint, to the stones in the original rebuilt fireplace, to the hand towels in the restroom.

### Human Resources

Hire for behavior and train for skill. Behavior is a must!

Every employee receives three interviews: human resource screening, peer reviews, and a general manager interview.

View of staffing: If we take care of them, they will take care of the guests.

### Organizational Structure

The organizational structure is unique at this property. It is seasonally adjusted with flexible staffing and to the highest levels in the industry (averaging 3.5 staff members to each guest).

They have merged a concierge and assistant front-desk manager to create a guest relations manager, who is charged with overseeing the total guest experience during a stay and checking in with the guests assigned to them on a daily basis to ensure their satisfaction.

(continued)

They have merged a housekeeping supervisor, a room service server, and butler to create a floor valet, who is in charge of fifteen rooms and oversees two housekeepers. They take orders from guests and oversee all of the rooms on the floor. This saves on labor and gives the guests a face to recognize. These are entry-level management positions, which provide an incentive to learn the hotel and grow. They keep this person on the same floor and they form a relationship with guests. These managers check in with the guest at least once a day, making small talk, which can be the best form of survey, and provide a personalized experience. It gives the guests a chance to be heard, ask questions, and communicate with a manager.

## Meetings

Mr. Hostettler conducts employee round tables once a month. Employees are rotated through these meetings. Managers and employees voice their issues and concerns. This is a chance for employees to have direct contact with him. He asks direct questions of the employees such as, "Are the guests happy?" He elicits ideas and gains valuable feedback.

## Special Service Tips

The Ocean House asks questions when guests make reservations. Then they research and prepare for their guests. They Google everyone who registers and then call 10 days in advance of their arrival in an effort to learn how to better serve them. They ask if there is a celebration and which car they plan on driving. Guests are blown away when the valet identifies their car and greets them by name. If it is a family, they learn the gender of their children and prepare a toy, a crib, and a onesie. If it is assumed to be a romantic getaway, they fill the bathtub. All of this is done to help them achieve the highest level of guest satisfaction.

## Surveying the Guest

The Ocean House surveys the guests in many different ways: Trip Advisor website, e-mail comment cards, 5-star evaluations, and their guest relations managers who are charged with direct contact. Reports are sent in every night so that any potential issue can be immediately responded to.

## Gratuity

The Ocean House is a nontipping facility. All employees sign a contract stating they will not accept tips. Instead, a Shared Resort Gratuity of $28 per room per night is added to the guest folio. This helps to increase the guest experience because they don't need to worry about tipping. It adds more of a residential feel to the property. Money from the "Shared Resort Gratuity" account is shared and allocated based on comment card scores. They are divided among employees based on a 92% or above satisfaction rate. If above 92%, they get 100% of their allocated tips; if less, they get a lower score. This is viewed as a reward instead of a punishment. If the department improves for the next two months, they get the lost tip money back.

## Changes

Mr. Hostettler has seen many changes in his hotel career. Hotels have grown from guest index cards to the technology of cameras and Vocera to ensure guest service. He sees technology as a major driver of change in the near future.

He has seen changes in staffing culture to include more of a concern for quality of life and instant gratification. The reward system helps to accommodate this change. Mr. Hostettler explains that historically there was an employee culture of "paying dues" and advancing your career. Now he sees a division of those who are in it for a job as opposed to having a passion for it and wanting it to be a career. He wants the staff to feel as though they are a part of the hotel and take responsibility and ownership for their work.

He has also seen changes in the guests. They now want iPads and technology and are working much more during their stays. There is a distinct blend of work and leisure in their culture. There is also a trend for shorter vacations and a real desire to be sustainable.

# CHAPTER REVIEW QUESTIONS

1. How does the concierge help the guest service experience?
2. List and provide solutions for three common front-desk issues.
3. What is "walking a guest," and why is it done?
4. List the procedures common to checking out a guest.
5. What is the difference between EP, AP, and MAP?
6. Why might it be helpful to consider your grandmother visiting when relating to hotels?
7. Should housekeepers acknowledge the guest?
8. After reading the feature about Mr. Hostettler, how would you describe his idea and importance of a "brand"?

#  CASE STUDIES

### Walking the Guest

There is a phrase in the hotel business, "Heads in beds." Hotels must fill each room each night. Lost revenue from an unsold room can never be made up. Each night, a small percentage of reservations are either canceled at the last minute or simply deemed, "no-shows." This leaves hotels in a predicament because they may have refused others earlier or simply did not try to sell the room. As a result, many hotels overbook by a small margin. Some properties have taken to securing the first night on a credit card to be paid in advance. To make things worse, some guests stay longer. Also, hotels have rooms that are unexpectedly unavailable pending repair. When the calculations do not add up, and too many reservations show, the hotel honors the reservation at another hotel. This is referred to as "walking a guest." It is hoped that this happens very infrequently. When a hotel is overcommitted and overbooks to the point that it ends up walking people on a regular basis, it stands to lose many customers and much money. Business customers may have meetings scheduled at the hotel. Conference attendees may have an event at the hotel. This may change their travel plans, making it quite bothersome. There are also initial monetary losses. The hotel loses revenue from the guest, and some pay for their room at the competitor's property. They also lose the time transporting them to another property, writing a letter of apology, and so on.

1. What is "walking a guest"?
2. Why do hotels walk a guest?
3. How much does it really cost a hotel to walk a guest? (Consider the costs of losing a future customer as well.)

### Up-selling with a Price

Increasing average sales per guest has been a common theme in hospitality as well as all retail. Consequently, up-selling, or selling more to the customer, has become a popular push in most settings. There are several approaches to this:

Suggestions Method: "We have a nice king suite with a view of the pool."
Ask Method: "We have you in a bed in our standard room, is that suitable for your needs?"

Listen and Watch Method: Watch for guest needs. "We have a great restaurant and award-winning spa."

Top-Down Method: Starting with the highest-price rooms and moving down. "We have our diplomat room available for $195." If no, "We have a suite for $150."

Lowest-Plus Method: "Did you want to upgrade to a water view for $25 a night?"

Random-Choice Method: Present all available options at once. "We have a diplomat room for $195, a standard room for $75, and a suite for $150."

Properties mandate that their staff up-sell using these techniques. Front-desk and reservations staff are evaluated based on their use of these techniques, and their jobs are compromised if they do not "make the ask." Consequently, their heart is not in it. Other properties are motivated to up-sell by using contests, encouraging employees to sell at any cost. Sometimes this works and sometimes it does not. Average dollars per guest are increased, but at what cost? Guests are accustomed to sales pitches. Most are immediately turned off by high-pressure sales gimmicks. They are on guard and vigilant, cautiously scrutinizing the staff for hidden tactics during all their transactions. As a result, trust has diminished. Staff are placed in awkward positions, and the guests feel taken advantage of if they are sold beyond their personal level of comfort. At this point, guest service has eroded and there is no opportunity for customer service. Some guests will change brands when presented with sales tactics.

On the other hand, the guests may enjoy the upgrade. They might never have experienced it if it had not been suggested. Perhaps they could receive it complimentary once and like it so much that they pay for it in the future. In these cases, everyone wins.

1. What are the benefits to up-selling?
2. What are the disadvantages to up-selling?
3. What are ways that hotels can up-sell but still deliver great customer service?

## Basic Hotel

The Basic Hotel is a generic, no-frills hotel that provides only the essential accommodations for a very reasonable price. The Basic Hotel brand strives to lead the economy sector by providing only the basics. Its motto is phrased with humor stating, "Basic rooms and basic service, at a basic price." It offers no restaurant, no spa, no business center, and no lounge. The rooms are small and clean, but basic. The beds are reasonably comfortable and the bathrooms offer only the essentials. The rooms offer a television, alarm clock, lamp, house telephone, bed, a desk, and chair. Guest interaction is kept to a minimum. The front desk has a sign on it that humorously reads, "Basic Hotel Service." Guests are encouraged to check-in and check-out at a kiosk. No Concierge Desk is provided, but the guests can ask the Front Desk "basic questions." A series of vending machines has a sign over it that reads, "Basic Essentials." It provides solutions to most needs, offering snacks, toiletries, ice, and beverages. Basic Hotel also offers an application for smart phones that serves as a concierge and can automate the entire check-in and check-out processes if guests wish.

After the stay, guests are electronically sent a basic survey. The technology and price are the two highest scores on the returned surveys. Guests receive basic service and accommodations at the Basic Hotel.

1. Describe the Basic Hotel's customer service concept.
2. How high are the customer expectations at the Basic Hotel?
3. Do you believe that the Basic Hotel meets customer expectations?
4. In your opinion, do you believe this a good thing?
5. Do you believe that guests are concerned with the level of service in the Basic Hotel?

### The Green Earth Hotel

The Green Earth Hotel is a concept that offers lodging in a sustainable manner, while striving to offer as high of a level of service as possible. They offer such common sustainable features as:

Earth-friendly construction
Paperless front desks
Air driers in place of hand towels
Options for changing towels and sheets on beds
Skin-care dispensers
Water-saving devices
Optimal use of natural lighting
Energy-efficient light bulbs

These Earth-friendly features have been a major selling point to the guests. It has also reduced labor and utility costs. In addition to being Earth-friendly, however, they also want to deliver the highest level of guest satisfaction possible. Because they are paperless, they collect comments from their guests verbally and electronically. Recent guest surveys have shown that guests at the Green Earth Hotel have considered the level of service to be lacking. The compost pile behind the hotel smells in the summer months and is attracting many pests. There have been several comments regarding the use of gray water in the toilets. Some guests are not accustomed to this and consider it to lessen their experience. The management is dedicated to providing a sustainable experience, but they also want the guests to feel appreciative of their cause while enjoying their experience.

1. Rate the guest experience at The Green Earth Hotel.
2. Is it possible to be both Earth-friendly and guest-friendly?
3. What changes could the hotel make to improve guest satisfaction?
4. What do you believe is the future of balancing these two qualities?

# The Guest Service of Events

## Chapter Objectives:

*After reading this chapter, you should be able to:*

Apply the five stages of ensuring customer service to an event.

Identify and explain the different types of meetings and events and their specific challenges as related to customer service.

Identify and explain the different types of customers or attendees and their specific challenges as related to customer service.

Describe how to ensure quality service during pre-event, event, and post-event activities.

## Terminology:

CMP
SMERF
Stakeholder
SWOT
Touch Points

# Introduction: Special Pressure from Events

The coordination of an event is very demanding. Even seasoned professionals have intense stress placed on them. Mostly, they thrive on it. They have the weight of the world and they can handle it. When planning or working an event, it is crucial to place yourself in the role of the attendee. With so many things to coordinate, true event professionals never lose sight of walking in the shoes of their guests. Consider the following:

- Nearly everyone is emotionally invested.
- This could be a once-in-a-lifetime event for the participants.
- Tens or hundreds of thousands of dollars or more will go into this event.
- It is on display for everyone to see.
- It typically happens once and cannot be redone.
- People's health and safety are at risk.
- Staff intensely plans for several months to over a year.
- All of the work will commence within a few hours to a few days.

In order to have a great event, there may be thousands of variables that need to come together. A formula for delivering quality service at events can help to ensure that your guests leave satisfied. A structure for managing these variables appears with five steps below.

# Pre-event Services: Setting Up the Event

There are five steps to consider when managing an event:

1. Assess the environment
2. Predict outcomes
3. Plan success
4. Monitor weaknesses
5. Assess quality

**A tented event.** Photo Courtesy of S. Markham.

## ❦ ASSESS THE ENVIRONMENT

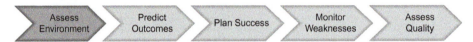

Assessing the environment is done using many different methods. To begin, it is important to understand the types of meetings and attendees. After that, you can begin to predict and manage by touch points. A SWOT analysis is also a helpful tool for understanding the good and the improvables of your offerings and that of the competition. It is also essential to review each of the customer touch points.

### TYPES OF MEETINGS

It is important to determine the venue. The type of event is often proposed by the client and will dictate many aspects of the event. It sets the expectations of the event for all. There are many types of meetings and events, each with a different name that will inspire a distinct tone in the minds of the attendees. Their tone may be formal or informal. They may be informational, educational, or even entertaining. The attendance may be small or tens of thousands. It may be hosted by an association, corporation, or a social group. One of the first steps is to determine and name the type or function of the event. Below is a list of common meeting or event types:

- Lecture: Formal, structured, speaker
- Forum: Multiple speakers, moderator, open to question-and-answer sessions with audience

- Retreat: Less formal, typically smaller in size and at a location remote from business offices, great for planning
- Convention: Meeting of delegates, cyclical scheduling, general sessions for all attendees and breakouts for smaller subgroups, may be in conjunction with exhibition
- Clinic: Specialized training
- Exhibition: Vendors display, in conjunction with another type of meeting, built-in audience
- Conference: Meeting, typically for specialty area to discuss advances
- Seminar: Smaller groups, leader, work on problems
- Trade show: Vendors display goods and services of a specific trade, open only to people in that specific trade
- Special events
  - Children's
  - Cultural
  - Group
  - Professional
  - Sporting
  - Themed
  - Tours
  - VIPs
  - Music productions
  - Spouse events

**Table setting at a tented event.** Photo Courtesy of S. Markham.

## TYPES OF ATTENDEES

There are many types of attendees. Below is a list of the primary categories. Each type of attendee has its own special set of needs and expectations:

- Corporate
- Associations
- General public
- **S**ocial, **m**ilitary, **e**ducational, **r**eligious, **f**raternal (SMERF)

**Social, Military, Educational, Religious, Fraternal (SMERF)**
An acronym and customer group that combines social, military, educational, religious, and fraternal organizations.

Each group of attendees comes with its distinct set of qualities, making each a very different experience. Within each of these is also a great variance of formality, skill, assumptions, and decorum. It is important to predict but not prejudge a type of attendee based on your past dealings with the market. Many event professionals have been surprised at how differently groups act. Also, groups change leadership and direction from event to event.

## ❦ MANAGING TOUCH POINTS

**Touch Points**
Each time that a guest has an experience with your organization, a representative of it, or an aspect the organization planned.

One great way to assess the environment is to look at things through the eyes of the guests. The moment of truth scenario by Jan Carlzon holds true for events. Think of an event as many smaller events, some in a series and some simultaneously. Now break down each of those smaller events into each time the guest has contact with you, your organization, or an aspect that you planned. We call these **touch points**. Managing by touch points allows you to plan, troubleshoot, and best serve the guest.

A **SWOT analysis** is another great way of assessing the environment. A SWOT analysis is a survey of the things that you control and the things that you do not control. It lists the good and the bad of each.

**SWOT Analysis**
An analysis of the strengths, weaknesses, opportunities, and threats of an organization, containing internal and external examination.

- *Strengths*: The positive attributes of the organization.
- *Weaknesses*: The negative attributes of the organization.
- *Opportunities*: The positive outcomes that may occur beyond the control of the organization.
- *Threats*: The negative outcomes that may occur beyond the control of the organization.

To perform an initial SWOT analysis, begin by making a bulleted list within these categories, and asking the following questions (here, followed by typical examples of answers).

- Strengths:
  - Q: Of the things that you control, which are positive?
  - A: Volunteers. Special content/product knowledge.
- Weaknesses:
  - Q: Of the things that you control, which are negative?
  - A: We do not have a specialty in this area.

- Opportunities:
  - Q: Of the things outside your control, which can have a positive effect on you?
  - A: New change in the market. Competitor now out of market.
- Threats:
  - Q: Of the things outside your control, which can have a negative effect on you?
  - A: Competition, poor press, weather.

## WHAT ARE YOU OFFERING?

To continue to assess the environment and expand on the idea of a SWOT analysis, it is important to realize that you are offering both goods and services to your customers. Examples of these are:

### Goods

- Rooms
- Pipe and drape (the curtains and their support used for backdrops and borders)
- Food
- Beverage
- Temperature
- Lighting
- Audiovisual equipment

**Food offered at an outdoor event.** Photo Courtesy of S. Markham.

**Services**

- Planning
- Support
- Information
- Advice
- Safety

As you realize what it is that you are offering, you will then want to begin to monitor and control it. Too many organizations take these things for granted. Also, the customer needs to be informed of your offerings so they can appropriately set their expectations, and you can meet them. The old adage holds true: What gets monitored, gets controlled, and gets improved upon.

**Hotel conference room set-up.** Photo Courtesy of S. Markham.

## ⁀ PREDICT THE OUTCOMES

Assess Environment ⟩ Predict Outcomes ⟩ Plan Success ⟩ Monitor Weaknesses ⟩ Assess Quality

After assessing the environment, predicting the outcomes is the next step. This can be done for good and for bad. You must have desired outcomes of the event, even if they are obvious or implied. This can be expressed in a few ways:

- Mission of the parent company
- The event description
- Event theme

These points will be monitored and evaluated in a later section.

It is also important to predict what might go wrong so that it can be planned for and reduced. This is referred to as risk management. There are professionals and entire companies that specialize in this area. Other times, it is done in-house. This is a way of assessing the "what-ifs." Below is a three-step model for achieving the objective.

## RISK MANAGEMENT

### 1. Identify the Issues

What are the possible risks? History is a great indicator, but also be sure to consider current conditions. The risks come from many areas within and outside of your control. Also see the weaknesses and threats from your SWOT analysis. Typical survey risk areas to identify are:

- Technological
- Legal
- Financial
- Natural disasters
- Safety
- Suppliers
- Entertainment
- Attendees

### 2. Identify the Likeliness

This may be more difficult to do. It is often a hunch or intuition. It will likely be based on a blend of:

- Past events of this type
- Current conditions
- Inside information
- Published reports
- Unpublished reports

### 3. Identify the Potential

What are the implications of this occurrence? To what degree would it impact the event? Would it be inconvenient, substantial, or devastating? Something may occur relatively often, but if it is of little or no consequence, then it may not be a huge priority. Consider rating the potential as low, medium, or high for initial categorization. Also, be sure to ask whether these issues interfere with other things, creating a larger potential for problems.

## ✦ PLAN SUCCESS

Assess Environment → Predict Outcomes → **Plan Success** → Monitor Weaknesses → Assess Quality

Now that the environment has been surveyed and the outcomes are established, the true planning can begin. Quality guest service is about meeting or exceeding guests' expectations. To do this, the first step is to set the expectations.

### SETTING THE EXPECTATIONS

The guests at an event have expectations. There are many things that have established this. It is crucial not to oversell, while not drastically underselling. If oversold, the expectations are too high and the attendee feels slighted. If undersold, you will overdeliver, but attendance may be low because you didn't accurately portray what the event was about. To take this a step further, you are planning and selling expectations.

The customer service experience is about meeting or exceeding the expectations. How do you set the expectations? Expectations are established from a well-orchestrated culmination of:

- Marketing efforts
- Past performances
- Word of mouth
- Meetings
- Location
- Price

Most larger events are planned years in advance. When designing the event you set expectations by establishing and setting up:

- A theme
- Site selection
- Site inspections
- Layout
- Suppliers
- Technicalities
- Catering and services
- An audience
- Financial plans
- Well-established program guidelines from which to work
  - Example: timing/schedule
    - Mealtimes
    - Event times
    - Free times
    - Transition times

- Regulation compliance
- Registration
- Confirmations
- Badges

**In addition to baseball games, the historic Fenway Park in Boston has been the site of many other sporting and cultural events.** Photo Courtesy of S. Markham.

## PROMOTIONS MARKETING

Promotions marketing is the main communication used to establish expectations and attract attendees. You must let potential attendees know what the event is about. You build anticipation. In order to market effectively you must be able to answer the following questions:

- What is the product?
- Who are the customers?
- What are the customers' needs and expectations? Are they:
    - Looking for a novel experience?
    - Learning?
    - Excited?
    - Scared?
    - Planning to purchase items?
    - Expecting to be entertained?
    - Getting away?

Once this is established, you can begin to tailor your promotions campaign to achieve your goals. The answers are mostly intuitive, and all of your promotions should be geared toward achieving these goals.

## ESTABLISHING JOB DESCRIPTIONS

As planning continues, it is important that everyone has a clear definition of their roles. Because of the ever-changing nature of events, roles are not uniform as in other parts of the hospitality industry. Many staff members will experience something new or different in each event. Despite this, clear roles and responsibilities must be established. There are keys to maintaining order, and hence customer service. There are similarities between roles from event to event, particularly if they are on-premise.

### Does Everyone Have

- Their job descriptions?
- An appropriate line of communication?
- Established procedures? (as much as possible)
- Checklists?

### Do They Know

- Their responsibilities?
- The chain of command?
- What is acceptable?

### There Are Key Skills That Each Role Requires. Do They Have

- Problem-solving strategies?
- Essential computer skills?
- Organizational skills?
- Clear descriptions of their areas of responsibility, even if the role may vary?
- Support to complete the expectations?

### Positions Common to Events That Require These Would Be

- Speakers and entertainers
- Information desk, point person
- Sales
- Community relations
- Box office
- Registration personnel
- Event supervisor
- Exhibition manager
- Operations manager
- Ushers
- Safety and security
- Concessions and catering

- Merchandising
- Facilities
- Intermediaries
- Volunteers

## ✧ MONITORING THE WEAKNESSES

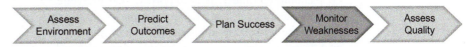

The surveying, forecasting, and planning are done. The guests are arriving. Everyone feels it in the air. The band is warming up. A thousand things race through your mind. It is now or never. It is showtime!

As you plan, work, or wrap up an event, issues will inevitably arise. Even the best-laid plans need monitoring and tweaking to be successful.

### ATTENDEE NEEDS

Guest service is about taking care of the attendees. The needs of the attendees can be overwhelming and resource-intensive. They require planning, labor, facilities, capital, patience, and time. To begin, consider all the things they need—anticipation based on the past is a great start. Next, let them know—communicate through sign-age, announcements, staff posted at stations, and electronically. Send them early mailings—address areas such as:

- Schedule of events
- Special events
- Weather and climate
- Dress/attire
- Lodgings
- Dining, special diets
- Special needs
- Changes
- Payment options
- Restrooms, floor maps, emergency care
- Information about the surrounding area
- Transportation
- Services offered at property
  - Valet parking
  - Spa
  - Accommodations for handicapped guests
  - Special allergies
  - Pets
  - Interpreters
  - Child care

## WORKING WITH VOLUNTEERS

Volunteers are essential to most events. Without them, the labor costs would make the event cost-prohibitive. They provide extra service and care that makes the event a success. They may serve in high-level positions. Some event managers are volunteers, although not likely as a full-time position. Volunteers primarily serve in lower and mid-level positions, such as:

- Ushers
- Door holders
- Referees
- Security
- First aid
- Information
- Customer relations
- Traffic control

Volunteers should be seen as co-workers, despite their lack of monetary compensation. This means that they should be given responsibility and held accountable for their actions as if they were paid employees. Tell them that you expect:

- As much from them as you would from a paid worker, not less
- Enthusiasm/belief in the organization/project/event

Remember, most patrons don't realize they are volunteers. Consider the following points:

- Make positions clear
- Make expectations clear
- Offer promotions within jobs
- Provide support
- Given suitable tools or materials
- Offer open two-way communication
- Treat them with respect
- Give them a token of appreciation, or involve them in a token-reward activity

In giving of their time and expertise, remember that volunteers are compensated in other ways. While not paid, they do receive many things in return. They receive:

- Social contact
- Feelings of usefulness
- Feeling a part of something larger, a camaraderie
- Satisfaction in helping an organization they believe in
- The opportunity to help in something worthwhile
- A token of appreciation

## POST-EVENT SERVICES

There may be congratulations, a celebration, or even a sigh of relief once an event is over, but the work is certainly not done. This is when the finishing touches are placed on the service provided. This includes social media, press releases, and all of the unresolved guest issues. Remember to thank the attendees for coming. Emphasize the highlights of the event. Let them know they had a good time. Follow-up is key to customer satisfaction and return business.

## CRISIS MANAGEMENT PLAN

In a previous section, the outcomes of a risk assessment were established. At this point, it is time to construct a plan. The first goal is to reduce the likelihood of crises occurring. For the instances that cannot be avoided, you can still plan to reduce the potential impact of their occurrence. You should be ready for almost everything:

- Plan.
- Have a back-up plan.
- Have a back-up plan for your back-up plan.

**Crisis Management Plan (CMP)**
A detailed outline of procedures that a Crisis Management Team enacts. A specialized plan to respond to a crisis or catastrophe.

A **Crisis Management Plan (CMP)** is a detailed guide describing the procedures in the event of an emergency. Typically, a CMP is assembled with a Crisis Management Team (CMT). This team consists of trained professionals in all possible areas. Ideally, many are on staff. Some may be on call. They should have a system of communication in place with a basic plan for almost anything including:

- Fire
- Bomb threat
- Evacuation
- Catastrophe

## ✦ ASSESSING THE QUALITY

The last step in the list of managing for quality guest service in an event is *Assessing the Quality*. This can be done by surveying the event. Without this, we have limited and perhaps biased feedback on the true success of the event.

## SURVEYING THE EVENT

Many events are surveyed. Guests are often asked opinions and many feel overwhelmed with the requests and disregard the surveys without a second thought. If the surveys are too long, they lose interest. Also, they can be a nuisance to complete,

and the guests wonder whether anyone even reads their responses. As a result, many people will not fill out a survey. A majority of those who complete the surveys do so because they are upset. Consequently, the responses do not accurately represent the general population. So, the questions are: What will you assess? Who will you assess? How will you assess? And, what will you do with the information?

### Content: What Will Be Assessed?

- Does the event or the organization have a mission/purpose statement to check it against?
- Who do we need to please?
- Is their image upheld?
- More than "How was it?"
- What are the take-away points from this event?
- What were the goals/objectives? Were they met?
- Are the sponsors pleased?
- Are the guests pleased?
- Is the parent organization pleased?

### Population: Who Will Be Assessed?

**Stakeholder**
Any person or group that would be affected if the event, company, or situation were to cease to exist.

To begin to answer this question, you must first determine the stakeholders. A **stakeholder** can be described as anyone who has interest in the event. It could be anyone who would be affected if the event were to cease to exist.

After the list of stakeholders is established, the groups become evident. Potential stakeholders may be:

- Attendees
- Spouses
- Parent organization
- Sponsors
- Purveyors

### Medium: How Will You Assess It?

This can be a formal, printed survey and it can be mailed, filled out electronically, or answered by telephone. It can be on a comment card or even at an on-site portal. Each medium has its own advantages and disadvantages. The qualities or characteristics should drive the decision of the medium. Here are some general tips:

- Make it easy to complete.
  - Encourage respondents to complete it.
  - Consider offering a reward.
  - Meet and ask prospective survey recipients personally.
  - Send follow-ups as necessary.
    - Let them know how and why it counts.

Avoid boilerplate or standard phrases such as "Your comments are important to us" or "We value your input." Be original and fitting to the group and the event.

### Interpretation: What Will You Do With It?

Evaluation is crucial, but only one piece of the puzzle. Ideally, monitoring and evaluation occur before, during, and after the event. As a result, findings should not be a surprise. They should be informative, validating, but seldom, if ever, shocking. Findings should be taken in context, and not disproportionately. A handful of poor comments is not great, but it does not mean that the entire event was a failure. Consider the bad with the good. When reviewing, consider the following:

- Who will look at it?
- To whom will it matter?
- What went right?
- What went wrong?
- What is at the root of the problem?
- What are the possible costs or damages?
- What can you fix?
- What will you do differently next time?
- What will you do the same next time?
- What are the take-away lessons?
- What are the immediate actions, or to-do's as a result?

In closing, meetings and events are a vital part of the hospitality industry. There is much that goes into effectively serving the guests. However, if handled with professionalism, planning, and appropriate responses to their needs, the events are likely to be a success.

 # CHAPTER REVIEW QUESTIONS

1. Describe why there is special pressure to perform well in events.
2. List and briefly describe three different types of meetings or events that are designed for smaller groups.
3. Why is it crucial to identify the importance of an issue when conducting risk analysis?
4. List and describe four ways that you can set the expectations of guests.
5. Explain the concept of managing touch points.
6. In events, you offer the customer both goods and services. Explain this concept.
7. How might a corporation consider a retreat to be a success?
8. What is a CMP?
9. What benefits might volunteers receive?
10. List three ideas for making volunteers feel appreciated.

# CASE STUDIES

## Can You Deliver?

Sales representatives are crucial to events. When they sell events, they earn commissions. They tell about how great the event will be. Typically, they are honest and accurate. Occasionally, they promise more than they can deliver—in some cases, they simply aren't aware, and in other cases they compromise to make sales quotas.

In this case, an event-planning company is trying to enter the market. Their goal is to gain 10 percent of the anticipated, local market share for the next year. This is an aggressive goal considering the market and the larger, established competition. They hire Christina, a sales manager who has worked for the competition prior to leaving the industry 5 years ago to raise her child. She was on top of her game when she left, and now she wants to regain her former title. She still has some leads in the area and remembers all of her training. She recruits two sales assistants and is promised a bonus if they make the 10 percent goal. After a slow, rough start, the sales begin to roll in. The calendar begins filling all at once. The business is now off to a great start and on track to meet the market-share quota. Because of Christina serving as such a great front person, the business leaders are excited. However, problems begin to arise when the rest of the company doesn't perform as well as the sales staff claimed they would. In fact, they are having a difficult time meeting most of the sales contracts Christina is selling. Christina hears about this from her customers. She sensed there was trouble with the disconnect between the sales department and the operations department, but she had no idea of the extent. Furthermore, she learns that the field support staff are very upset at her "for promising the impossible." She is terribly distressed because she believed that she didn't make any promises that were unreasonable. In fact, she believes the field staff are overreacting and incompetent. She stops by the director of operations' office to discuss the matter, but he is out in the field troubleshooting an event. Christina decides to devise a strategy for dealing with this based on what she remembers from her past employer. She knows that she has to be tactful.

1. How important is it to deliver what is promised?
2. What are the discrepancies between the sales and the operations departments?
3. How should Christina approach the situation?
4. Outline ideas for assessing and improving the disconnect at the company.

## What's Going On?

5-A's Event Planning is a medium-sized event planning group. They have five full-time and three part-time event planners. Allison, one of the newest full-time event planners, has just been assigned to an event that had originally been assigned to another part-time event planner who resigned after difficulties with the event and pressure from 5-A's. Allison welcomes the challenge. She is competent and energetic and full of new ideas.

The event is a corporate promotional dinner to thank the business's customers. The corporation typically handles small events in-house, but is enlisting the help of a professional meeting-planning company to ensure that this event goes off as planned.

As soon as Allison receives word of the event she immediately calls Sam, the direct contact person at the account to set up a meeting. Allison quickly finds herself deep in the project. She realizes the company has many different ideas and very high expectations for the event. They were promised many great things that Allison keeps finding out about. She wonders how this is even possible with their budget. She listens to everything they say and diligently takes notes. Then, she reports back to her supervisor, the director of operations. She explains the dilemma. Allison is told to make it work or they will get someone else who can make it work. She feels unsupported. She goes to the purveyors to review the pre-arranged details. They explain that they cannot deliver what she is asking. She continues to negotiate and tries to determine what exactly the purveyors can offer and all of the real possibilities for the event. Armed with this information, Allison calls Sam to discuss the issues. Sam tells Allison that the customer is always right. Sensing that this will be an involved issue, Allison sets up a meeting with Sam and the director of operations for the following day. When Allison arrives at the meeting, she finds that Sam is only one of four people at the company making the decisions, and all of these people have different ideas.

1. List the issues regarding the promotional dinner event.
2. What would you guess happened with the planner that Allison replaced?
3. How could the director of operations be more helpful?
4. What are Allison's options at this point?
5. How should Allison handle this meeting?

## Different Interests

Weddings are wonderful and joyous events. It is the perfect day for the bride. For many, it is the day that she has dreamed of since she was a young girl. Everyone will look forward to it. It will be perfect. They will love it!

Now let's talk about the mother of the bride (MOB). The MOB is a very strong-willed woman. She was present at all of the planning meetings and is paying the bill for the wedding. The MOB was resistant to any suggestions and kept changing the plans without communicating with others. "It's all about the bride. I just want it to be perfect for my baby," she says. Not really. In truth it is all about the MOB taking control and intimidating everyone else. The bride-to-be (B2B) was mostly timid around her mother, although she would occasionally let others know that she didn't like her mother's choices. The groom is easygoing and non-confrontational. Even after hints and interventions, the MOB continued to be adamant and argumentative. Consequently, the MOB got precisely what she wanted.

The setting of the wedding was a tent in the yard at the private estate of the MOB. It was a beautiful setting with many great offerings. The MOB insisted that there not be alcohol at the event. She was a religious woman who was opposed to alcohol. The MOB was irate when it was revealed that the groom's family had brought alcohol and was drinking it in the parking lot and out by the horse stables. She immediately went to the wedding planner and complained. She insisted the wedding planner go get rid of the alcohol immediately. The wedding planner wanted to keep everyone happy and was fed up with the MOB.

1. Is it possible to please everyone?
2. How do you please many guests with competing interests?
3. Who should the planner satisfy first?

**4.** Should the planner have stuck up for the bride during the planning?

**5.** How should the planner handle the alcohol situation?

## Turf Battle

The All-Sport Arena is a multiuse facility that accommodates two minor-league sports teams in addition to numerous other sporting events and functions. The arena is always busy, and everyone must follow a strict schedule of when each team can and cannot be on the field.

One Friday afternoon the two minor-league teams were both scheduled to be on the field for practice at the same time. The field had inadvertently been double-booked. Typically, this type of conflict is settled with the arena director. A few game changes and practice shifts combined with the director leaving early due to a stomach bug caused the situation to occur and flare out of control. To add to the situation, the assistant director was on vacation and no one else in a position of authority was available.

At this point, the two teams needed the facility at once. Both have rights to it, and no one else could be reached for a decision. The coaches have figured it out in the past, but this time neither would back down. There had been some field changes in the past and a war was on. Both coaches felt as if the other was pushing. Both teams were backing their coaches and the mood was quickly escalating. Both sides claimed to have rights to the field and they both refused to share it. The direct line of control could not be established. Fans were issued special passes to watch one of the teams practice. The other team had the press on site for promotion and interviews for the upcoming game.

**1.** How did the problem occur?

**2.** What happens if the direct line of control is unavailable?

**3.** What could have been done to avoid this problem?

**4.** What could be done at this point?

# The Guest Service of Travel and Tourism

## Chapter Objectives:

*After reading this chapter, you should be able to:*

Define the dynamics of tourism, as they relate to service, in an in-depth manner.

Identify and describe types of travel and the specific wants and service needs of the travelers in the segments.

Define and identify the three components of providing quality service to travelers.

Identify and explain the dynamics of the macroenvironment of tourism.

Explain the changes in tourism and detail how it affects the service of guests.

## Terminology:

Accommodation

All-Inclusive Tour

Carbon Footprint

Charter

Code Sharing

Conservation

Convention and Visitor Bureau (CVB)

Destination Management Organization (DMO)

Eco-Tourism

Excursion

Hub and Spoke

Incentive Travel

Niche Travel

Open Jaw

Pension

Tourism

Yield Management

# Introduction

Travel may be essential for business; it may be for fun, or even life-enriching. A professional in the field of travel and tourism must realize what they are offering in an effort to best serve the guests. Consider the following statements:

- You are selling the world.
- You are selling memories.
- You are selling bragging rights.
- You are competing against every other memory and experience the guest has ever had.

# Definition of Tourism: The World

The product of tourism has always been the world, so it cannot be easily defined. An official definition of **tourism** is everything associated with the traveling of more than 50 miles from home.

To expand, tourism includes all activities in a complex system involving everything that goes into awareness, searching, traveling, accommodations, activities, and post-travel experiences. With such a broad definition, it makes tourism very difficult to quantify and control for a favorable outcome. Much is demanded of you, and you must always be vigilant of vulnerabilities that are largely outside your direct control. This chapter relates the delivery of quality service management in travel and tourism using four main points:

**Tourism**
Everything associated with traveling more than 50 miles from home, typically for leisure.

Know Product → Know Guest → Know Yourself → Blend for Goals

1. Know your product.
2. Know the people.
3. Know yourself.
4. Blend the three together to best meet the desired goals of all.

This order may seem contrary to standard product-marketing, but a travel professional is selling and servicing existing products. The property, event, or city is typically outside of their control. It is unchangeable. Instead, the travel professional must know the specifics of the product and the wants and needs of their customers in order to make the most appropriate match.

## ✲ STEP 1: KNOW THE PRODUCT

This first step is unlike marketing, where you must first know your customer. In most aspects of travel, you must know the product first, then match people to your product. The most difficult part of this is that your product is the endless possibilities of the world. You must be able to calculate the odds of success with many variables that are out of your control. To begin, the variables outside your control are:

- The people
- Transportation
- Cycles of rates
- Crowd flows
- Calendars
- Health factors
- Social climates
- Personal safety
- Pricing strategies
- Major players
- Cultures
- Governance
- Societal norms
- Laws
- Reviews
- Classifications
- Lodging

These are all aspects to consider when serving the traveler. Remember, although these are outside your control, they are predictable. With experience, you will get better at working with your predictions.

## TYPES OF TRAVEL AND TOURISM

Business Travel

Leisure Travel

There are many types of travel, but the two most common categories are business travel and leisure travel. Each of them has many subcategories and each tends to balance the other out depending upon the day of the week, the season, and the venue. For example, a hotel may cater to business travelers during the week and to leisure travelers on the weekends.

## WHOSE GOALS ARE WE MEETING?

There are no distinct lines between the goals of everyone involved in travel and tourism. It is hoped that the goals will cross over into each other. This point of intersection or overlapping of goals is the key to pleasing the customers. It will surface and plague the customer-service system if any single other entity is left.

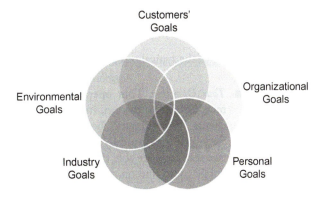

### Customers' Goals

The goals of the customer should always be placed first. Phrases such as, "The customer always comes first" proliferate in the literature in nearly every industry. The idea of focusing everything around the customer is referred to as customer-centric. While the goals of the customer are certainly important, it would be unwise to consider only them, without taking everything else into consideration. Thus, a common ground should be established. Let's understand the customer goals and find the common areas that are easily shared with the other constituents.

Understanding customer goals requires an understanding of what motivates them. What are their true goals? Once understood, the next step is to prepare the customer. This is done both logistically and psychologically.

- Understand the goals
  - What motivates them?
- Preparing the customer
  - Logistically
    - Itinerary
  - Psychologically
    - Setting the appropriate expectations
    - Making the venue tangible (websites, pictures, essential readings, etc.)

### Organizational Goals

Without meeting the organizational goals, you will go out of business very quickly. To blend this into the equation is essential. The profits cannot be eroded. Fees must be collected. Too many comps will eat away at profits, so these should be monitored. Labor costs must be scrutinized. Some services require immediate attention, while others can wait. Prioritization and automation are key.

## Personal Goals

All too often this lies in an imbalance. Either it is all about the customer, all about the business, or all about the employee.

If a position is too demanding:

- What are the labor-intensive components? Can they be altered?
- Is it a certain customer or profile? Can these be altered?
- What is the true value of the customers' business?
- Are they worth the disproportionate allocation of resources?

You must satisfy your own realistic needs in order to be truly happy and naturally able to please others. If you are not happy, it will show. Of course, there will be times when you simply need to endure, but those times should be few and the rest of your work should be a consistent, reasonably satisfied flow. If not, the customer will know long before anyone else even realizes it.

## Industry Goals

Every industry sets up guidelines. The travel and tourism industry is no different. The World Travel and Tourism Council (WTTC) establishes guidelines to promote and protect responsible travel and tourism growth throughout the world. There are several other organizations that have similar goals uniting the industry through research and collaboration of their members. Ethics, greening, and sustainability are particularly large topics of the industry. All travel professionals should be involved and current with industry associations such as the WTTC to unite and help perpetuate the industry that so many depend on.

## Environmental Goals

**Eco-tourism**
Travel to, or promotion of, environmentally conscious actions, typically based around awe-inspiring natural resources.

**Conservation**
Reasonable and responsible use of natural resources in the environment to ensure optimal current and future appreciation.

**Carbon Footprint**
A person's effect on the amount of carbon dioxide released into the atmosphere. Also used in more general terms as being environmentally conscious.

Environmentally conscious travel is a huge trend throughout the travel industry. **Eco-tourism** is a term describing the travel to, or promotion of, environmentally conscious actions, typically based around awe-inspiring natural resources in tourism. It implies **conservation**, or the reasonable and responsible use of resources in the environment to ensure optimal current and future appreciation. Another term that follows this is **carbon footprint**, which is the effect of one's carbon dioxide released into the atmosphere. It is also used in a general way as being synonymous with environmental consciousness. All of these terms together are generalized under the term *green* or *greening*. Without consideration of greening, there would not be a future.

The key to meeting the goals of all is understanding them and concentrating on the areas where they overlap. Realize where all are coming from and try to find a common ground.

*Prepare* the customers.
*Understand* that business must be conducted.
*Take care* of yourself.
*Align with* the industry.
*Protect* the environment.

This is how customer service is delivered in the travel and tourism industry.

# CHAPTER REVIEW QUESTIONS

1. Why might a client want an open-jaw flight?
2. Why is eco-tourism good for the community?
3. What is the difference between a tour guide and a tour operator?
4. Why is tourism so difficult to define?
5. List and briefly describe five types of leisure travel.
6. How does intangibility and heterogeneity apply to travel and tourism?
7. What is niche travel, and how can it be an effective means of pleasing your client?
8. How has the field of travel and tourism changed in the past few years?
9. What are some of the essential qualities of a travel professional?
10. What are the three main things that you should know in order to provide quality service to enhance a customer's travel experience?

# CASE STUDIES

### Glowing Algae Tours

Many tourists come to the Bahamas for sun and relaxation. They also dine, shop, and snorkel by day. At night comes more dining, parties, and perhaps gambling. As an excursion, tourists have come to long for something unique. A niche tour for those who want to experience a wonder of nature is a guided kayaking tour through the glowing algae. It has an intriguing allure to tourists, and many inquire about it.

In order to do this, tourists are shuttled to a remote spot near the beach around 9 P.M. They watch a small instructional film and demonstration. Then, they are given gear and kayaks. They carry or drag the kayaks down to the beach, get in the water, and are acquainted with the boats and paddles. Once everyone is in and adjusted, they paddle together out to the reef. This paddling takes about 45 minutes and is done in the near-total darkness.

Finally, they reach the glowing algae and, for most, it all seems worthwhile. It lights up and glows as the kayaks pass over the top of them. The bio-luminescent awe is tranquil.

As great as it is, the experience is not for the weak, and the tour company receives complaints. It seems that people either love it or hate it. Despite stating upon making reservations that it is a kayak tour and tourists should be in good physical shape, not everyone is prepared for the tour. Occasionally, paddlers tire and need to be towed or assisted. Some tire from dragging the kayaks down to the water.

Occasionally, the tide is strong and the water rough. Sometimes a storm blows in unexpected rains, making it miserable. On rare occasions, sharks are spotted, and although no attacks have ever been reported, it scares the tourists.

1. List the inherent issues with Glowing Algae Tours.
2. What is outside their control?
3. What is within their control?
4. How could the company reduce the number of guest complaints?

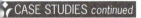

## Establishing Bus Protocol

Garrison Bus Lines offers several types of tours. Many of these are assisted travel trips aboard their buses. They offer transportation to many different venues, from ski trips, to casinos, to theaters, to ballgames. They are an older, established transit company with a pricing strategy that offers a real value.

Occasionally, the guides encounter issues on the bus. Sometimes they can resolve it well. Lately, the guides are having more trouble, and the old-school styles of being strict are simply not working. The owners wonder whether this can be attributed to the changing demographics of the clients. The guides attribute it to the lower prices of the chartered trips. The owners want the guides to be kind to the patrons and let them have fun, but fear that some are wrecking it for the others.

As a solution, they have hired a college intern to help them develop a protocol for preventing and handling customer service scenarios. The deliverables are a training guide and a small set of demonstrations accompanying each type of common incident.

The company has several logs from the drivers and incident reports from the tour agents. From those, a list of the most popular and difficult guest service situations have been produced. The list is as follows:

- Late passengers
- Misinformed passengers
- Smoking demands
- Intoxicated guests
- Rest stop requests
- Unusual items aboard the bus

1. Devise tips for avoiding these scenarios.
2. Devise methods for dealing with these scenarios after they have occurred.

## Offering a Service

Travel agencies have undergone many hardships in the past few years. The advance of technology has placed the power of travel arrangements into the hands of the consumer. Anyone with an Internet connection can locate and compare fares, availability, and predictability. Travel agencies have lost the power of exclusivity in travel arrangements.

It is now about more than price. The leisure traveler is typically shopping for the lowest price but also needs the service that accompanies it. It is a balancing act with trade-offs that some customers learn the hard way.

As travel professionals witness this change, many have done more than just complain. They have begun to alter their marketing efforts. They have begun a challenge of retraining the general public on what they offer.

When a traveler plans a trip, things don't always go as planned. Travel professionals assist people with their knowledge of what works and what does not. They are more familiar with rates, airlines, charters, and many other logistics that can make or break a trip.

1. What has happened to travel agencies in the past few years?
2. How are some agencies changing their marketing tactics?
3. How is service a distinguishing factor?
4. List ideas of how a travel professional can use service as an advantage.

❖ CASE STUDIES *continued*

### Corporate Travel, LLC

Corporate Travel, LLC is a corporate travel agency that strives to serve its customers. It offers many services and technologies to its clients, who seem to really appreciate it. It has recently instituted a technology that it believes will give it even more of an advantage over the competition. It has adopted a new technology called air2youNOW. This proprietary technology enables the clients to speak with a travel associate in a call center via SMS or live video chat. The business clients like it because they do not have to open their laptops, and can even text when they need to.

They also overhauled their website to permit live video and text chats between the agents and the business travelers on the go. They have also instituted a new automated request technology that helps with nonessential, but timely, requests. These requests can be placed into the system and submitted to corporate for approval within 24 hours.

They also depend on great customer service. In every survey, service rates at the very top along with cost and ease of travel. Despite having these technologies, the travel agents aren't as productive. Their sales have actually lowered. They seem to spend more time solving small problems on the edge of their responsibility or listening to complaints from angry, stranded travelers. In short, what had been rated as the highest priority is becoming overwhelming.

1. Outline the issues with service at Corporate Travel, LLC.
2. Why are the agents busier than ever?
3. Do the new programs really pay off?
4. What is the real problem at Corporate Travel, LLC?
5. What could be done to remedy the problem?

# The Guest Service of Casinos

## Chapter Objectives:

*After reading this chapter, you should be able to:*

Describe types of casinos as they relate to customer service.

Identify and describe types of floor positions typical to casinos.

Describe the unique characteristics of a casino property.

Explain and apply the concept of guest service to various casino guests.

## Terminology:

Comps
Low Rollers
Player-Tracking Systems
VIPs
Whales

# Introduction

Casinos are unlike any other facet of the hospitality industry. The average guest will lose more than they will win. How then, do you make them leave happy and want to return? It is the experience! The casino experience is very difficult to replicate outside a casino. The guest is provided with some of the best services available. The more they spend, and lose, the better the services. The lights, the energy, the spirit behind it can be a real thrill. Guests crave this experience. It is up to the casino professionals to make it happen.

## ⚜ TYPES OF CASINOS

Casinos offer much more to guests than gaming. Casinos may be freestanding or on a riverboat, but quite often they are part of a larger entity. Many casinos are within hotels. Some casinos are part of a hotel complex or a destination resort experience. Casinos are linked to hotels, food and beverage operations, meetings and convention halls, entertainment arenas, golf courses, and even cruise ships. Gaming is typically considered the money-maker, and other offerings support the casinos. The hope with regard to the extra amenities is to contain the spending within the property by offering guests everything they need. Once they leave, the money goes with them.

## ⚜ FROM CRIMINAL TO RESPECTABLE

In the past, casinos were viewed as criminal enterprises. Now they are very respectable and are owned by major companies; they are highly regulated. Anyone who wants to own part of a casino can simply buy shares in their stock.

Casinos also have an interest in responsible gambling. They have made great progress in helping guests with compulsive gambling behaviors. Many work with agencies like the National Center for Responsible Gaming and the Responsible Gaming Council.

## ⚜ COMPLEX ENTITIES

Hospitality is a unique industry. Its casino segment is heavily regulated and requires a unique model. Casinos are typically not stand-alone units; they are part of a larger offering of services and amenities, making their existence quite complex. This alters the typical operations of the other departments. The environment, the views toward profitability, and the customer profiles are all unique to this segment.

# Floor Positions

Front of the house (FOH) casino games are typically split into two primary divisions: slot machines and table games. Table games require much more support so the organizational chart is more layered. Typically, every employee on the floor must be state-licensed. Table games are:

- Blackjack (21)
- Roulette
- Craps
- Baccarat
- Poker

A dealer runs the table. He or she is given responsibility for an individual table. Several tables together in an area are referred to as a pit. Floorpersons oversee a group of games within a pit. Pit managers oversee all of the groups of games within the pit. Shift managers oversee most or all of the pits, and a games manager is in charge of all games.

Dealers get the most guest interaction. They must be completely fair and honest and have no prejudice. Dealers cannot give advice. People in this position are typically friendly and talkative, but they have a job to do. They are highly scrutinized. They have pit bosses and cameras observing every move. It may seem exciting, but most of their actions are routine. They must keep up the pace and deal a certain number of hands or spin a certain number of times in order to keep the game moving and earn the casino a profit. They are constantly pressing to keep the players going, and some of the players may not always appreciate this or view it as unfriendly.

Common back of the house (BOH) casino departments that support customer service may include:

- Accounting
- Cashier's station/cage
- Countroom
- Bookkeeping
- Surveillance
- Security

Most money is tracked using electronic cards. When money is moved, teams of three people are common.

Slot machines have staff positions as well:

- *Slot manager*: Also called "Director." Responsible for overall management
- *Shift manager*: Responsible for slots during a given shift
- *Slot mechanic*: Responsible for repair and maintenance of slots

- *Slot Attendant*: Also called "Floor Person." Responsible for verifying payouts, and supervising change attendants
- *Cashiers*: Located within "Main Cage." Responsible for completing payment of payouts and making change

The front office of the hotel is staffed with bell staff and reservations staff. The sales and marketing department are the administrative staff that deal indirectly with the guests. The housekeeping, maintenance, security, and room service staff also play key roles in customer service.

# Unique Environmental Characteristics

## ⚜ MAIN GOAL

The primary goal of a casino is like that of any other business—to earn a profit. In order to do that, the casino must provide a service and retain the customer. Once the customers leave the property, they are no longer spending money there. Much goes into keeping the casino customer within the casino. Consequently, many casinos have evolved to become everything to the customer. They offer food and accommodations without the guests ever leaving the property. Additionally, they are designed to reduce the interference of the attention to the outside world, making time appear irrelevant.

## ⚜ HIGH-TECH

Most patrons of casinos desire technology. State-of-the-art technology is part of the competitive mix in offering a guest a great experience. Competition pushes casinos to embrace the latest technologies. Casinos must be on the cutting edge of everything from lighting, to entertainment, to communications. These new technological innovations are assisting the casino side of hospitality to achieve efficiency of service as well as overall cost savings. The tools come in the form of both hardware and software enhancements that allow for more efficient operation in player tracking, cash acceptance, and jackpot payouts.

Most players are also tracked on **player-tracking systems** through reward cards. Customers are rated. **Comps**—free food, beverage, lodging, or prizes—are given according to the amount they gamble. Comps may be done with a point system. Casinos can also share information with each other regarding profiles in the case of cheats.

It isn't just one person who has knowledge, it is a team equipped with customer relation management (CRM) and database technologies.

## ⚜ FREE DRINKS

It is customary for drinks to be offered free of charge on the casino floor. This keeps customers there longer so they don't have to leave for a drink. This also helps them to

**Player-Tracking System**
A system that monitors the frequency and usage of gamblers. Used to give rewards or comps.

**Comps**
Free compensation for food, beverage, rooms, or other gratuities to reward guests.

feel welcomed and as if they are valued and receiving something, even if they may be losing money at the machines or at the tables.

## ⁒ FOOD AND BEVERAGE

Meals are offered in all styles so that the customer does not have to leave the property. Some are quick meals so that they can get back to a "hot" slot machine they believe will pay out soon. Other restaurants give them a chance to relax and enjoy before returning to the games. Originally, restaurants were "loss leaders," meaning they were only there to support the gaming function. They offered $2.95 prime rib dinners as an attraction. The food and beverage operations lost money that was quickly regained through the casino. Things have changed, and while the food is still considered a support department, it is now also offered and expected to earn a profit. It is also common nowadays to have every possible type of food outlet. Some casinos may offer as many as 20 to 30 or more, while smaller ones may have only a handful. Some are chains and others are named after celebrities. A wide variety brings in the gamblers and meets the demands of the rest of the players. The restaurants see different traffic patterns, increased comps, and different demographics than non-casino operations, but quickly learn to adjust and accommodate to the overall plan.

## ⁒ ROOMS

Casino hotels are some of the largest in the country and the world. Some have 3,000 to 4,000 rooms, and some have as many as 6,000. A casino hotel is for VIPS, frequent players, and tourists. It also supports conferences and conventions. A casino hotel operates as a lodging facility, but it is intended to facilitate the casino. Many comps are given. It is not uncommon for as much as 90 percent of the rooms to be comped. Occupancy patterns may also be different from those of other hotels. The casino hotel is not designed for the locals unless they are medium or high rollers. The hotel keeps players on premise so they spend their money there. Free rooms, or comps, are given to the frequent players and VIPs to draw in and maintain these crowds. Upgrades are also common. These are billed directly to marketing. These demographics can be very demanding, so the hotel has to be ready to consistently deliver a high level of guest service. Since it is a festive environment, extreme and occasionally questionable events can occur. People are celebrating and a few are less than scrupulous so caution must be maintained. As with other great hotels, it is also common for a few guests to take up permanent residence at the casino hotels.

**VIPs**
Celebrities, high-profile, or high rollers who receive special attention and services from the casino.

**Whales**
Gamblers who spend very large amounts gambling. They are accustomed to receiving very high levels of service.

## ⁒ VIPS

**Very important people (VIPs)** are celebrities, high-profile people, or high rollers (very high rollers are also known as **whales**). They are crucial to the industry because they represent a high percentage of total gaming revenues. They tend to wager very

large amounts that can be in the millions. Medium and high-rollers also spend great amounts, although less than whales.

Entire departments may be dedicated to the care of these customers. Interpreters, concierges, chefs, and the like are at their immediate disposal. They have all of their personal needs met. Whatever it takes is done for them. They want for nothing. They are provided with privacy and given special areas in which to gamble. Casinos keep rooms set aside for unexpected VIPs. They are given large suites on separate floors with many extras and have personal attendants dedicated to them. Their suites may have separate bedrooms and a dining room so they can invite guests and entertain. All of these things create overall value of which the players feel they have earned through their gambling expenditures. As a result, the players feel appreciated. The medium and high-rollers also receive many perks, although in lesser amounts than the whales.

## MEETINGS AND EVENTS

Many casinos are associated with meetings, trade shows, exhibitions, and conference centers. Casinos are a great draw for attendees of meetings. Meetings and events attract new customers to the casinos. In fact, Las Vegas can be considered a conference city. Without conferences, the city could not support itself on individual gamblers. Conference attendees are compelled to stay there because of the conference. While they are there, they typically patronize the property, including buying food and beverage, attending shows, retail purchases, and gambling. When they stay and eat, they pay nearly full price. There are few comps given to these crowds.

**Low Rollers**
Guests who spend very little on gambling.

Casino shows attract many different types of people. It is not uncommon to see a rodeo, a computer trade show, and a business meeting all being held simultaneously. Lately, sports teams are being integrated into show arenas, bringing yet another type of new crowd. Meeting the needs of this crowd is very different because their primary goal is different from that of typical gamblers. They may be non-gamblers or very **low rollers**, who spend very little on gambling. Casinos are an extra perk for them. They can be enticed into spending if they feel the need for adventure or a splurge. These attractions can bring in business during the week, when the casino might be slow, so they are advantageous to the property.

## ATMOSPHERE

Casinos appeal to the senses. Every casino is a party. No matter what day or time of day that you are there, the atmosphere is festive. Lights of all colors and the sounds of bells fill the air. It looks very similar whatever the time of day or weather, and most casinos do not display clocks which makes it very easy to lose track of the outside world. All of this helps to provide an escape into a fantasy land where fun is the theme. Guests feed off of this energy. It fills the senses.

## ✦ OTHER ACTIVITIES

Some casinos are even resorts with golf, spas, shopping, shows, and many other activities. They offer alternative activities for gamblers to spend or to occupy the non-gamblers in the party. Like the restaurants, medium and luxury brand names have been lured to open shops, making the overall offerings very attractive.

## ✦ SECURITY

Security in casinos is at a much higher level than at most other hospitality operations. Surveillance is very big. Everything is monitored on video. Cameras cover nearly every angle and every square foot. You literally cannot go anywhere without being on camera from many views. Profiles are established. Customer levels are monitored. Facial recognition programs are in place. Cheater information is available and shared to track them globally. The casinos work with each other so that information can be shared anywhere.

Security officers are visible, controlling access, cash drops, counts, and all physical assets. A director of surveillance oversees the surveillance department, games, compliance, and conduct.

## ✦ OUT-OF-TOWN GAMBLERS VERSUS LOCAL GAMBLERS

When visiting a casino, the valet or doorman is the first to assess and welcome the guests. There is a wide blend of people who come with very different needs and expectations. It might be a local who just finished a shift, or a group celebrating a special occasion or even a vacation getaway. Visits to casinos may be frequent and the guests have very specific wants and needs. Or, they seldom travel and aren't fully aware of their needs and expectations. Whatever it might be, it is important to discern or size-up these guests immediately because they arrive with very different sets of needs and expectations. Marketing studies have shown that out-of-town guests spend significantly more per person; however, locals spend less but visit more often.

The local gambler isn't as impacted by the glitz and the glare of casino atmosphere. They have become accustomed to it. They avoid the places that do not specifically fit them for a variety of reasons. It could be small things like parking or clientele. A casino quickly learns if it is attracting local gamblers. This crowd has different and lower, yet quirky expectations. It likely isn't a special occasion for them, just casual entertainment. They spend less but make up for it in frequency.

## Jeffrey Hartmann
President and Chief Executive Officer of Mohegan Sun Casino, Hotel and Entertainment Resort

Photo Courtesy of Jeffrey Hartmann.

### Property

Mohegan Sun is a $2.5 billion facility located in Uncasville, Connecticut. It is a full-service complex that includes casino and a resort hotel, including meeting spaces, restaurants, golf, spas, shopping, and an exhibition arena.

I MOHEGAN SUN BOULEVARD · UNCASVILLE, CT 06382
WWW.MOHEGANSUN.COM · 888.226.7711

Photo Courtesy of the Mohegan Sun Hotel.

**The Mohegan Sun Hotel.** Photo Courtesy of the Mohegan Sun Hotel.

### Interviewer Background Highlights

**1984**—Began as a CPA at PriceWaterhouseCoopers
**1991**—Became the Director of Finance at Foxwoods Casino
**1996**—Came to Mohegan Sun as Executive Vice President and Chief Financial Officer
**2004**—Became Executive Vice President and Chief Operating Officer of Mohegan Sun, reporting to Corporate Chief Officer, where he worked on growth of the property, raising $2.5 Billion for Mohegan Sun building project.
**2011**—Became President and Chief Executive Officer of Mohegan Sun.

### Business Strategy

To be the premier resort experience; not just a casino.
They want to be the best by providing a unique, all-encompassing environment as a resort.

### Vision

To be the preferred entertainment destination by delivering memorable experiences and unmatched personalized services.

### Core Values

The business strategy must be aligned with the vision and core values.

- Blowing away the customer.
- Bottom-line performance.
- Developing passionate and dedicated employees.
- Continuously striving for perfection.

### Business Management Style

Mr. Hartmann explains that his idea of leading at his level involves setting and following a vision.

Mohegan Sun created the "Time to Shine" campaign, in which employees are encouraged to create special moments for the guests. This idea has helped the employees to recognize the individual guest-contact moments.

He has also instituted "Breakfast with Jeff," when he invites employees to a monthly breakfast to get to know each other, share experiences, and gain insights. He asks these questions of all of the employees at the breakfasts:

- Tell me about yourself.
- What do you like most about Mohegan Sun?
- What can I do to help you in your job?

The answers are very empowering. Employees generally want recognition for their performance.

In his role as CEO, he wants to eliminate "silos," or departments that operate without communicating. He believes that it is his job to set the vision and get employees to follow enthusiastically. He sends a weekly e-mail on Fridays, entitled "What's Happening," that briefs managers.

He responds to guest letters personally and follows up with employees and operations. He sends thank-yous and shout-outs daily. He wants managers and employees to remember the vision and feel a part of the organization.

## Human Resources

Mr. Hartmann explained that it all starts with the hiring process. Because of the poor economy and the demands for a high level of service, Mohegan Sun can be more selective in their hiring process. The human resources department has moved to behavior-based interviews. They place individuals in groups and briefly leave them alone to observe their group interaction. It was modeled after the airline industry interviews and has been proven to be very successful.

The training is unique. Because of the Native American tribal ownership, training is based on the "Spirit of Aquai," which involves four Mohegan standards:

1. Welcoming
2. Mutual Respect
3. Cooperation
4. Building Relationships

## Surveys

Mohegan Sun uses a service called Market Metrix, which sends out 1,000 customer surveys a month. It assesses 43 sections covering all areas of the property. Results are reviewed weekly and also during monthly meetings. Their goal is 90 percent customer satisfaction. Results under 75 percent are flagged and warrant a follow-up.

## Special Service Tips

Valet parking is free and automatic. The valets can bring the car to anywhere the guest desires on property. They act as a first point of contact. They scan cars, recognize levels, and draw upon their tact and technology to appropriately handle all requests.

## Guest Services

A Guest Recognition Program tracks the guests and segments them into four tiers:

- Player's Club
- Wolf
- Sagamore
- Sachem Guests (invitation only)

The Sachem guests are the highest level. The guests in each level are updated every 6 months. Mohegan Sun has a VIP Services Department that is tasked with ensuring that guests are treated with the level of service and accommodations they desire. This department also handles all in-bound calls and appropriately routes them to the rest of the property.

(continued)

Mohegan Sun also does an outstanding job of catering to their Asian market. They have Asian hosts who operate like point guards, ensuring that everything is in place to provide the best experience for them. These hosts have a very good understanding of the wants and needs of the Asian market and the offerings of Mohegan Sun. They arrange everything from language translations to special menu offerings.

### Trends

Mr. Hartmann states that the biggest change ahead will be the maturation of the baby-boomer generation. Generations X and Y are going to be surpassing them in terms of disposable income, and they must be marketed to and entertained differently. He predicts that handheld software will become bigger and will drive the future of

the business. With this technology, people are changing how they socialize. This change in the social aspect will be very important for casinos and resorts, and they must be ready to react to it. This will require casinos to change how to interact with and cater to them. Table games may see the biggest change with this interaction. The technology is out there, and it is only a matter of time before it will be fully integrated.

### Acknowledgment

Mr. Hartmann would like to acknowledge the contributions of the late Mr. Bill Velardo. He created guest services at Mohegan Sun and is considered to be the Father of Guest Services and Operations. Mr. Hartmann considers himself to be a steward and caretaker of these original works.

# CHAPTER REVIEW QUESTIONS

1. How are the guest services different for high-rollers versus low-rollers?
2. Why does a casino hotel give most of its rooms away?
3. Why do casinos typically serve free drinks?
4. Explain how food and beverage service is different at a casino.
5. How are conference attendees different from typical casino guests?
6. Why do casino hotels give so many comps to high rollers?
7. What types of services do whales receive?
8. How important is casino security?
9. Why do casinos offer so many services to the guests?
10. What is the "Spirit of Aquai"?

# CASE STUDIES

### Catering to the Low-Rollers

Casinos have much competition. The smaller, older properties cannot compete with the newer, bigger properties. Some casinos decide to go after the low-roller market and take the fast-food approach by decreasing costs and sales-per-customer but increasing customer counts.

The High-Stepper Casino is one of the oldest properties in the area. It has been renamed a couple of times and has seen a few different owners and management

companies over the years. Originally in a great location, the area had once seen a boom of business, then lost out during a downturn in the local gaming community. Over the past 10 to 15 years, it has seen a rather steady growth of new entrants into the market, but they are building in an area about a mile away from this location, making it less likely to be visited.

The management of the High-Stepper is trying to determine a new direction. The management must report this new idea to the board of directors and the asset managers in a formal presentation next month.

After looking at what the casino has to offer, they decide to be a casino that accommodates to low and medium-rollers. Basically, they want to make all new gamblers feel at home. They want to be there for the guests who don't have as much to spend. They want to attract the local traffic. They also want to cater to the medium rollers, making them feel like high rollers.

1. Evaluate what the High Stepper has to offer to its customers.
2. Will the new strategy work?
3. What will they have to change at the property to better serve their target guests?
4. What would you change about the strategy?

## Spain, Inc.

Spain, Inc. is an upscale dining chain. They have several free-standing units. They run a tight operation, with a strict operations protocol. They train their managers to operate the business in the Spain, Inc. manner. They adhere specifically to the methods of customer service that have served them well for many years. As a result, they are known for their old-world hospitality. From the food and décor, to the staff and customer service, they provide a consistent and exceptional experience.

As they continue to grow, the corporate office development team has decided to open a new location in a full-scale hotel, casino, and resort. They will be 1 of 35 food-service operations on the premises. They believe this move will further the exposure of Spain, Inc. and provide the company with much additional revenue.

Jason is a Spain, Inc. store manager who has been with the company since he graduated from college. He has been through all of the rigorous training. He has advanced from waiter to dining room manager, to assistant manager and finally to store manager. He won an award for best new store manager this past year. His operation runs well, but is relatively small and has limited bonus potential. Jason accepted an offer to become store manager of the new unit located within the casino.

As they open the new Spain, Inc., Jason soon learns that his restaurant within a casino is very different. Everything from the employees, to the customers, to the hours are different from the restaurants located outside the casino.

One of the first things that Jason notices is that his recruitment efforts have been attracting a different type of employee. Next, he is caught off guard by the peak and non-peak hours. His customer counts had always varied depending on the weather. Now, things are different. His outside seating is really inside the huge, climate-controlled building. It is as if they had brought the outside in with a perfect climate. It is never too hot or too cold. His deck is now the preferred seating. He also notices that the busy days aren't the same. The new place followed the typical Friday and Saturday nights, but also saw strong counts on other days and whenever there were special events held at the casino.

He also saw a change in the wants and the needs of the guests. As a result, many of his former customer-service strategies were not working. Many of the guests were receiving comps. Jason quickly noticed that customers don't behave the same when their meal is free. Many order differently, so their menu mix has been very atypical. It seems like people are either extravagant or cheap. To add to that, they either take a long time with their meal or want it quickly, so that they can get back to an event, gambling, shopping, or their room.

Spain, Inc. typically hosted many special occasions, such as birthdays. It was something that people made reservations for, and the restaurant was ready to accommodate them. These demands had decreased in this unit. Jason also noticed that parties arrived together instead of waiting for the rest of their party to join them. Also, the groups were smaller, and many didn't have reservations.

Jason also noticed that more of the customers desired to be respected and receive special accommodations. The casino's VIP Team would frequently accompany these people behind the scenes to ensure their needs were met. Jason had never before experienced this type of intervention in his operation. He also witnessed some wild and crazy characters that were very atypical to Spain, Inc. patrons.

All of these changes came as a surprise to Jason. Much of what Spain, Inc. had done in the past had ceased to apply in a casino operation. His marks on his comment cards were lower from anything that he saw in his former store. He tried to make small adjustments, but his standard operating procedures were not ready for this drastic change. The staff wasn't ready, and Jason was becoming frustrated. Jason's district manager was aware of the situation and decided to visit Jason along with the director of operations.

1. How might operating a food-service establishment within a casino be different?
2. Why wasn't Spain, Inc.'s customer service training working?
3. What questions should be asked at the meeting?
4. What should Jason do differently to accommodate these changes?

## Meeting the Needs of Meetings

Skytop Hotel and Casino is an established, older property. For years, it has offered gambling, accommodations, food and beverage, and meeting space to its patrons. Most recently, the hotel has decided to gain additional revenue by revamping its meetings and events. Its hope is that it could bring new groups to benefit the entire property. It has undergone a recent change in its director of sales (DOS) position. The new DOS has replaced many of the sales staff and implemented an additional profit-sharing incentive system. Everyone must work together to fill the hotel, the casino, the restaurants, and the meeting spaces. If all are successful, the sales staff will receive an additional profit-sharing bonus.

Generally, this has worked out quite well. The entire property has been quite busy. One of the new strategies was to develop a pursuit for the SMERF (social, military, education, religious, fraternal) market, resulting in a few new groups booked at the property. With it, a couple of religious and educational groups brought in very different customer profiles. In short, they were frugal and didn't like gambling. They didn't spend as much at the restaurants. They went off-property to eat for less. Many would not even enter the casino. They did not patronize the shows unless they were free, and some voiced that they were offended at the content. To add to this, most did not drink, and the bars were empty. In fact, some of the people from the groups scoffed at other casino guests. The employees wondered why or how these

groups were even booked at a casino property if they didn't like to gamble. Consequently, the groups, the employees, and the other patrons were upset.

The director of operations (DOO) met with the DOS and the food and beverage director (FBD) to understand and resolve the situation. The FBD explained that food and beverage sales were down, except for banquets. The DOS explained that the sales staff made their sales quotas. The DOO explained that as a result, the property now had new groups that they did not know how to service. The FBD admitted that they could provide different options. The DOS admitted that they needed a new system for sales quotas. They all admitted that the current situation was not working.

1. How are these groups different from their other meeting groups?
2. Can non-gambling groups attend meetings at casinos?
3. Can a casino property still earn a profit from these groups?
4. How can the property best accommodate to the needs of these new groups?

## The Glitz and the Glamour

Ron is an employee at a casino on the local casino strip. He grew up in a nearby town and had always aspired to be part of the limelight associated with casinos. He always found gambling to be an interesting hobby. He enjoyed the casinos on the strip as fun places to visit. The action never stopped, 24/7. There was always an event with people and lights and everything else that filled all of the senses.

When it became evident that his other job did not have a future, Ron decided to make a career shift. Looking to gain more enjoyment and satisfaction from future employment, he decided that a job working with people topped his wishlist. He also considered his hobbies and how he spent his spare time. Finally, he listed local businesses in his general area that were hiring and most closely matched his newly developed career profile. Casinos quickly climbed to the top of the resulting list.

Ron began in the back of the house as part-time support staff. After his state qualifications were met, he began working the casino floor. He enjoyed helping people. He enjoyed the atmosphere and the steady pay. He learned to deal cards and became a dealer at one of the blackjack tables. He began getting regular shifts and regular customers. Tips quickly grew and then became consistent. He enjoyed his job.

Now, after a few months, the glitz and the glamour is beginning to wear off. Despite the fun casino atmosphere and the pay, it is a regular job with some downsides. He always liked to please people. Some of the players weren't happy unless they won, and a few people had obvious gambling issues. By policy, he could not even give them advice. He had to stand there and watch people gamble away more than they should. He could report it, but his involvement ends there. He also realized that the glitz and glamour of a 24/7 environment isn't as glamorous when he occasionally had to rotate through the night shifts and holidays. Gaming wasn't turning out to be nearly as attractive as the movies led him to think. It is a regular job, with good points and bad points, ups and downs.

Ron's personal life has also been impacted. He is working more than before, and his hours varied at times, compromising his social life. He is finding it difficult to sleep and is watching more television than ever on his time off.

All of this has had an impact on his work. Ron's pit boss realizes that he hasn't been as cheerful as he was when he first began. He doesn't seem to be as welcoming to his regular

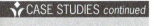

customers. Ron was even warned once about his attitude. He thought that he would enjoy this job at a place that he loved, but working in his field of hobby is very different than enjoying his hobby.

1. What were Ron's original expectations? Were they realistic?
2. Was Ron a good fit for the job?
3. What should the casino do to help Ron stay motivated and best serve customers?
4. What can Ron do to motivate himself?

# Section III

# Assessments and Planning

# Research and Tools

## Chapter Objectives:

*After reading this chapter, you should be able to:*

Apply the basic procedures of research methodology for service research.

Identify and apply various quality research tools and techniques.

Compare and contrast service quality external awards and certifications.

Construct a research assessment using appropriate quality tools and techniques.

Assess and improve a process properly using quality techniques.

## Terminology:

| | | |
|---|---|---|
| Affinity Diagram | Fishbone Diagram | Quality Assessment Tools and |
| Baseline Measurements | Flow Chart Diagram | Techniques |
| Benchmarking | Focus Group | Root-Cause |
| Brainstorming | Force-Field Analysis | Analysis |
| Check Sheets | Gantt Chart | Scatter Diagram |
| Control Chart | Multi-voting | Secret Shopper |
| Cost–Benefit Analysis | Pareto Chart | Six Sigma |
| Cost of Error | Poka-Yoke | Star-Rating |
| Delphi Method | Process Reengineering | Surveys |
| Diamond Rating | Pros–Cons Sheet | Survqual |

# Introduction

In the management of service, you will have to do much research. It isn't usually formal and you probably won't be wearing a white lab coat. The term *research* means investigating, thinking logically, and determining a solution. Quality tools are the vehicles for doing just that. Tools are the keys to unlock the doors of mysteries. They provide organization, logic, clarity, and insight well past what the mind could do on its own.

This chapter is divided into three main sections. The first discusses the foundations of performing research. The second discusses the use of tools and techniques used in the service industry. The third covers external awards and certifications common to the hospitality industry.

# Setting Up for Research

Research is anything but haphazard. It is a formal process. It is scientific. It follows a set of steps that allow it to be standardized and critiqued for validity. In setting up for research, there are criteria that need to be established to ensure a successful experiment. We can refer to these casually as the why, what, who, and how of research experiments (Figure 10.1). Their more formal labels and explanations are listed below.

**FIGURE 10.1　The Why, What, Who, and How of Research.**

## ✝ WHY: COLLECT BACKGROUND INFORMATION

Collecting background information is crucial to any research. It identifies areas of concern that help to establish a starting point and build a case for the direction of future investigation. Without it, you are guessing or 'shooting in the dark'.

You can begin an analysis by asking questions such as:

- Are you providing wants and needs?
- What's involved in your service?
- What is good, what is bad, and what can be changed?
- How consistent can you be?
- What are the newest trends?

You should also take **baseline measurements**. These are "before" measurements that describe a situation or condition prior to intervention. Baseline measurements are helpful in monitoring growth or change after you make improvements.

---

**Baseline Measurements**
"Before" measurements that describe a situation or condition prior to intervention.

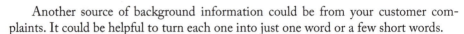

Another source of background information could be from your customer complaints. It could be helpful to turn each one into just one word or a few short words.

You could also hold a focus group or simply just listen to your staff, because they probably have some great suggestions.

## WHAT: DETERMINE WHAT TO MEASURE

After background information has been collected, the information must be sorted and analyzed. This is when the real direction takes place. The end product of this step is having the primary areas to measure. All suggestions should be considered in determining the primary areas.

Examples of this could be:

- Empowerment
- Customer service
- Communication
- Job security
- Price

## WHO: CHOOSE THE POPULATION

After you know what to measure, you need to determine who, how much, or how many to measure. This may seem straightforward, but the details need to be considered and rules must be established. Something as simple as measuring the customers may become an issue:

- Do you want former, current, and potential customers?
- What if they are repeat customers?
- Can you measure every customer every time?
- What if you cannot reach them or they refuse?
- What if they purchase a lot, or a little, or their transaction is voided?

As you are setting this up, you should also determine how the population will be divided. For example, it could be divided by demographics or psychographics:

- *Demographic*: Age, income, marital status, education, stage in family life cycle, home ownership, gender, ZIP code, occupation, household size and type, travel patterns, ethnicity, religion
- *Psychographic*: Lifestyles, mode of living, needs, attitudes, reference groups, culture, class, family influences, hobbies, political affiliation

## HOW: CHOOSE THE METHOD AND MEASUREMENT

After laying the groundwork and determining what and who to measure, the rest of the research typically follows a logical path. The "how" completes the classic research methodology format (research is typically conducted using this method). It has six steps and will take much diligence to complete, but will likely yield superior results.

1. Choose instrument type
   a. Tools
   b. Techniques
2. Adapt tool or technique
3. Pilot test
   a. Trial run of your experiment
   b. Smaller scale
4. Revise based on results of pilot test
5. Administer experiment
6. Interpret data

# Tools and Techniques

There are many **quality assessment tools and techniques**. These can be used in experiments and in every step of the quality service process.

Quality assessment tools and techniques can be divided into four main groups by their purpose. They are used for specific reasons depending on your needs. The four main purposes (shown in Figure 10.2) are to:

**Quality Assessment Tools and Techniques**

A research instrument used to target, analyze, develop, or evaluate a service system.

1. Target an opportunity for improvement
2. Analyze the area targeted for improvement
3. Develop and implement improvements
4. Evaluate improvements

Some tools can be used in more than one group.

**FIGURE 10.2   Quality Assessment Tools and Techniques.**

### Target an Opportunity for Improvement

- Define the process, identify and describe the problem.
- These tools analyze processes or determine current conditions.
- These tools help to write a problem statement or specify areas for improvement. They help to prevent misunderstandings. This forms a foundation for objective analysis.

### Analyze the Area Targeted for Improvement

- These are tools that assist in understanding the areas for improvement. They could also help to classify quality issues and analyze the preliminary data.

- These tools help to assess:
  - ○ Importance to guests
  - ○ Importance to management
  - ○ Importance to staff
  - ○ Control over the improvement area

### Develop and Implement Improvements

- Determine and implement solutions to remedy the problems.
- These tools help to identify, select, and implement potential solutions.
- These tools can help to develop an action plan that has:
  - ○ Acceptance by guests.
  - ○ Acceptance by management.
  - ○ Acceptance by staff.
  - ○ Cost-effectiveness.
  - ○ Timelines for implementation.
  - ○ Practicality of implementation.

### Evaluate Improvements

- Assess the changes.
- These tools assist in evaluating the impact of the changes or solutions. They include many different sources of feedback to assess questions such as:
  - ○ Did the changes work?
  - ○ Am I asking the right questions?
  - ○ How do I know?
  - ○ Can I trust this information?

The next section will detail many of the quality assessment tools and techniques common to the quality service research process. The tools are listed alphabetically. A brief definition is provided, including a display of their place in the research process, along with tips of when they are most useful. In addition, basic instructions are provided, along with an example of most. This should help to place them into a context of how, where, and when they could best be used.

**Affinity Diagram**
A process that sorts ideas into categories for further interpretation. not in terminology lists.

## ❖ AFFINITY DIAGRAM

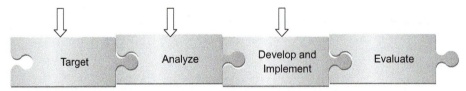

**Definition:** A process that sorts ideas into categories for further interpretation.
**Helpful when:** Analyzing verbal data or too many facts or ideas are in need of sorting.

| Time | Cost | Labor | Difficulty |
|------|------|-------|------------|
| Low | Low | Medium | Low |

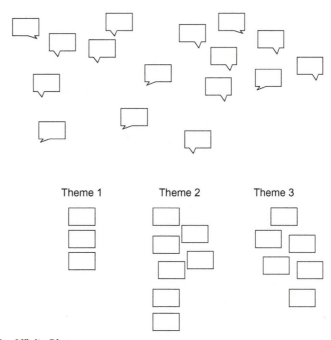

**FIGURE 10.3    Affinity Diagram.**

**Instructions (see Figure 10.3):**

1. Brainstorm, collect, or assemble different ideas for potential problems, causes, errors, or underlying reasons for the problems.
2. Record each idea on a sticky note, on a white board, or in some similar fashion.
3. Begin to place in groups. Look for relationships and commonalities.
4. Begin to develop and refine labels for groups. Look for primary groups and subgroups. Make duplicates if ideas belong in more than one groups.

**Benchmarking**
A comparison of best-practice methods.

# ❧ BENCHMARKING

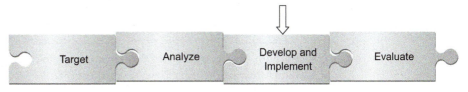

**Definition**: A comparison of best-practice methods.
**Helpful when**: You need to find the best way to perform a process.

| Time | Cost | Labor | Difficulty |
|------|------|-------|------------|
| Medium | Medium | Medium | Medium |

**Instructions:**

1. Determine process that needs improvement.
2. Determine who will be compared (benchmarked). This should ideally be with another business that is the "best-in-class" at this process. They may be a competitor or even in another industry.
3. Analyze what makes them best.
4. Adapt and adopt findings.

**Example:** In the past, the restaurant industry has had a difficult time with customers waiting for tables. The wait times could be long, and the customers were bored and uncomfortable. The restaurant industry searched across all industries to see if other businesses did a better job with customer wait-times. They discovered that Eye World Vision Centers handed out pagers to customers waiting for their eye glasses to be made. Benchmarking of this best-practice was applied and the rest is history. The restaurant industry quickly adopted this practice. Customers are no longer bound to a small area, and calling them is much less disconcerting.

## ✢ BRAINSTORMING

**Brainstorming**
Free-form thinking to generate ideas.

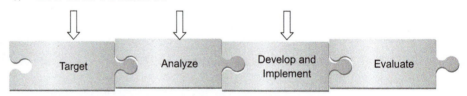

**Definition:** Free-form thinking to generate ideas.
**Helpful when:** When trying to obtain a wide range of ideas or options.

| Time | Cost | Labor | Difficulty |
|------|------|-------|------------|
| Medium | Low | Medium | Low |

**Instructions:**

1. Gather participants. Any size group will work, but a group with over 20 participants is more difficult to give all a chance to participate.
2. Present participants with issue for thought.
3. Give participants 2 to 5 minutes of silence to think and make notes.
4. Give everyone a chance to speak at least a few times.
5. Accurately record all ideas on board without judgment.
6. Process answers by seeking trends, eliminating duplicates, and so on.

**Check Sheets**
Tabulation list of frequency for repeated data.

## ✛ CHECK SHEETS

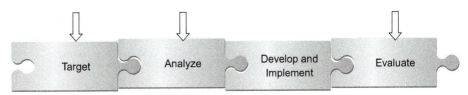

**Definition**: Tabulation of frequency for repeated data.
**Helpful when**: Collecting and analyzing repeated data, such as tabulating the guest complaints regarding renovation during a given week.

| Time | Cost | Labor | Difficulty |
|------|------|-------|------------|
| Low | Low | Low | Low |

**Instructions (see Figure 10.4):**

1. Determine what data will be observed.
2. Determine how the data will be observed. It should be measured the same way at the same location, at appropriate and consistent times.
3. Trial test for measuring or methodology errors prior to actual use.

| Renovation Complaints | | | | | | |
|---|---|---|---|---|---|---|
| | | | Day | | | |
| Reason | Mon | Tues | Wed | Thurs | Fri | Total |
| Noise | 6 | 3 | 2 | 1 | 0 | 12 |
| Mess | 3 | 2 | 3 | 7 | 2 | 17 |
| Eyesore | 3 | 3 | 1 | 6 | 1 | 14 |
| Congestion | 3 | 0 | 0 | 3 | 0 | 6 |
| Other | 2 | 0 | 0 | 3 | 0 | 5 |
| Total | 17 | 8 | 6 | 20 | 3 | 54 |

**FIGURE 10.4   Check Sheet for Renovation Complaints.**

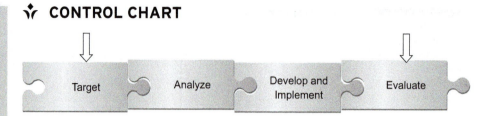

**Control Chart**
Graph that measures deviations of processes over a period of time. Other name: statistical process control (SPC).

## ✌ CONTROL CHART

**Definition**: Measure of deviations of processes over a period of time. Other name: statistical process control (SPC).

**Helpful when**: Looking at data that vary over time.

| Time | Cost | Labor | Difficulty |
|------|------|-------|------------|
| High | Low | Medium | Medium |

### Instructions (see Figure 10.5):

1. Determine data to be measured.
2. Determine control (average or ideal) line.
3. Determine upper control limit (UCL) and lower controls limit (LCL) that indicates when measurement is unacceptable or out-of-control.
4. Trial test for measuring or methodology errors prior to actual use.

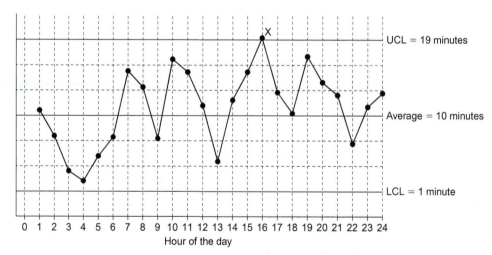

**FIGURE 10.5   Control Chart for Room Service Times.**

# ❧ COST-BENEFIT ANALYSIS

**Definition**: Used to decide whether an idea or project is cost-worthy.

**Helpful when**: Financial implications are a main priority. It answers whether it is worth doing from a financial standpoint.

| Time | Cost | Labor | Difficulty |
|------|------|-------|------------|
| Medium | Low | Low | Medium |

**Instructions (see Figure 10.6):**

1. Determine total costs associated with idea. Consider costs at all levels, present and future. Some of these may be difficult to quantify, such as time and satisfaction.
2. Determine total benefits associated with idea. The same qualities apply to these as in costs. Some of these areas, such as frustration, may be difficult to quantify.
3. Compare the results of each total against the other. This can be done as one cost and savings, annual costs, or both.
4. When comparing, you will encounter a break-even point. You must decide what is acceptable. In the case below, it is just under 3 years, which is likely acceptable since the system has a projected life of more than 10 years.

| New Property-Management System | |
|---|---|
| **Costs** | |
| System | $25,000 |
| Installation | $2,300 |
| Training: 200 staff hours @ $12/hour = | $2,400 |
| Training: 70 staff hours @ $20/hour = | $1,400 |
| Trainers: 15 hours @$45/hour = | $600 |
| Ancillary costs | $1,200 |
| **Total costs** | $32,900 |
| **Benefits** | |
| Reduction of incorrect orders voided | $5,000 / year |
| Improved inventory efficiency estimate | $2,000 / year |
| Improved ordering efficiency estimate | $3,000 / year |
| Reduction of system maintenance costs | $1,200 / year |
| **Total benefits** | $11,200 / year |
| **Payback** | $32,900 / $11,200 = 2.9375 years |

**Figure 10.6  Cost–Benefit Analysis for New Property Management System.**

**Cost of Error**
The total amount of costs associated with a customer service mistake or losing the customer.

## 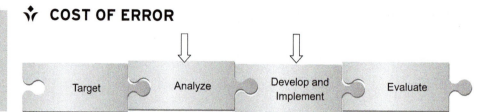 �__ COST OF ERROR

**Definition:** The total amount of costs associated with a customer service mistake or losing the customer.

**Helpful when:** Reviewing consequences of errors in processes.

| Time | Cost | Labor | Difficulty |
|------|------|-------|------------|
| Medium | Low | Low | Medium |

### Instructions (see Figure 10.7):

1. Determine process to be measured.
2. Calculate amount of errors in set period of time.
3. Calculate total costs associated with error.

---

Problem: Lines too long for customer to wait.

**Example 1:**

Occurrence: 2 patrons per night.

2 patrons × 315 days open per year = 630 lost customers per year.

630 × $15.38 check average per person = $9,689.40 per year.

(*Note: Other expenses that are more difficult to quantify: poor word of mouth, loss of tips.*)

This can also be done in a hotel setting based on a percentage of error.

**Example 2:**

0.5% of hotel customers leave because of a type of error.

0.5% × 400 rooms = 2 room per nights per day with uncleaned room issue.

2 rooms per night × 365 days = 730 nights.

730 nights × 80% occupancy = 584 room nights per year.

584 room nights × $89.65 average daily rate = $52,355.60 per year.

(*Note: There are typically other expenses that are difficult to quantify, such as loss of reputation.*)

**FIGURE 10.7  Cost of Error.**

**Delphi Method**
A method of gaining group consensus.

# ✿ DELPHI METHOD

**Definition**: A method of gaining group consensus.

**Helpful when**: You need to get a group to make a decision. Members avoid having to publicly defend themselves and they are free to speak their minds after reading the responses of others.

| Time | Cost | Labor | Difficulty |
|------|------|-------|-----------|
| Medium | Low | Medium | Medium |

**Instructions:**

1. Expert participants are selected and given a problem or situation in need of a decision. They are asked to provide comments in bullet form and not share responses.
2. The results are collected, tabulated, and handed out anonymously in summative form.
3. The participants review the group responses and consider revising or updating their own responses in light of the other opinions.
4. The new responses are collected from the participants, tabulated, and handed out anonymously in summative form.
5. This process continues for two or more rounds until a group consensus is formed or a vote is taken.

| | Rating: (1 = strongly disagree; 5 = strongly agree) Second Round Scores [first round scores in brackets] | | | | |
|---|---|---|---|---|---|
| **Comment** | **1** | **2** | **3** | **4** | **5** |
| New logo has retro appeal | | 1 [3] | 5 [3] | 1 [2] | 2 [1] |
| New logo has fresh look | 1 [2] | 5 [3] | 2 [1] | 1 [3] | |
| New logo mimics competitors | 1 [1] | 5 [6] | 3 [2] | | |

**FIGURE 10.8  Delphi Method Example Group Tabulation.**

## Service Insight

### Group Consensus

Not everyone in a group will always get their first choice. When a group must make a decision, it is unlikely that everyone will agree on precisely the same choice. The idea of group consensus means that everyone doesn't have to believe a choice is perfect or that it is their top choice. Instead, they believe that the choice is reasonable. They understand that the group as a whole believes it is the best choice or blend. Consensus means they will support it and they will not stand in the way of the choice at this time or in the future. Sometimes, group consensus is the best that we can hope for.

## ❀ FISHBONE DIAGRAM

**Fishbone Diagram**
Identifies potential
causes for a problem
in categories. Other
names: Ishikawa
diagram, cause-and-
effect diagram.

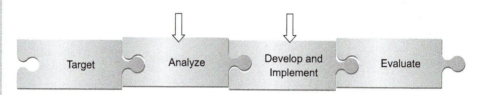

**Definition**: Identifies potential causes for a problem in categories. Other names: Ishikawa diagram, cause-and-effect diagram.

**Helpful when**: Identifying problems or causes for a multi-faceted issue.

| Time | Cost | Labor | Difficulty |
|------|------|-------|------------|
| High | Medium | Medium | High |

### Instructions (see Figure 10.9):

1. Write down problem or effect.
2. Set up with generic headings as applicable to your situation. Make them branches from the main arrow (problem). Typical headings are: Methods, Materials, People, and Equipment. Measurement and Environment are also sometimes used as additional headings.
3. In each heading, ask, "Why does this happen?" and record the reason.
4. Continue to ask, and broaden the branch as the reasons expand and deepen. The branches extend to indicate causal relationships.

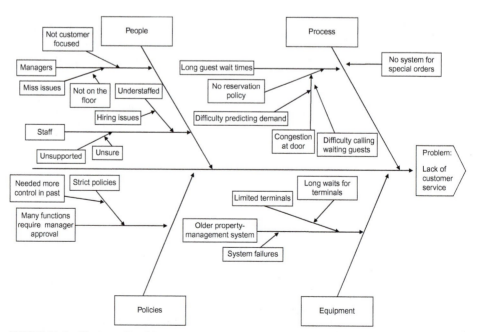

**FIGURE 10.9  Fishbone Chart Example of a Lack of Customer Service Problem.**

## ❖ FLOW CHART

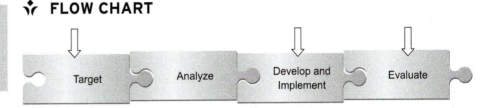

**Definition**: A graphic account of sequential steps in a process.
**Helpful when**:
○ Breaking down each step to analyze a process.
○ Understanding a process.
○ Showing where a process speeds up, slows, and has other issues.
○ Training new employees.

| Time | Cost | Labor | Difficulty |
|------|------|-------|------------|
| Medium | Low | Medium | Medium |

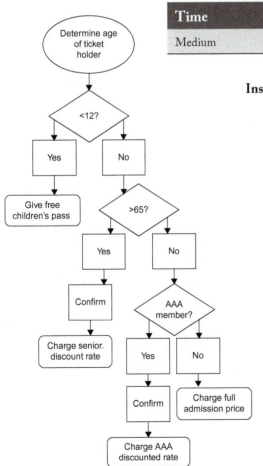

**Instructions (see Figure 10.10):**

1. Define process or interrelating processes.
2. Determine beginning and ending points of the process.
3. Determine all steps and options within the process.
4. Diagram each step and option using the appropriate symbol.
5. Connect using appropriate symbols.
   There is no universally accepted legend of symbols but commonly accepted meanings of symbols are as follows:
   ○ Ovals or circles = beginning and endings
   ○ Rectangles = typical processes
   ○ Diamonds or triangles = decisions
   ○ Arrows = demonstrate flow of the process

**FIGURE 10.10  Flow Chart of Determining Ticket Price.**

***Bottleneck***

A bottleneck is a metaphor used to describe a type of issue in flow charts. Just like the neck of the bottle constricts, forcing the liquid to gather and slow before exiting the bottle and completing the pour, so does a bottleneck slow the process in a flow chart. If you look around, you will notice many bottlenecks, like many people waiting to check out with only one register open.

## ✦ FOCUS GROUP

**Definition**: Qualitative (verbal) research in which a group (usually 4 to 10 people) is surveyed regarding their ideas and opinions on a certain product, company, or field.

**Helpful when**: You need in-depth data from respondents.

| Time | Cost | Labor | Difficulty |
|------|------|-------|------------|
| High | High | High | High |

**Focus Group**
Qualitative (verbal) research in which a group (usually 4 to 10 people) is surveyed about their ideas and opinion about a certain product, company, or field.

**Description**: **Focus groups** are typically conducted by a focus group facilitator, a trained professional who has superior communication and group skills. It is qualitative research in which a group (usually 4 to 10 people) is verbally surveyed regarding their ideas and opinion regarding a certain product or company. This method generates in-depth data from individuals that is difficult to obtain through alternative methods. A trained moderator leads the discussion. The group usually meets in a specially-designed room so that ideas can all be recorded and later interpreted. Each group typically lasts 30 to 120 minutes. Focus-group participants are usually given a token gift in appreciation of their time. The moderator may conduct one or several different focus groups on the same topics.

**Force-Field Analysis**

A technique for analyzing the forces that help and hurt a decision.

##  FORCE-FIELD ANALYSIS

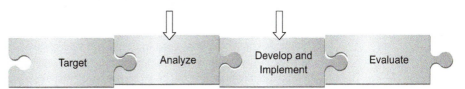

**Definition**: A technique for analyzing the forces that help and hurt a decision.

**Helpful when**: Determining and examining what is beneficial and detrimental regarding a decision. Pros–Cons Sheet examine the product of a decision while this examines the other factors that may enable or disable your efforts in pursuing the decision.

**Instructions (see Figure 10.11):**

1. List the decision in the middle of the page.
2. On the left, label: Forces for Change.
3. On the right, label: Forces against Change.
4. Brainstorm and fill in both sides of the page with bullet statements (forces).
5. Rate each of the forces from 1 (weak) to 5 (strong).
6. Tabulate and interpret your findings, deciding whether or not your plan is sufficient given the forces for and against it.

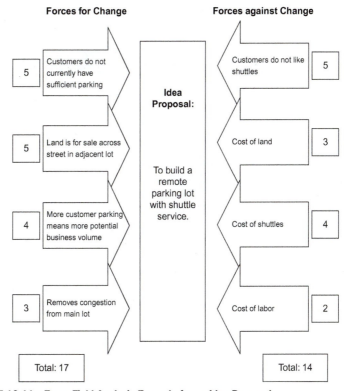

**FIGURE 10.11   Force-Field Analysis Example for an Idea Proposal.**

# ❧ GANTT CHART

**Definition**: A project planning tool that clarifies what is done and by when. It can also include who is responsible for the task.

**Helpful when**: You are setting up a project that requires coordination with others.

| Time | Cost | Labor | Difficulty |
|------|------|-------|------------|
| High | Low | Medium | Medium |

**Instructions:**

1. Determine tasks of project.
2. Determine order of tasks and which tasks need to be completed before others can begin.
3. Determine due dates of tasks.
4. Determine who will be responsible for each task, if applicable.
5. Apply steps 1 to 4 to the chart.

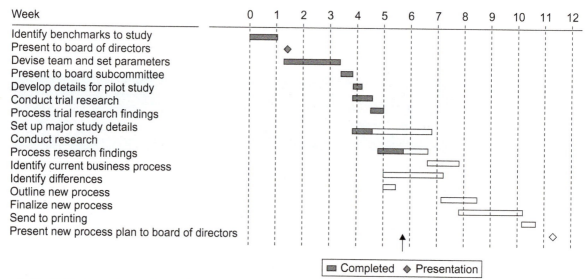

**FIGURE 10.12   Gantt Chart of Typical Research Project.**

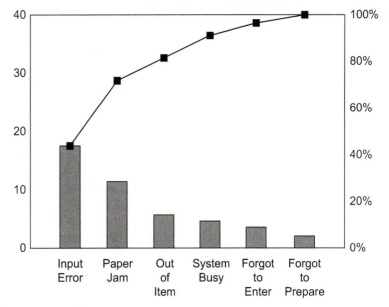

**FIGURE 10.14   Pareto Chart Example.**

# ❧ POKA-YOKE

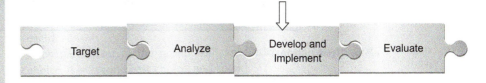

**Definition**: A system that helps to self-correct itself. Poka-Yokes are everywhere that you look. We take most of them for granted. They are engineered fail-safe systems.

**Other names**: Fail-proofing, mistake-proofing.

**Helpful when**: A process, function, or system is prone to a certain error.

| Time | Cost | Labor | Difficulty |
|------|------|-------|------------|
| Medium | Medium | Medium | High |

**Instructions:**

1. Observe the system for errors.
2. Select an error.
3. Revise the system to avoid or disallow the mistake to be made.

**Example**: A safety window prompting you to fill in missing information on a computerized reservation form before confirming.

## ✮ PROCESS REENGINEERING

**Process Reengineering**
A dramatic redesign of a system, process or business.

**Definition**: A dramatic redesign of a system, process or business that can have the most impact on achieving goals.

**Helpful when**: You require out-of-the-box thinking. When a process fails to the point at which it can no longer be patched, reengineering could be a great alternative in developing a plan.

| Time | Cost | Labor | Difficulty |
|------|------|-------|------------|
| High | High | High | High |

**Instructions:**

1. Observe the process.
2. Extract the main purpose of the process.
3. Seek or engineer alternative methods to achieve main purpose of process.
4. Thoroughly review every step, asking fundamental questions such as:
   a. Why it is done?
   b. Does it have to be done?
   c. Is that the only way it could be done?
   d. Is that the best way it could be done?

**Example**: A student cannot afford a car and rides his bicycle to school every day. It has been very rainy lately, so he purchases a rain coat. His pants kept getting wet so he buys fenders for the bike. His backpack still gets wet so he waterproofs it with a trash bag. With process reengineering, he looks at his goal: to get to school. He realizes that he can sell his bicycle and take the bus.

## ✮ PROS-CONS SHEET

**Pros–Cons Sheet**
A technique that compares the benefits and drawbacks of a given idea or solution.

**Definition**: A comparison of the benefits and drawbacks of a given idea or solution.

**Helpful when**: A decision has many points to consider.

| Time | Cost | Labor | Difficulty |
|------|------|-------|------------|
| Low | Low | Low | Low |

**Instructions:**

1. Begin with two separate sheets, one for pros and one for cons.
2. List all of the benefits of the idea on the pros sheet.
3. List all of the negative aspects on the cons sheet.
4. Devise a system to weight each of them. This can be stars or numbers in order of importance.
5. Compare results. Keep in mind not only the number of lines on each list, but also the priority or weight of the individual items.

## ✴ ROOT-CAUSE ANALYSIS

**Root-Cause Analysis**
Determining the underlying reasons why something happens.

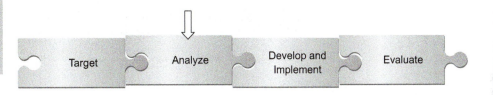

**Definition**: Determining the underlying reasons why something happens.
**Helpful when**: You want to explore why something happens so that you can solve it at the cause.

| Time | Cost | Labor | Difficulty |
|------|------|-------|------------|
| Medium | Low | Medium | Medium |

**Instructions (*Note*: This is sometimes done with a group.) (see Figure 10.15):**

1. Determine the problem. Write it on a board or in a similar fashion. This will typically become the effect.
2. Ask, "Why does this happen?" (*Note*: There may be more than one reason. Record any and all responses.)
3. State the response from step 2 and ask, "Why does this happen?"
4. Record the response(s)
5. Repeat asking why until it cannot be answered. This may be three, four, or five times. This is likely your root cause.

| Question | Answer |
|---|---|
| Why were we overcommitted on reservations? | Online reservations lost. People showed up that we didn't know about. |
| Why were the online reservations lost? | Our network went down and we couldn't retrieve the information. |
| Why did the network go down and lose information? | Our network administrator was on vacation and we couldn't reach him or his backup. |
| Root-cause answer: So we were overcommitted because we don't have a reliable backup for our network administrator? | |

**FIGURE 10.15  Root-Cause Analysis Example: Problem: Overcommitted on Reservations.**

## ᚃ SCATTER DIAGRAM

**Scatter Diagram**
A graphing of pairs of numerical data. Other names: scatter plot; X–Y graph.

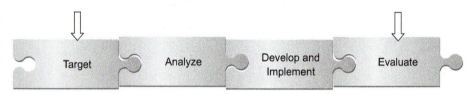

**Definition**: A graphing of pairs of numerical data. Other names: Scatter plot; X–Y graph

**Helpful when**: Examining for trends. Initial display and interpretation of coordinate data.

| Time | Cost | Labor | Difficulty |
|---|---|---|---|
| Medium | Low | Medium | Medium |

**Instructions (see Figure 10.16):**

1. Collect or gather pairs of data believed to be related.
2. Plot on an X–Y graph.
3. Observe for patterns. Run regression analysis if warranted.

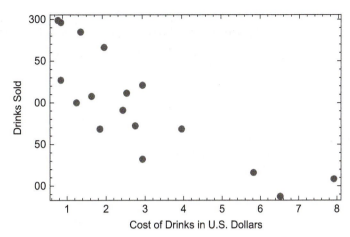

**FIGURE 10.16  Scatter Diagram Example of Contrast between Drinks Sold and Cost of Drinks.**

## ❖ SECRET SHOPPERS

**Definition**: Evaluators who pose as customers and report findings to the management and owners.

**Helpful when**: Owners or managers want to test and ensure that operational procedures are followed.

| Time | Cost | Labor | Difficulty |
|------|------|-------|------------|
| High | High | High | Medium |

**Secret Shopper**
Evaluators who pose as customers and report findings to the management and owners.

**Discussion**: A **secret shopper** is a customer in disguise. Outside contractors are sent to evaluate food, accommodations, services, and various other products in a covert fashion. Companies often change or rotate shoppers so as not to be discovered. Secret shoppers typically receive a reimbursement for the meal, show, treatment, or service and a small token of appreciation for their time. A standard form is devised for each type of situation. The shoppers must follow a strict protocol, shopping at certain times, and ordering certain items. Shoppers hide the forms and fill them out immediately after the transaction (see Figure 10.17). Owners use secret shoppers as a control device for operations. Managers usually have bonuses tied to shopper scores, and employees sometimes view it as spying. Nonetheless, it is relatively common, especially in chain establishments.

**Quality Evaluation Company - Customer Service Evaluation Form**

Last Name: _____ First Name: _____ Employee ID Number: _____

Property Number: _____ Property Location: _____

Date of Evaluation: ____/____/____ Arrival Time: ____:____AM/PM Time of Departure: ____:____AM/PM

**Property:**

|  | Poor | Below average | Average | Above average | Excellent |
|---|---|---|---|---|---|
| External |  |  |  |  |  |
| Dining room |  |  |  |  |  |
| Kitchen |  |  |  |  |  |
| Counter |  |  |  |  |  |
| Bathroom |  |  |  |  |  |

**Order:**

|  | Poor | Below average | Average | Above average | Excellent |
|---|---|---|---|---|---|
| Greeting |  |  |  |  |  |
| Accuracy |  |  |  |  |  |
| Timeliness |  |  |  |  |  |
| Quality |  |  |  |  |  |

**Staff:**

|  | Yes | No | Unsure |
|---|---|---|---|
| Was someone present at the door? |  |  |  |
| Was it busy? |  |  |  |
| Was the manager present? |  |  |  |
| Did all staff have proper uniforms? |  |  |  |

| Attendant's name: |  |
|---|---|
| Description of your order: |  |
| Additional comments: |  |

Please complete, affix your receipt to the bottom portion of the page and fax to 1-800-432-12XX

**FIGURE 10.17  Secret Shopper Evaluation Form Example.**

## ✤ SERVQUAL

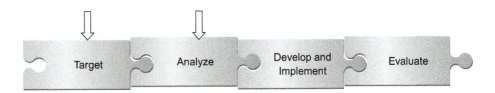

**Definition**: Measures five dimensions and assesses five different types of gaps in service organizations.

**Helpful when**: Owners or managers want to test or ensure that quality service is present.

| Time | Cost | Labor | Difficulty |
|------|------|-------|------------|
| High | Medium | Medium | High |

**Discussion**: Zeithaml, Parasuraman, and Berry developed SERVQUAL in 1985. They compiled the literature and blended it with practical use in industry. The SERVQUAL model was widely used throughout the 1990s and after. The dimensions are widely accepted and the gaps have strong real-world application. It has received very little press in recent years, but the dimensions and gaps are widely understood to be a classic contribution to service research.

**SERVQUAL** was originally developed with 10 dimensions: Tangibles, responsibility, responsiveness, communication (credibility, security, competence), courtesy, understanding/knowing customers, and access. It was later reduced to RATER, which stands for:

**R**eliability: Ability to perform promised service accurately and dependably
**A**ssurance: Employee knowledge, courtesy, ability to inspire trust and confidence
**T**angibles: Equipment, facilities, appearance of personnel
**E**mpathy: Individualized attention and care to customers
**R**esponsiveness: Prompt service, willingness to help

(*Note*: The last two dimensions combine the others previously mentioned in the original instrument.)

After measuring these dimensions, a measurement of five different potential gaps in the quality service process are determined:
○ Gap 1: Management expectation and customer exceptions
○ Gap 2: Management perceptions and service specifications
○ Gap 3: Service specifications and service delivery
○ Gap 4: Service delivery and external communications
○ Gap 5: Customer expectations and service delivery

**SERVQUAL**
Measures five dimensions and assesses five different types of gaps in service organizations: reliability, assurance, tangibles, empathy, and responsiveness (RATER).

## ❦ SIX SIGMA

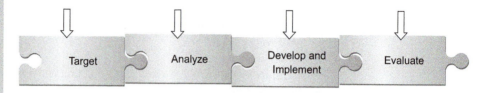

**Definition**: Quality program aimed at reducing defects to less than 3.4 in 1 million. Define, measure, analyze, improve, control (DMAIC).

**Helpful when**: A full embrace of quality control in a product is desired.

| Time | Cost | Labor | Difficulty |
|------|------|-------|------------|
| High | High | High | High |

## ❦ SURVEYS

**Definition**: A polling of a group. Can be formal or informal. Works well with small to large groups.

**Helpful when**: You need to obtain a brief response from a broad audience.

| Time | Cost | Labor | Difficulty |
|------|------|-------|------------|
| Medium | High | Medium | Medium |

**Could be administered to:**

- Employees
- Managers
- Customers (Existing, Potential, Lost/Dissatisfied)

**Types of questions (*Note*: Offer "no opinion" when appropriate.):**

- Close-ended questions: Have specific options for an answer
  Example: How old are you? ____ <18 ____ 18–29 ____ 30–49 ____ 50–65 ____ ≥66
- Open-ended questions: Have no specific options for an answer
  Example: How old are you?_____

## Types of scales:

- Likert scale
  Example: 1 = strongly disagree; 2 = disagree; 3 = neutral; 4 = agree; 5 = strongly agree
- Verbal frequency
  Example: 1 = always; 2 = often; 3 = sometimes; 4 = seldom; 5 = never
- Forced ranking
  Example: ____ Bud ____ Coors ____ Miller ____ Amstel ____ Guinness
- Semantic differential
  Example: Hot ____ ____ ____ ____ Cold

## All surveys should have:

- Introduction briefly describing the situation: Who? What? Why?
- Body including the survey questions
- Closing
- Thank you

## All surveys should be:

- Brief
- Focused directly on the subject
- Simple to follow
- Focused without extraneous information

## Effective survey questions should be:

- Clear/unambiguous to ensure consistent interpretation. (Poor example: What do you do?)
- Grammatically correct and free from spelling errors
- Free flowing and easy to understand
- Ordered so that sensitive questions come last

## Effective survey questions should not include:

- Leading questions that introduce bias or lead to a particular answer
  Example: Would you favor random searches to keep people safe from bombers, assassins, and drug smugglers?
- Inapplicable or overly sensitive questions
  Example: What are your children's names?
- Overly demanding recall questions
  Example: When learning to ride your bicycle, how many times did you fall off?
- Double-barreled questions—two questions in one
  Example: Do you enjoy going to an event and getting a program?

**Effective survey writing should avoid:**

- Technical language or terminology
- Asking questions that you already have the answer to
- Too many questions assessing the same point
- Embarrassing/personal questions
- Too many questions
- Multiple changes in response patterns
- Questions that cannot be answered with the options provided

---

## Service Insight

### *Correlation Does Not Imply Causation*

Your research may show that variables are seemingly related. Be careful of your interpretations and claims.

- Claim: Odd-numbered days yield fewer complaints.
- Claim: A recent rise in male travelers caused a lowering of guest complaints.
- Claim: A rise in gas prices relates to a decline in pool usage.
- Claim: An increase in service staff has led to a decline in room service delivery times.

When conducting research, be aware that just because two variables may be correlated, one does not necessarily cause the other. They may not be related at all to each other.

- Incorrect: If the value of A rises as the value of B lowers, then A's rising causes B to lower.
- Reasoning: Many things could cause B to lower in value. Just because the two values have correlation does not mean that one causes the other. Seemingly related or not, we cannot imply that.

Now let's review the previous claims:

- Incorrect: Odd-numbered days yield fewer complaints.
- Reasoning: Scheduling? Service staff? Property maintenance?
- Incorrect: A recent rise in male travelers caused a lowering of guest complaints.
- Reasoning: Did the manager/staff change? What other factors changed?
- Incorrect: A rise in gas prices relates to a decline in pool usage.
- Reasoning: What was the occupancy? Clientele? Weather?
- Incorrect: An increase in service staff has led to increased room service delivery times.
- Reasoning: That's illogical. The opposite might happen. There were likely other issues.

## FORBES STAR EVALUATIONS

**Star-Rating**
Forbes Mobil Guide rating system of 1 to 5 stars. Unannounced inspectors rate hotels, restaurants, and spas, assessing over 550 standard aspects for its 4- and 5-star applicants.

Forbes Travel Guide evaluates hotels, restaurants and spas in the United States, Canada, and Asia. Forbes has been evaluating since 1958. In 2009, Forbes merged with Mobil Travel Guide, another industry leader, and assumed its **star-rating** system. In it, hotels, restaurants, and spas are evaluated using a 5-star rating system. Forbes primarily concentrates on 4- and 5-star properties. In 2011, Forbes Travel Guide awarded 54 hotels, 22 restaurants, and 21 spas the prestigious honor of 5 stars. The same year it also awarded 172 hotels, 150 restaurants, and 111 spas the 4-star award.

Ratings are determined by the combined scores of a facility inspection (25 percent) and a service evaluation (75 percent). Facility inspection is up to 3 days and 2 nights and reviews 17 major areas of the hotel, including reservations, room service, laundry, and concierge. Service evaluation is performed incognito and assesses over 550 points.

*Five-Star Hotels*: These are the most exceptional of all properties. They are nearly flawless, the staff is passionate and eager to deliver guest satisfaction beyond their expectations. The properties exhibit fine craftsmanship, comfort, and quality and are a destination unto themselves. Examples: Montage Beverly Hills, Mandarin Oriental NYC.

*Four-Star Hotels*: Distinctive setting, many interesting and inviting features, strong attention to detail in all aspects, prideful and accommodating staff, personalized service. Examples: Wynn Las Vegas, St. Regis Deer Valley Resort.

*Three-Star Hotels*: Are held to lesser inspection and evaluation standards than the 4- and 5-star candidates. They are still very nice properties with a strong sense of location, distinguishing style, ambience, functionality, and ease of access to meetings or tourist attractions.

In 2005, Forbes began offering an additional consulting practice that shares the extensive inspection criteria with the hotels. This allows them to more appropriately gauge what they need to change in order to achieve the 4- and 5-star ratings.

## ❦ AAA RATINGS

| Features | Ratings of hotels, restaurants, campgrounds |
|---|---|
| Input | AAA unannounced inspectors |
| Award | Diamond rating of 1 of 5 |
| Difficulty | High |
| Customer recognition | High |
| Field recognition | High |

## AAA DIAMOND RATINGS

The American Automobile Association (AAA) approves and rates hotels and restaurants. They cover more entities than any other rating association. AAA began

**Diamond Rating**
AAA rating system of 1 to 5 diamonds scoring hotels, restaurants, and campgrounds. The largest guide of its kind.

approving hotels in 1937 and added the rating system in 1963. The lodging ratings evolved into the currently known **diamond rating** system in 1976. Diamond ratings were rolled out to restaurants between 1986 and 1991. They rate hotels and restaurants on a scale of 1 to 5 Diamonds. One is the lowest and 5 in the highest. The ratings assess extensiveness of services, amenities and décor. The diamond rating is highly coveted. Only 179 have ever been awarded (in the U.S., Canada, Mexico, Caribbean) which equals 0.3% of the 31,000 hotels and 28,000 restaurants evaluated in those areas. Candidate properties for diamond awards undergo multiple evaluations and an expert panel. In 2011, 124 hotels were awarded the diamond rating. AAA inspectors visit every property and rate them every year.

## Hotel diamond ratings:

- *1 Diamond*: The lowest level. This is a no-frills property, but satisfactorily meets the basic requirements. It is suitable for the budget-minded traveler.
- *2 Diamonds*: A modest designation of a property. It has more to offer than a 1-diamond property, and offers modest accommodations.
- *3 Diamonds*: A property for a traveler with more needs.
- *4 Diamonds*: Properties that are located in upscale areas. They are refined, stylish, and feature a high level of quality throughout.
- *5 Diamonds*: Properties that offer the highest level in all manners. These properties offer the best of everything. They are the pinnacle of luxury, with impeccable service and amenities. Names like Ritz Carlton and St. Regis are common in this category.

Restaurants must first meet a criterion of having set minimum requirements to be evaluated. Diamonds represent levels of food, décor, and service. A total of 55 restaurants scored 5 diamonds for 2011. The restaurant with the longest-standing 5-diamond rating is The Inn at Little Washington Dining Room in Washington, Virginia, which has held it since 1988.

## Restaurant diamond ratings:

- *1 Diamond*: "Good food" meets basic, essential requirements of food, management, and overall quality. Limited food selection, limited service (or self-service), basic décor and surroundings. Lower-priced.
- *2 Diamonds*: "Family fare" reasonably priced. Better dishware, garnishes, familiar surroundings with a theme, elevated level of food and service. Up-graded.
- *3 Diamonds*: "Entry-level fine dining," has a chef and highly trained cooks and a menu that reflects it, complementing beverages, dining room manager, skilled service staff, fine-dining, comfortable, typically adult-oriented.
- *4 Diamonds*: "Fine dining," has an executive chef, highly trained kitchen and dining room staff, fresh market ingredients, first-class impressions in all respects.
- *5 Diamonds*: "World-class dining," the best in every aspect. Renowned, world-class cuisine, "haute cuisine." The best of everything from the staff, to the menu, to the beverages, to the décor, to the food. Typically very expensive.

—newsroom.aaa.com/wp-content/uploads/2011/09/5D_Facts_2011.pdf.

# CHAPTER REVIEW QUESTIONS

1. List the basic procedures of the classic research methodology format.
2. At what point in the research process are people surveyed?
3. What are the four parts of setting up for research?
4. How is the research process begun?
5. What are the four different groups in which a tool could be divided?
6. What is the purpose of a Secret Shopper?
7. List three tools that could be used for evaluating improvements.
8. Why do think that the Ritz Carlton was the only hotel to receive the prestigious Malcolm Baldrige Quality award?
9. What is the difference between a star rating and a diamond rating?
10. What substantiates a 5-diamond rating for a restaurant?
11. What substantiates a 5-star rating for a hotel?

# CASE STUDIES

### The Riverboat

The Riverboat is a casino on the Mississippi River. It has enjoyed years of a loyal local following. The staff and management have been in place for many years. It ran a great operation, but recently its revenues have been falling. It has witnessed 5 consecutive years of 1 to 2 percent declining revenues. Although this is a slight decline each year, the trend continues. The owners of the boat visit occasionally and are obviously beginning to get nervous. The management company that runs operations is also very concerned. The future is unsure. Many of the employees have rumored that the management company needs to turn business around within the next year or the owners will not renew its contract. Overtime hours and customer comps have been eliminated and the company is tightly monitoring the other expenses. Employee and customer moral has diminished and is evident in the service. Employees and lower-level management are nervous and trying to do the best they can.

One day, the new district manager of the management company came aboard for a visit. Everyone knew she was there and was on their toes. She spent the day on The Riverboat observing and talking to as many employees and customers as possible. After a series of informal discussions, she met with the boat management, and a plan was devised to conduct research to determine the issue behind lost revenue and to seek a solution.

1. Did the new district manager begin the process correctly?
2. Outline the next research steps that The Riverboat should take.

### José's Travel

José's Travel is a small, private company that prides itself on serving the people of the greater Los Angeles area. It is a full-service travel company with a strong clientele speaking mostly Spanish. To assess his customer service, José e-mails all of his customers an electronic survey 1 week after their trip. It groups questions into main areas, such as accuracy of service, friendliness of service, and price/value of service. Four questions are listed in each area, each approaching the topic from a slightly different point of view.

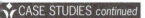

Of the surveys sent out, Jose realizes that only about 25 percent of his customers reply. When analyzing the responses, he sees two trends emerge. One group loves everything and is quite pleased with all aspects of the service. Another, yet smaller group is displeased with nearly every aspect of the service. He believes that customers generally appear happy and quite pleased in the store and on the telephone, so he is unsure how they could have received such poor ratings across the survey from a few of the customers.

In an effort to rectify the bad experiences of his customers, he has historically e-mailed them back, offering a coupon, although he has seldom ever received a reply to his e-mail offer. To probe further, José has recently begun calling each of the customers who responded with an average of less than 60 percent satisfaction. He has been unable to reach most of these people on the telephone. He leaves messages, but continues to receive little or no information as a result.

1. List the research steps that José has taken up to this point.
2. In what step might José have failed?
3. Outline tips or advice that you would give to José' to help him better gauge his customers.

## The Suggestion Box

The Operations Department at the Van Arena consists of 15 full-time help, with several others brought in on an as-needed basis. Jeff has recently been promoted to director of operations and of the department. He has been at the arena for 7 years. He began as a part-timer in high school, eventually working his way to a full-time employee after graduating from a local college. He has always gotten along well with the other members of the department, and considers many of them close friends.

In the storage room, Jeff noticed a comment box gaining dust in the back corner. He decided to place it on the wall outside his office with blank cards in a rack above it. He didn't know what would happen, and he didn't really think about it until he decided to open it one day.

To his surprise, it was quite full. Jeff spent the next 2 hours in his office poring over the comments. He was very upset, but decided to wait until the next weekly staff meeting.

Jeff could barely stand waiting, but the meeting finally came. He walked into the room last and stared at everyone. He took out a folder containing the comment cards from the suggestion box. He then proceeded to read all of them, one by one. The room was silent and the air was heavy. Jeff was obviously mad. Everyone froze as he began:

"You stink."
"You give preferential treatment to your friends."
"We could use new uniforms."
"Sometimes people sneak in over the fence after dark."
"We could save money by getting automatic devices in the restrooms."

Overall, there were many good suggestions, but there were also two very negative ones. Jeff could not get over how someone could write those two. He looked around the room to survey their faces. He had a few ideas who it was. It even looked like the two negative comments were in the same handwriting. Jeff was mad at everyone.

1. Was the Comment Card Box a good idea? Explain.
2. Rate the responses that were read. Overall, what did they say?
3. If you were Jeff's boss, what advice would you give him regarding the comment card box?

# EXERCISES

## Exercise 1: Conducting Service Research

**Directions:**
Your objective is to develop a plan, employing quality service improvement tools to help the company in the scenario move through the improvement process.

**Assignment to be submitted:**
1. Assuming the role of consultant, choose two tools to help the company in the case scenario below. Complete the chart explaining which two tools you chose, what they will measure, who will be measured, and the purpose of the tool, such as target an opportunity for improvement, analyze the area targeted for improvement, develop and implement improvements, or evaluate improvements. Your response must contain answers to each area in the chart below. Further think this through and predict the anticipated outcome of each tool.
2. Determine the prediction of outcome for tool 1.
3. Determine the prediction of outcome for tool 2.

**Case Scenario:**
Your institution is receiving complaints regarding student parking.

|  | Name of tool: | What will it measure? | Who will be measured? | Purpose: |
|---|---|---|---|---|
| Tool 1 |  |  |  |  |
| Tool 2 |  |  |  |  |

## Exercise 2: Analyzing a Survey

**Directions:**
1. Obtain a survey of a hospitality business in a field that interests you. This may be local or national.
2. Print out the survey and staple to the back of your assignment.
3. Reference the survey and fill in the example and indicate whether or not it is correct in the chart below:

| Component | Example | Was it correct or incorrect? |
|---|---|---|
| Introduction provided |  |  |
| Clear instructions |  |  |
| Type of scale used |  |  |
| Free from introducing bias |  |  |
| Avoids technical terminology |  |  |
| Directions provided |  |  |
| Thank you included |  |  |

## Exercise 3: Diamond Rating

**Directions:**

1. Choose a local hotel or restaurant that can be observed for this assignment.
2. Review it according to the Diamond Standard Rating according to AAA.
3. Provide examples to support your decision.

Name of Property: _____

Location of Property: _____

Number of diamonds awarded according to your review: _____

**Justification:**

List at least seven aspects of the property that substantiate your Diamond Rating:

| Aspect |
|--------|
| 1. |
| 2. |
| 3. |
| 4. |
| 5. |
| 6. |
| 7. |

# Strategic Planning for Service

## Chapter Objectives:

*After reading this chapter, you should be able to:*

Define and apply strategy as it applies to a service operation.

Outline and apply the three main facets of strategy.

Implement four parts of a strategic service system.

Analyze the internal and external aspects of a service organization in a SWOT analysis.

Understand vision, mission, and statements of purpose as they relate to service.

## Terminology:

| | | |
|---|---|---|
| Champion | General Competition | Service Process Implementation |
| Change Theory | Indirect Competition | Service Strategy |
| Continuous Improvement | Mission | Silo |
| Coproduction | Problem Statement | Strategic Service System |
| Credo | Resource Viewpoint | Strategy |
| Customer-centric | Service Guarantee | SWOT Analysis |
| Direct Competition | Service Mission and Service Vision | Vision |

*"Failing to plan is planning to fail."*

*"Service doesn't just happen; it must be planned. You need a strategy."*

This chapter focuses on strategic planning for service. It is divided into three parts:

- Introduction to Service Strategy
- Analyzing Position and Market
- Integration: Implementing a Service Strategy

In the first section, the premise of strategy is introduced as it relates to hospitality management and a foundation is established. The second section discusses the internal and external evaluations of the SWOT analysis in an effort to analyze the position and the market environment. The final section covers writing objectives and implementation of the strategy.

# Introduction to Service Strategy

## ❦ STRATEGY DEFINED

**Strategy**
A calculated plan to achieve a common, chosen objective.

The science of strategy can be quite complex. Numerous books, courses, and even college majors are devoted to this subject. Consultants and professionals devote entire careers to the study of the topic. As complex as it may be, it is also a very basic concept at its roots. Simply put, a **strategy** is a calculated plan to achieve a common, chosen objective. This definition sounds simple. However, each word and phrase has distinct meaning. Let's dig more deeply into the three main facets of strategy.

### CALCULATED PLAN

We aim to develop a strategy through methodical means, to structure a well-thought-out plan with direction. This is anything but ad hoc. It involves self-analysis and external input to make the best possible plan with the information available. Any and all progress will be monitored and revised as needed.

### COMMON, CHOSEN

The framework is agreed upon and supported at all levels of the business. Everyone is made aware of the plan, the direction, and the commitment involved to get to the objective. Upper-level management supports low-level management and line staff in all of their efforts. Everyone is working together.

### OBJECTIVE

The desired outcome may vary greatly in nature and scope based on the organization and the goals, but it is always present. Objectives ultimately help to achieve goals. Most objectives involve a plan for improvement. Some examples of aggressive objectives include being known as having the absolute best service or gaining market share.

Others are to develop a unique characteristic, in order to create a distinction from the rest of the competition. In bad economic times, a few strategies enable a business to merely survive a forecasted, unstable economic period. In the end, everyone is working together, with a plan, in an effort to reach a common goal or objective.

## ✦ STRATEGY IS NATURAL

Strategy is a natural way of thinking. We are all programmed to think strategically about many things in our lives. We have a want or a need (objective and goal). Formal or not, we perform research and decide how we will achieve it (plan). We, and others, agree to follow, support, and monitor the plan and direction (common, chosen).

For example, a student in this course has an objective to complete it and other courses so they can graduate from college. The goal is to obtain a job, position, or career. The objectives (graduation) are part of a plan to help them reach the goal (job). They did the research and decided on a college, which courses to take and which professors to take them with, when to take the courses, and how to balance other priorities to obtain a degree. They allocated the resources (time, money, and effort) and made a plan to make it happen. The objective is graduation. The goal is a job. The plan (strategy) makes it happen.

## ✦ IMPORTANCE OF STRATEGY

Strategy creates many benefits to the organization. Strategy is the underlying premise to delivering quality guest service. Every Fortune 500 company uses strategy. Below are some of the benefits:

- Increased communication
  - Planning and monitoring facilitates communication.
  - Everyone hears about and knows what is happening.
  - Grapevines and rumors are minimized.
- Increased understanding
  - Promotes a deeper understanding between departments.
- Established common direction
  - Everyone is working the same way toward the same goal.
- Increased efficiency and productivity
- Ease in decision making
  - It provides a basis for making decisions.
- Increased commitment
  - All are committed to a common purpose.
- Reduction of stress
- Reduction of anxiety
- Awareness of competition
- Awareness of marketplace
- Awareness of internal operations

## ❧ LACK OF STRATEGY

Failing to plan is planning to fail.

- *Crisis management*: A great manager can fix problems as they arise.
- *Optimistic management*: Just do the best that you can.
- *Mental management*: It is all in my head.

Strategy has many pitfalls. The wrong approach or lacking in just one aspect could spell disaster. Some organizations may have a direction, but are not in agreement on how to proceed. The intentions may not be well communicated. Some only have an idea in their head and don't see value in outward planning. Some have a plan but are monitoring progress in their head. Some are reasonably pleased with the current situation and become complacent. Others see a need for a plan but lack knowledge on how to proceed. Or, worst yet, some are simply burnt out or lazy. Whatever the reason, a business that fails to plan is planning to fail.

## ❧ STRATEGY APPLIED TO THE CUSTOMER MINDSET

Consider this. You have a strategy. It leads you to objectives and goals. Your intentions are well constructed in the procedures and processes. Conflicts arise when processes and procedures don't meet the demands of the customers. Suppose the customer arrives at 9 A.M., exhausted from an international flight. They only have sleep on their mind. You follow the process. You tell them that check-in is at 3 P.M. and offer to hold their bags. Now you have a process and they have a process. Their timing isn't always your timing. Why should the customer have to pay you to accommodate to your ways? If you truly care about the customer, a process should accommodate these instances if at all possible. This doesn't mean giving away the hotel, but processes shouldn't be so formal that they conflict with the customers needs.

## ❧ CONTINUOUS IMPROVEMENT

The hospitality industry is very dynamic—technology changes, expectations change, economic conditions change, and the marketplace changes, so companies must always be on their toes and be ready to identify areas in need of improvement or change. As these areas are outlined, care must be taken to prioritize objectives. In order to maximize the return on available resources, there should be a structure in place for planning, executing, and monitoring, then revising, executing, and monitoring again.

**Continuous Improvement**
A premise of instituting quality through a cycle of planning, monitoring, interpreting, and revising.

**Continuous improvement** (see Figure 11.1) is an essential premise of instituting quality. It is a cycle of planning, monitoring, interpreting, and revising in a constant effort to improve something. The hospitality industry is very dynamic—technology changes, expectations change, economic conditions change, and the marketplace changes, so companies must always be on their toes and be ready to identify areas in need of improvement or change. As these areas are outlined, care must be taken to prioritize objectives. In order to maximize the return on available resources, there should be a structure in place for employing these steps. It is an unending cycle. It is an adaptation process in a continually evolving environment.

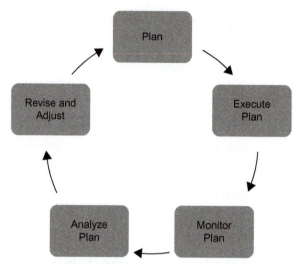

**FIGURE 11.1  Continuous Improvement Cycle.**

Continuous improvement is analogized in the common idea that *quality service is a journey, not a destination.*

## CHANGE THEORY

"It is not the strongest of the species that survives, nor the most intelligent, but the ones most responsive to change."

*—Charles Darwin*

**Change Theory**
A science behind helping businesses transition through changes.

**Change theory** is the idea that there is a science behind change. Several theories exist and organizational behavioral professionals dedicate careers to specializing in helping businesses succeed through transitional periods.

There are many things that make instituting changes difficult. Preconceptions, habits, insecurities, past practices, fear of failure, and jumping to conclusions all affect instituting change.

There is an analogy of change management as being periods: frozen, thawing, whitewater, and refreezing, as shown in Figure 11.2. The initial frozen state is the status quo, the usual, the expected, or the norm. It is the way that we have always done things.

Changes will come in many forms. They may be a new technology system, a new service procedure, new management, or a myriad of other things. When this occurs, a

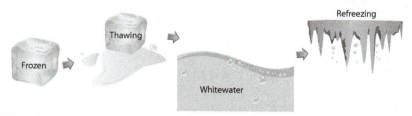

**FIGURE 11.2  Analogy of Change Management.**

period of unfreezing occurs. To extend the analogy, this may even seem like whitewater. It will be very problematic. Stress and disorganization will likely occur. Everything is unsettled.

Then, eventually, the whitewaters will calm, and it will refreeze. Things will also settle in the workplace. It will not freeze in the same way as before. In fact, it will probably be much different, but things will settle down. Then it will again become a new definition of the term *frozen*.

These changes with unsettling middle points and different end results will continue to cycle throughout business and life. The cycle times may be a few weeks to several months, and even a few years. People specialize in smoothing these transitions, but just realizing the cycle and the current stage helps you to see it and manage it more effectively.

# Analyzing Position and Market

Does your business currently have a strategy? If so, what is it? If not stated, where is the company currently headed? What would a silent observer guess is the strategy? In other words, what does the 'writing on the wall' tell you? Follow your intuition. That is probably the current strategy, by design or by accident. It is likely focused on objectives such as:

- Sales
- Fixing or avoiding an error
- Reducing a cost
- Forming an alliance
- Adjusting staffing levels
- Retraining or retooling

**Problem Statement**
The root problem or fundamental cause of why something is happening. Often the results of both internal and external analysis.

This will help you to develop a **problem statement**. This is the underlying reason why something is occurring. Often this is made clear through the SWOT analysis, as described below.

It may have come from the top administration or from the line staff. It may be based on feedback from return customers, perceptions of new customers, a desire to outpace the competition, or developing new sales opportunities. A lack of communication could be a result of a **silo**, a metaphor for departments and groups within the company that do not communicate well with each other. Instead, they all work in their specific areas instead of working together. There could be multiple or overlapping reasons. In any event, it is important to know where your business stands.

**Silo**
A metaphor used to describe the separate departments of an organization that work independently and fail to communicate with each other, thus replicating processes, working inefficiently, and causing frustration.

## ❦ SWOT ANALYSIS

A **SWOT analysis** is a valuable tool commonly used to establish a starting point in strategic development. It evaluates both internal and external attributes of a business

and is very useful for observing the big picture also known as the macro view. It allows you to know where your company stands, where the competition stands, and how the outside variables influence your business. The letters of the SWOT stand for:

**SWOT Analysis**
An analysis of the strengths, weaknesses, opportunities, and threats of an organization, containing internal and external examination.

**S**trengths
**W**eaknesses
**O**pportunities
**T**hreats

The SWOT analysis has two primary components: internal and external. The strengths and weaknesses make up the internal analysis and the opportunities and threats make up the external analysis. The internal components represent the areas of the operation that are within the direct control of the business, such as operations, marketing, staffing, management, and finances. The external components represent the areas of the business over which the business has little or no control, such as competition, economic conditions, and changing technologies.

The attributes are roughly sorted as:

- Internal or within their control + good = Strength
- Internal or within their control + bad = Weakness
- External or outside their control + good = Opportunity
- External or outside their control + bad = Threat

The business has no direct control over the external influences; it can only adjust to them.

A SWOT analysis reviews each of these areas. A statement within your control is internal and is either good or bad. If it is good it is a strength, and if it is bad it is a weakness. If it is not within your control it is external, and its effect on you is either good or bad. If its effect is good, it is a known as an opportunity, and if its effect is bad it is known as a threat.

Other tools such as the Internal Factor Evaluation Matrix (IFE) and the External Factor Evaluation Matrix (EFE) rate and assign points to the categories for comparison.

The following tables show questions to ask as a starting point of SWOT analysis.

| Internal | | Strength | Weakness |
| --- | --- | --- | --- |
| Operations | What standards do you have in place? | | |
| | How do your costs of operations compare to industry standards? | | |
| Finance | How favorable are your financial ratios? | | |

*(continued)*

| Internal | | Strength | Weakness |
|---|---|---|---|
| Marketing | Can you make your service tangible to the customer? | | |
| | Do you have a strong brand image? | | |
| | Are you different from the competition? | | |
| | Do you want to be different? | | |
| Staffing | Do your employees know your strategy? | | |
| Management | How does your business support this strategy? | | |
| Research and development | Are you innovative with new products and services? | | |
| Management information systems | How strong is your ability to gather, control and manage information? | | |

| External | | Opportunities | Threats |
|---|---|---|---|
| Culture | How has the mindset of the population changed? | | |
| Market—customers | What are the growing demographics in your marketplace? | | |
| | What does the market look like? | | |
| | How do the customers perceive you? | | |
| | How do they perceive the competition? | | |
| | What are their needs? | | |
| | Why do the customers come to your business instead of the competitor's? | | |
| | Do your customers know your strategy? | | |
| Technology | How is the technology changing? | | |
| | Have you leveraged the available technologies? | | |
| Competition | What is the competition doing well? | | |
| | Are you a leader or are you catching up to the industry leader? | | |
| | Are there barriers to entry? What prevents new entrants into the market? | | |
| | Benchmark—Look at best-practice methods. Observing the best-in-class at methods or products, or services. | | |
| | Retaliation—How will they respond to your changes? | | |

*(continued)*

| External | | Opportunities | Threats |
|---|---|---|---|
| Economy | Unemployment rate, gross domestic product (GDP), inflation rate? | | |
| Legal/political | Are there any new laws that will affect your business processes? | | |

## ❧ IDENTIFYING YOUR COMPETITION

Determining your competition is highly subjective and often misunderstood. In one sense, your business is unique in what it offers to its customers in at least one way. It is unique either by location, by marketing, by service, by product, or by delivery. In another sense, it shares many of the same qualities as other businesses and competes with those businesses on one or more levels.

**Direct Competition**
Other businesses who compete for the same clientele, in the same industry, delivering similar goods and services.

### DIRECT COMPETITION

An interesting planning exercise is to ask a small business owner to name his competition. He will typically come up with a handful of competitors in the same geographic area delivering similar products and services to the same customers. He is naming what we refer to as **direct competition**.

**Indirect Competition**
Other businesses who compete for the same clientele, delivering related, but not identical, products and services.

### INDIRECT COMPETITION

If you were to ask the same small business owner about businesses that provide a slightly different product, the owner might claim, "They don't touch me. They aren't my competition at all." In one sense he is correct, but in every other sense he is terribly wrong. Other businesses may be delivering a different product or service, but they are still competition. A business offering a slightly different product to the same market is an example of **indirect competition**.

Here is another thought. Have you ever been on your way out to dinner at a nice restaurant and decided to eat at a quick-service restaurant instead? How about the opposite? What changed your mind? What were the other options?

Indirect competition is still competition. In poor economic times, fine dining has lost customers to upscale-casual dining. Upscale-casual dining has lost customers to casual dining, who lost customers to limited-service dining, who lost to quick-service dining. Some customers jump even two or three levels on a whim.

**General Competition**
Businesses that compete for the same clientele's time and/or dollar.

### GENERAL COMPETITION

Also, consider a getaway destination package for $299.00. You would love to go. You may even have the time, but you don't have the money. Where was it spent? Who else was competing for your time or your dollar? In **general competition** (see Figure 11.3), businesses compete for the same time and/or dollar of the clientele, but with very different products and services. It may not be directly related, but it still hurts the bottom line.

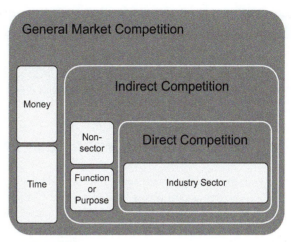

**FIGURE 11.3   General Competition.**

# Integration:
# Implementing a Service Strategy

"The need to have everyone on the bus is only part of it. It needs to be the right bus, headed in the right direction, and the right people need to be in the correct seats."

*—Adapted from Jim Collins, "Good to Great," Fast Company*

There is much to this quote:

- Having everyone "on the bus" means that you need to have the company together in a united effort.
- The "right bus" means that you need to have the right, or most suitable, objectives.
- The "right direction" means that the bus (strategy) needs to be properly implemented.
- And everyone in their "correct seats" means that you need the right people in the right places. This may mean moving, retraining, or even replacing people.

Good intentions are not enough. Plans are great, but implementation and follow-up are crucial for even the best-laid plans. The employees are the resource that is key to making service happen. Employees and management must share the same values.

Implementation is the process. It is the art of transforming plans and potential into practice. It needs to go from paper into practice, from a service strategy to actual service. All of this is part of the strategic service system.

## ❧ THE STRATEGIC SERVICE SYSTEM: PURPOSE, PRODUCT, PLAN, PEOPLE

**Strategic Service System**
A four-part system that involves purpose, product, plan, and people.

The **strategic service system** involves four main components: purpose, product, plan and people (see Figure 11.4). All are prerequisites; all must exist simultaneously, and all are equally important in the strategic process. Each will be discussed in depth.

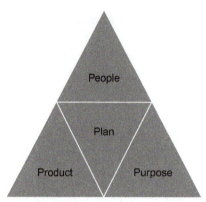

**FIGURE 11.4   The Strategic Service System.**

### PURPOSE

**Customer-centric**
The premise of placing the customer first in all a company does. Focusing on pleasing the customer and organizing the company with that as a primary goal.

> "Our mission statement about treating people with respect and dignity is not just words but a creed we live by every day. You can't expect your employees to exceed the expectations of your customers if you don't exceed the employees' expectations of management."
> —*Howard Schultz, CEO, Starbucks Coffee*

What do you stand for? What do you want to change? What do you want to focus on? **Customer-centric** is an idea that the business should focus every decision with the customer as the main priority, outranking all others. While this view may seem drastic, the customer should certainly be a consideration in decisions.

**Credo**
Originally used for professing religious beliefs, was adopted by companies as a passionate label to describe what the organization stood for.

In defining the purpose, objectives will likely follow. Objectives come from having a well-developed purpose. These tools are known as mission and vision statements. Other objectives come from similar statements, such as a **credo**.

A **mission** statement is written for the customers and employees. It is helpful when evaluating the direction of the company. Topics typically mentioned in mission statements are:

**Mission**
A statement that explains the purpose of your business. It is usually a paragraph and states the core purpose of the organization. It should be the origin and foundation of all other decisions for the business.

- Products or services
- Markets
- Technology
- Profit/growth
- Philosophy
- Employees
- Customers

**Service Mission and Service Vision Statement**
Similar to a traditional vision and mission statement but targeted toward service.

A mission statement for the overall business typically answers the question: Why are we in business? **Service mission and service vision** are similar to a traditional mission and **vision** statement, but are targeted toward service. The *service mission* is also known as the *service concept*.

### Service Insight

**MGM Mirage Mission Statement**

Our mission is to deliver our winning combination of quality entertainment, luxurious facilities, and exceptional customer service to every corner of the world in order to enhance shareholder value and to sustain employee, customer, and community relationships (MGM Resorts International).

**Vision**
A statement, usually a sentence or two, that explains where a business is striving to go or be in the future. Typically inspirational and sometimes a bit lofty, it is used in strategic planning.

### Service Insight

**Tyson Foods' Vision**

Tyson Foods' vision is "to be the world's first choice for protein solutions while maximizing shareholder value, living our Core Values, and fostering a fun place to work." The company's mission is to produce and market trusted, quality food products that fit today's changing lifestyles and to attract, reward, and retain the best people in the food industry (Tyson Foods, Inc.).

### Service Insight

**Ritz-Carlton Credo**

Ritz-Carlton's Credo: "The Ritz-Carlton Hotel is a place where the genuine care and comfort of our guests is our highest mission. We pledge to provide the finest personal service and facilities for our guests who will always enjoy a warm, relaxed, yet refined ambience. The Ritz-Carlton experience enlivens the senses, instills well-being, and fulfills even the unexpressed wishes and needs of our guests (The Ritz-Carlton)."

**Service Strategy**
Formula for delivering a service that defines the practical interpretation.

A **service strategy** is a formula for delivering a service. It is a plan that defines the practical interpretation of service. A strategy is a means of obtaining an objective to fulfill goals. General business strategies are classified by function. Service strategies are more focused on achieving a specific service objective or goal so they are geared primarily toward better serving the customer. Service strategies and general business strategies should complement each other. Both are important in hospitality.

Example: We are committed to delivering superior customer service that meets the needs of the customers in a consistent manner of professionalism. Our commitment to our guests is **SERVICE**:

Satisfaction
Ethical
Respectful
Versatile
Innovative
Communication
Empathy

## PRODUCT

**Service Guarantee**
A promise of satisfaction for your products and services.

In many instances within the hospitality field, the product is a service. By changing the staff and the systems, you are, in a sense, changing the product. In other situations, better seats, larger screens, or better amenities may be needed.

A **service guarantee** is a promise of satisfaction for your products and services. This is something the customers will see. The staff will be required to memorize it, and it will probably be posted somewhere obvious. Examples of this are:

"We will meet the expressed and unexpressed wishes of customers."
"Total customer satisfaction, guaranteed."
"If you're not happy, we'll fix it."

## PLAN

"How do you eat an elephant? One bite at a time."

—*Bill Hogan, Lluimna Press, 2004*

**Service Process Implementation**
The overall mechanics of implementing actual standards in the guest service process.

How does it meet the objective? The same principle applies; you break it down and begin. It has been said that every great journey begins with a single step.

A plan is filled with careful thought and good intentions, but is never a sure thing. Instead of thinking of a plan as a "must," think of it as trying to shoot arrows at a target on a windy day. Conditions keep changing, and you need to adjust as you go.

**Service process implementation** is the overall mechanics of implementing actual standards in the guest service process. It might be a customer relations plan, how will guests be served, or the actual changes the employees will make.

When developing a plan, you must first break it down into pieces. It must be based on the desired objectives and fit with the overall service strategy. It must have a timeline, communications, guidelines, and many other characteristics.

### Timeline

All plans must have a timeline. Each procedure should be calculated and an order of completion clearly stated. It should be realistic, and provide for a margin of error.

### Communication

How will everyone know? Everyone must be able to recognize and comprehend the goal. Progress toward objectives cannot be monitored, measured, and

achieved if there is a lack of comprehension. Have a slogan. Make it identifiable. Hold a contest or a campaign. Report the status.

### Guidelines

Revise the employee policies. Outline, ensure the details are described and that all are aware.

### Leadership

Develop a task force. Have a champion.

### Measurable

You must have some way of measuring outcomes. It can be speed of service, comment card averages, or a reduction in the number of complaints.

### Relatable

The objectives should relate to and support the service mission.

### Obtainable

It must be possible to achieve the goal. Target points set too high can cause the staff and management to become disheartened and frustrated. This leads to a reduction in motivation.

### Challenging

Too easy of a goal is inefficient, wasting staff and management's full potential. The total cost of the objective should be within reach.

---

**Service Insight**

**We Have Changed Our Services**

Occasionally, businesses will have to change the way that they offer services. Changing employees is difficult enough, and you pay them! Changing the way that customers transact is even more difficult. Most customers can be placed into three different groups:

1. Customers who mind little or not at all.
2. Customers who need assistance with the change.
3. Customers who want it the old way.

Every change is different. Some are smooth and some create a big headache for all. Some businesses incur so much grief that they revert back to the old way. It is trial and error.

What seems obvious to you may not be obvious to others. No matter the change, whether it is self-check-in, a new rule, or a different pattern, customer service representatives should always be readily available for assistance. Don't assume that signage and mailings regarding the change will be noticed or understood.

## PEOPLE

### Training

Staff must have the proper skill sets. Training or retraining is often needed with changes. Many successful organizations promote on-going employee enrichment.

### Attitude

A service culture must be evident. Evoke passion, emotion, and a sense of belonging.

Cultivate in staff a feeling of importance. Let them know how their job supports the overall quest to fulfill the objective. Let them know where the business would be without them. Only admit those who instill a sense of pride in their work and take a sense of ownership. Do they call it "theirs"? Do they refer to it as "their hotel"? They should.

Build their confidence. Train, monitor, and reinforce it.

When a staff member is given personal responsibility for achieving a specific goal, they are referred to as a **champion**, or service champion. They would be responsible for organizing all of the efforts to achieve the goal.

### Motivation

What are the motivators to change? Incentive? Performance? Bonus? It's your job?

Encourage and support employees in doing their jobs. They must be empowered. Make sure they buy in to the service strategy. They must see a need.

### Customers

Don't forget about your customers in this process. How much are they involved in the service process? Some customers prefer to control their service experience. When they are substantially involved, as in the case of self-service, this is referred to as **coproduction**. For this to occur, customers themselves need to be comfortable with this process. They must be trained and aware.

## ☥ RESOURCE VIEWPOINT

A resource is something that can be tapped into and worked with to create something else even more valuable. Consider crude oil in the ground. It is worth marginal value per barrel, but if you refine it you can do so many more things with it. It can become diesel fuel, gasoline, jet fuel, or even a multitude of plastics and other petroleum-based products.

Resources in business and hospitality are the same way. The **resource viewpoint** states that every hospitality business has three main resources (see Figure 11.5):

- Human resources
- Financial resources
- Physical resources

**Champion**
A person commissioned with the task of achieving a desired goal. This individual would be responsible for organizing all staff, systems, and procedures to align the organization in its efforts to achieve the assigned goal.

**Coproduction**
The extent to which the customer should be involved in the process of service, which gives the customers a sense of control and tailors their service, contributing to the success of the encounter. Customers must be trained, and the instructions obvious and clear and support given.

**Resource Viewpoint**
The idea that every business has three resources with which to work and to use to their benefit.

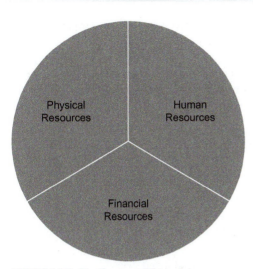

**FIGURE 11.5 The Resource Viewpoint.**

Human resources is the most important resource of all. It is also the most variable, the least controllable, and the least efficient.

Financial resources are the dollars that move through the business. They are the most closely regulated resource. Bank deposits are made daily. Financial accountants and revenue managers precisely calculate, predict, and control every facet of the stream of revenue through a business.

Physical resources consist of all of the tables, seats, beds, planes, rooms, buildings, screens, monitors, and technology in a business. They are controlled and monitored to produce optimal efficiency while balancing costs and demand.

Every decision involves the allocation of resources in some sense. In a way, the manager is constantly managing and balancing resources. Increasing guest service is not free. It involves retraining and monitoring. Sometimes, an increase in staff is necessary. It usually involves a demand in physical resources for nicer seats or infrastructure, which in turn places a greater demand on financial resources. Ideally, the manager should be working with each of the three main resources to build them up just as you would refine crude oil to make other more valuable products.

# CHAPTER REVIEW QUESTIONS

1. List the three components of strategy.
2. Explain why strategy is both important and natural.
3. Outline the basic concept of continuous improvement.
4. What is the strategic service system?
5. What are the three resources common to most all businesses?
6. What does the "O" in SWOT stand for?
7. What is the benefit of conducting a SWOT analysis?
8. What is the difference between internal and external components of the SWOT analysis?
9. What are five of the characteristics you should consider when developing a plan?
10. What is the best advice that you could provide for a property about to change or alter its services?

# CASE STUDIES

### Emily's Farmhouse Chicken

Emily's is a small restaurant located in the Midwest. It features fried chicken in an old farmhouse. Locals and those from the surrounding area patronize Emily's for homemade chicken and dumplings. White gravy is a specialty. It offers a very limited menu that has worked well in the past. People who are fortunate enough to find a seat in the small dining room/living room

CASE STUDIES *continued*

are served family-style, all-you-can-eat chicken for one low price. Places like Emily's populated the Midwest and South for many decades. They were successful until cities developed and chain restaurants offered many more choices at competitive prices. While Emily's still holds a loyal clientele, the experience of eating homemade cooking in a small, old farmhouse is slowly beginning to lose the interest of some patrons. Carol, Emily's daughter and long-time employee of Emily's, noticed this change. She mentioned it to Emily who told her, "Don't fix it if it ain't broken." Carol tried to explain that it was beginning to be broken and that if they didn't look toward the future now, it would soon be too late.

1. Evaluate Carol's mindset.
2. Was Carol thinking strategically? Explain.
3. At this rate, predict the future of Emily's in 10 years.

## Rusty's Emporium

Russell (Rusty) Donovan loved having fun. He scraped together enough money to buy an old factory and begin Rusty's Emporium 15 years ago when he was in his 20s. Rusty's motto has always been, "Have fun." Rusty's Emporium is an entertainment center. Over the years, Rusty had filled his Emporium with a multitude of attractions. He went to auctions and acquired many items. Some are used, and some are displayed, while others are sitting out back with large blue tarps over them.

Rusty began with laser tag and an arcade, but has grown to include a skateboard park, paintball, rock climbing, a pool with a slide, four hot tubs, miniature golf, a foam pit, a carousel, and a snack bar. Most recently, he began hosting kids' birthday parties.

Things have become busy with the parties and all of the other attractions, but the growth has also brought problems. Very different crowds of people attend the different attractions and they don't always blend. He is having difficulty maintaining the different attractions, and they often spill over from one to another. He can no longer oversee the Emporium himself, so he has had to hire more staff and incur more expenses. It is difficult to predict what attraction will be busy, so staffing and training has become difficult. His revenue has increased, but is becoming overshadowed by his costs. This was originally a fun place that Rusty enjoyed; now it is a disorganized mess.

1. Evaluate Rusty's strategic plan.
2. What has Rusty done correctly?
3. What advice could you provide for Rusty at this point?

## Sheila's Spa

You could say that Sheila's whole life was about spas. Her mother owned one when she was younger. Sheila had worked in spas since high school. She went to a local college and took classes on spa management. She delighted in traveling to destination spas for vacations, and now she finally has her chance at owning and operating her very own spa.

She has spent countless hours exploring the options. She wanted just the right combination of everything! She had kept a journal detailing her experiences at various spas around the world. She had saved all of her plans from her class projects during college. She went to the bookstore and bought every book available on spas. She even found a few computer programs that allowed her to play spa simulations. It was a labor of love. Everything would be perfect!

Sheila decided to begin the hiring process, so she set up a series of interviews. She interviewed all candidates at least twice. She used a behavioral interview for the finalists, then went to their past employers and clients to verify their skills firsthand. Some candidates had as many as six interviews.

She went to trade shows and warehouses and shopped on-line, observing literally every product on the market relating to spas.

She used a computer program to lay out the spa and projected her earnings for her business plan. Her banker asked her when she planned to open. Although her financial situation was still in great standing, Sheila told him that she did not yet want to open until everything was perfect. She believed that if you open and it isn't perfect, then customers will not return. During the next few weeks, a few of her new hires took positions at competing spas. Things were very close to opening, but Sheila feared they weren't quite perfect.

1. Assess Sheila's planning technique.
2. What issues do you foresee in Sheila's planning?
3. What advice would you provide for Sheila?

## Hal's Diner

Hal is a veteran of the food-service industry. He is self-taught, beginning his career washing dishes at age 9 in his father's diner. Everyone knew this because he told them about it nearly every day. Hal recently opened Hal's Diner with his own savings. He served typical diner Greek food that he had always known and served. He knew it all very well. A few other diners also scraped out a meager existence within the downtown area, but Hal believed that his would be the best.

Jason was hired as a waiter. He waited tables, but was much more than a waiter. Jason was in college studying to be a food-service manager and was a very bright and talented young man. He was working his way through school and took on night shifts to learn more of the industry and pay the bills. Late one evening when things were slow, Hal struck up a conversation with Jason. He asked him if they ever taught anything like this at his school. Jason wasn't sure what to say because Hal was very outspoken. Hal pressed further, "I see you watching everything. How do you think I am doing?"

Jason decided to speak his mind. "Hal, you are a veteran of the industry and I respect that, but times are changing and you must plan for it. Customer service and monitoring the competition are important. You cannot simply think that you are unique with what you are doing."

Hal's face turned bright red and his fists clinched. "I have been doing this for 53 years. You kids think that you know so much. The competition has nothing on me and the customers who don't like it can go down the road."

1. Who was correct, Jason or Hal?
2. Assess Hal's Diner compared to the competition.
3. What can be done to help Hal?

# EXERCISES

## Exercise 1: SWOT Analysis

**Directions:** Choose a local hospitality company and fill in the SWOT Information Chart below:

**Company Name:** _____

| Internal Components | Strength or Weakness? | Substantiation |
|---|---|---|
| Operations | | |
| Marketing | | |
| Employees | | |
| Management | | |
| Research and development | | |
| Market—customers | | |
| Technology | | |
| Competition | | |
| Economy | | |
| Legal/political | | |

## Exercise 2: Vision/Mission Review

**Directions:** For the purpose of this exercise, use the vision, mission, credo, motto and any other narrative that the company publishes. Choose a hospitality company that interests you. Review their vision and mission statements and other narratives and attach them to the back of this assignment. Complete the questions below.

**Company Name:** _____

1. What is the one line that describes what the company stands for?
2. What is the main priority of the company?
3. How many times is customer/guest service mentioned?
4. What would you change, remove, or add to the statements?

## Exercise 3: The Strategic Service System

**Directions:** Relate the Strategic Service System to a business in the local area. Outline your responses below:

Business Name: _____

Type of Business: _____

1. Purpose:
2. Product:
3. Plan:
4. People:

# Developing a Staff

## Chapter Objectives:

*After reading this chapter, you should be able to:*

Identify hiring attributes for quality service.

Describe the role of verbal and nonverbal communication in delivering quality service.

Explain and apply the concepts of successful nonverbal communication.

Explain the importance of corporate culture in developing a brand.

Identify the attributes of successful hospitality candidates.

Embrace the concepts behind guest service terminology.

Contrast the importance and different views of training, managing, and developing.

## Terminology:

Body Language
Cross-Functional Teams
Employee Turnover
Empowerment
Internal Customer

Job Description
Job Specification
Organizational Culture
SOP
Synergy

"The magic formula that successful businesses have discovered is to treat customers like guests and employees like people."

—*Tom J. Peters*

# Introduction

The employees are at the front line of the company. They are what the customer sees. They are the ones interacting with the customer. They can seize or lose opportunities. How well you hire, train, and develop your employees determines your future as a manager. If you could hire, train, and promote precisely the right people:

- You would have little or no employee turnover.
- You would have excellent customer service.
- You would work a lot less, and smile a lot more.

# Hiring

Today's society is filled by design with positions at hourly rates for which employees clock in and out, performing duties with little sense of responsibility for true guest satisfaction. Managerial positions are overly controlled by financial goals. Numerous policies and procedures inundate staff, and management is overwhelmed with forms and reports. Everyone has talents; most employees can be really great with customers if trained, supported and empowered.

Developing a staff is something that is crucial to any hospitality business. We can't train employees for every unique situation, but we can give them the resources or "tools" that could apply to most situations.

Businesses aim to hire for attitude and traits and then train for precise skills. Policies and procedures, stories, examples, demonstrations, and corporate culture are all ways to indoctrinate employees, who could then use their discretion in their application. Through practice, they monitor them and the employees hone their craft.

While hiring for attitude may be true to a certain extent, candidates must also present the satisfactory level of mental abilities such as judgment and comprehension skills. They must be familiar with basic procedures and methods or at least have transferable skills. They also need to possess organizational skills to work on projects alone and with others. But in the end, the hospitality industry has little use for candidates with poor attitudes and poor people skills.

**Job Description**
Details what the position does: duties and responsibilities.

**Job Specification**
Details what the position requires: knowledge, skills, and abilities.

## ❧ WHAT DO HOSPITALITY COMPANIES LOOK FOR?

Standard forms for the hiring process include the job description and the job specification. The **job description** explains what they do in the position, the duties and responsibilities. It is often used in interviewing, training, and evaluation. The **job specification** explains what they need to successfully complete the job. It is primarily used in hiring. It includes knowledge, skills, abilities, education, and certifications. It gives much insight into the qualifications of the ideal candidate. Occasionally, these two

documents are blended into one and referred to as one name or the other. The important thing is that a business has this information and uses it appropriately.

Most hospitality companies seek similar traits and ask themselves similar questions when hiring someone:

- How do they appear?
- Do they get along with others?
- Can they communicate?
- Are they sensitive to others?
- Can they foster customer relationships?
- Do they know and understand your business and your customers even if they're not from the same background?

### Service Insight

**An Attitude to Please**

It takes a very upbeat person to genuinely serve. A person with an attitude to please has satisfaction in knowing they did a great job. Guests can tell when someone wants them to have a good experience at an establishment and can tell when they are faking a concern for their experience. It is easy to recognize. To have an attitude to please others is almost like a calling.

**Only about 10 percent of the general population is born to serve others and have an attitude to please (see Figure 12.1). About 60 percent can be trained to serve, and about 30 percent don't belong in hospitality. Seek out and hire the 10 percent, sort through the 60 percent and train them to act like the 10 percent, and then run from the other 30 percent!**

Successful hospitality professionals share certain common qualities. Some are innate, while many can be developed. As you read the following list, you will begin to see a model of an ideal candidate to hire.

- Have a genuine desire to please others; find reward in a job well done
- Are motivated from within—an energetic personality
- Bring a positive attitude to work, leaving personal issues behind
- Able to adapt to situations, but are consistent in performance
- Able to anticipate needs and demands before they occur
- Feel a duty of loyalty to the company
- Are sensitive and consider the needs of others
- Are sincere
- Have knowledge of procedures, and products (which is different from rules that can or cannot be broken)
- Have a thirst for continuous learning
- Have knowledge of themselves
- Have pride in themselves
- Have knowledge of standards of excellence, what to strive for
- Have positive habits
- Have great listening skills
- Have great communication skills

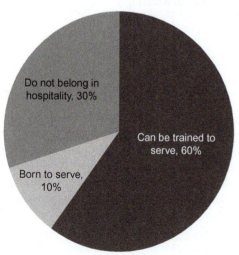

**FIGURE 12.1 Classifying Interviews in Hospitality.**

**Service Insight**

*Duty of Loyalty*

It is probably in the manual. Employees should have a duty of loyalty to their company. That means that they should always be acting in the best interest of the company.

This means at work and sometimes extends to outside work. Most companies agree and are doing something about it. Companies are cracking down on employee social media presence. Companies can and do terminate employees for lessening the reputation of the company.

**Employee Turnover**
A measure of the rate of employee losses and gains during a given period.

Hiring correctly is crucial for guest service. Your staff will be more content, they will perform better, and a momentum will develop that will make the manager's job much easier. Another benefit of this is lowered **employee turnover**—a measure of the gains and losses of employees. It is typically expressed as a percentage during a given period, such as a year. A higher turnover percentage means that employees work at the business for a shorter amount of time before leaving or being terminated. Lowered turnover means less time spent training, and therefore, fewer training expenses and less aggravation that comes along with it, hence causing even more turnover. Reducing turnover means more content employees and is a general indication that your operation is well-run. All of this contributes to successfully implementing customer service.

To calculate employee turnover:

1. First, determine the period of time to be used (month, quarter, or year).
2. Determine the number of the separations (number of employees that have left and been replaced). Each full-time employee counts as 1. Adjust accordingly for part-time employees who will equal a fraction relative to their hours (e.g., 2 half-time employees equal 1 full-time employee).
3. Divide the number of separations by the total number of employees during that same period (again, adjust for part-time employees).
4. Multiply this figure number by 100 to get a percentage. (*Note*: Sometimes, the calculation is simplified by only including full-time workers. It can also be calculated for management, employees, or new hires separately. You may also need to adjust for adding new positions or downsizing.)

# Communication

When you communicate, you are revealing much more than you might initially realize. As a customer approaches you, an identity of them begins to form. Without them saying a single word, you have formed a detailed biography of who they are. Consciously or subconsciously, this often directs how you will react in a situation. It will direct your questions and their responses. Be conscious of this. Your guesses are often correct, although you continue to hone this skill throughout life. You can expound and put together such descriptors as:

- Confidence
- Education
- Knowledge of surroundings

- Mood or demeanor
- Accent—country or region
- Gender
- Sexual orientation
- Social status
- Respect for others
- Energy level
- Age
- Personal lifestyle
- Ambitions
- Health

It can also have a counter-effect. As they look at you, they are doing the same thing. This changes the service experience. It alters their expectations. A certain profile will cause customers to assume and thus change how they are going to react or "play it." A profile may remind them of someone or they may associate a communication/presence with a certain outcome. Not everyone is open and nonjudgmental.

## ❦ VISUAL

You only have one chance to make a first impression. Your dress and appearance are important. What works well for one situation may be very inappropriate for another. Although people may have been taught not to judge one another, they often do; they make these snap judgments about others. A business must control what it is able to, and the employees' initial appearance is something that can be controlled. Customers are approaching frontline service staff with needs that often have to do with their trust in them for their health, safety, money, entertainment, status, and comfort. The first impression can make a big difference.

## ❦ BODY LANGUAGE

Many ideas are communicated without ever speaking a word. Because many people mistrust the spoken word alone, they look for other clues in body language. All must be synchronized in order to do this. People pick up on these clues very quickly, often without realizing it.

Hidden feelings and thoughts may be revealed through body language. This could help to interpret a customer's needs or help them to gain trust in or establish a professional image for you.

**Body Language**
Nonverbal communication that gives clues to one's underlying premise.

Because humans use many senses, **body language** can give subtle clues as to the underlying premise of a person's motivation. Communication occurs in many ways, and verbal is only a part of the equation of communication. In other words, you can tell what someone is thinking by watching how their body reacts. The same is true for the customer. You could be saying all of the correct things, but if your body tells a different story, you are sending a mixed message. Your words and your body language must be synchronized.

*Eyes*: People often desire eye contact during a conversation. They are comforted by another giving them this. Looking away when someone is speaking conveys an attitude of disrespect or insincerity. You want to give them your undivided attention or they may feel unimportant.

*Head*: Nodding of the head also conveys active listening skills. Shaking, bobbing, and facing any other direction than directly at the guest should be avoided.

*Face*: Avoid blank looks. Smile whenever possible. Be aware of whether you naturally scowl or frown and try to avoid this.

*Hands*: Avoid excessive hand gestures. Pointing with an open hand conveys trust. Avoid waving continuously, using a tightened fist, putting your hands in your pockets, or fumbling with keys, a cellphone or jewelry.

*Arms*: Never fold your arms. Keep them at your sides. Behind your back is fine. Never lean.

*Torso*: Turned toward the guest, as straight as possible. Note your posture. Be professional.

*Legs*: Stance should be about shoulder-width apart. Avoid leaning on one side or shifting back and forth. When sitting, crossed or together for women; together for men. They should always be bent at the knees while sitting and never apart.

*Feet*: Should be flat to the floor and pointed at the customer. Avoid shifting and tapping.

*Distance*: How close is too close? This depends on the occasion: closer for personal (24 to 48 inches). Further for social, formal, or public occasions. Watch whether the guest gets closer or backs away or appears uncomfortable.

Remember that your body communicates. All must be instinctive or it will look rehearsed or contrived. You must practice these principles to appear genuine. When dealing with customers, it is important for you to be able to discern their body language. It is also important for you to convey the appropriate body language. Once you are aware of it, you will typically know when you get it right.

## ❧ VOCAL

Vocal expression is even more difficult to control. Few people focus on it, but it is essential. Have you listened to yourself on a recording? It is probably very difficult to do this. If you are serious about your presence, you should. When doing so, observe:

- Inflection: Variation in voice
- Pitch: High, low, or monotone
- Timing: Fast or slow
- Volume: Loud or quiet

Ask the following questions:

- Is it strong enough to resonate confidence?
- Is it firm enough to command a presence?
- Is it distinctive?
- Do you enunciate?

As an exercise, try listening to others for these qualities. It quickly makes you aware of your own vocal abilities. Also try to learn phrases that parallel the organizational culture. Examples of training responses are:

- Please and thank you.
- May I?
- It is my pleasure.
- That would be great.
- With your permission.
- Would you consider?
- I regret to inform you that.
- Great question.
- That makes sense.
- Have you considered?

Also consider integrating other key words that identify with the organizational culture such as:

- Opportunity
- Challenging
- Options
- Fine
- Well
- Outstanding

There are also words that should be discouraged and removed from your vocabulary. It is difficult to remove them just while you are at work. Instead, remove them from your personal life as well. Otherwise, they will creep in when you are relaxed or in times of stress. Avoid these words such as:

- Vulgarities
- Profanities
- Religious, political, and sexual references
- Honey, babe, sugar, dude, chick
- Kid, kiddo, kiddies
- Axe (a question)
- You's
- Fittin'
- Fixin'
- OMG

Also remember to be optimistic and avoid negative phrases such as:

- Hang on.
- You have to.
- Not my job.
- I don't know.

- I don't have time.
- I haven't had the time.
- I can't.
- I won't.

## ❧ ANSWERING THE TELEPHONE

Everyone speaks on the telephone. It is very natural, but the rules change at the workplace. A business must train their employees to use a protocol. These tips can truly make a difference when answering the telephone:

- Use the standard greeting.
- Identify yourself by name and company, and thank them for calling.
- Minimize background noises.
- Listen, and do not interrupt.
- Be patient and don't rush them.
- Pretend that you are looking at them.
- Envision them as being in front of you.
- Smile—it will come through in your voice.
- Avoid multi-tasking, most people can tell that you are doing something else.
- Take note of their name and use it if possible.
- Restate and reply to each comment or question individually.
- Apologize for any inconveniences.
- Tell them what you are doing to satisfy their need.
- Apologize, give estimated time, and ask permission before placing them on hold.
- Ask whether you have answered their question.
- Ask whether there is anything else you can do to help them.
- Keep notes, follow up as needed, and do what you said you would do.

### Initiating a Call

- Have a plan, script, or flow chart to follow.
- Greet and identify yourself by name, company, and department.
- State your reason for the call.
- Ask whether you are speaking to the correct person.
- Refer to them by name.
- Write down notes; have a phone record sheet.
- Remember that you are repeating this many times, but it is the first time they have heard it.
- Have the computer system, calendar, and telephone directory available.

**Leaving a Message**

- Speak slowly and clearly.
- Leave date and time of call.
- Identify yourself and company.
- Leave basic information.
- Suggest options or tell them there is nothing else for them to do at this time.
- Leave a number and contact information.
- Leave a pleasant closing.

# Training, Managing, and Developing

Employees may come and go. A few need to move on, but many can and should be developed. It is your job as a manager to keep the momentum. Your job as a manager will be much easier if you have a great staff but hiring the right people is only half of the battle. You must properly train, manage, and develop them. In doing so, you will surely be rewarded.

This section details a four-step process for training, managing, and developing employees (see Figure 12.2):

1. Demonstrate personal and procedural expectations.
2. Integrate and initiate into the culture.
3. Demonstrate service standards.
4. Monitor, assess, support, and reward.

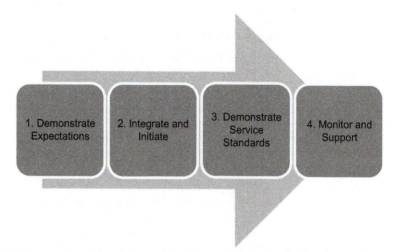

**FIGURE 12.2  Four-Step Process for Training, Managing, and Developing Employees.**

## ❖ DEMONSTRATE PERSONAL AND PROCEDURAL EXPECTATIONS

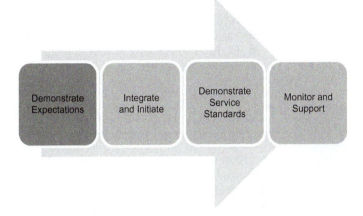

## GOAL SETTING

Everyone should be challenged. Setting goals helps establish expectations. It also helps to ensure that objectives are completed and goals are met. It keeps employees on track and allows management to fulfill its expectations from the ranks above.

Let the employees know what is expected of them. This should be detailed in the job description. It is continued through orientation and initial training. It also comes up in reviews. As simple as it is, using ABC prioritizing is quite successful.

### ABC Prioritizing

- Record all of your tasks on a list as bullet statements.
- Rank each of them as A, B, or C.
- A = the tasks that must be completed today.
- B = the tasks that are important, but could wait a day if necessary.
- C = the tasks that can wait.
- If something is of utmost importance, label it a AA, or even a AAA. Work on those first.
- Tasks labeled B may soon become AAA, but still do not have to be done on the present day.
- Now, begin the day working on the A's first. Then completing the B's. And, as time permits, work on the C's.
- Place a line through items as you complete them.
- Write up and revise a new list at the end of each day while it is still fresh in your mind.

As a manager, you should also set goals. Keep a close notice of what consumes the majority of your time. Delegate whenever appropriate and don't be embarrassed to ask for help. You will be setting employee expectations. Keep them informed and promote cross-training. Consider your role as an enabler of customer service.

## USE OF TERMS

Nearly every business has terminology. A great example of this is Walt Disney World, which uses the terms to help demonstrate expectations:

### On-stage and off-stage

- Similar to front of house and back of house.
- Everyone is to perform a role when in front of the customer.

### Cast members

- All employees should assume they are in a performance of some type while in front of the customer.
- Employees are all dedicated to the same cause.

### Guests

- All customers are really guests of ours.
- They are invited to join us in the performance.
- They aren't a nuisance, they are welcomed.

**Standard Operating Procedure**
A formalized method. Crucial in training to achieve consistency.

## STANDARDS

Every business needs standards for control and consistency. For example, "Try to refer to a guest by name whenever possible." Standards are used in training and evaluation. Without them, employees would have no idea what to do, or even whether they are doing it well. It may seem contradictory and controlling, but the employee discretion is not possible without **standard operating procedures (SOP)**.

## ✌ INTEGRATE AND INITIATE INTO THE CULTURE

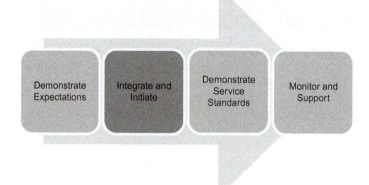

Demonstrate Expectations | Integrate and Initiate | Demonstrate Service Standards | Monitor and Support

## ✌ INTERNAL CUSTOMERS

"If you're not serving the customer, your job is to be serving someone who is."
—*Jan Carlzon*

**Internal Customers**

Staff who are served by other employees. This mindset helps employees to recognize that they are serving those who serve the customer and the importance of assisting them in their roles.

The concept of **internal customers** is that staff who serve other employees should think of those other employees as customers who are internal to the organization. Those employees go on to serve the customer. By contrast, typical customers outside the organization are referred to as *external customers*. This mindset helps employees to recognize that their service to other employees can have a direct impact on the customer. The idea is that an employee will deliver better service to another if they think of them as a customer. Employees also need to get along with each other when in front of customers. The public can easily notice when employees are fighting, and it makes them feel awkward.

## DEVELOPING A CULTURE/MANAGING AN IMAGE

An **organizational culture** is the personality of a business. It answers many of the questions that are difficult to place in procedure manuals. It can be designed and managed, and it has a life of its own. Your business can have a culture of helping customer service or hurting customer service.

Do your staff feel as though they are part of the family?

A culture directs many of the small details that cannot easily be expressed or managed. It should be facilitated at all employee contact points, including in orientation, in training, in the policies and guidelines, and in the verbiage or terminology. It should dictate:

**Organizational Culture**

The personality of a business—its style, pace, and attitude. It can be managed while also having a life of its own.

- Work pace
- Work style
- Attitude toward each other
- Attitude toward customers
- Presentation/appearance
- Skill sets
- Accountability
- Activities
- Priorities

## Corporate Culture at the Marriot International

Marriott International is an example of a company with a strong corporate culture. If you've ever spoken to an employee, you will know this is true. In the words of J.W. Marriott, Jr., "Culture is the life-thread and glue that links our past, present, and future."

Marriott is committed to fair treatment of associates and to providing training and advancement opportunities to all. Marriott's reputation for superior customer service rises out of a long tradition that started with J. Willard Marriott's simple goal for his small, fast-food stand called Hot Shoppes to provide:

- Good food and good service at a fair price.
- Do whatever it takes to take care of the customer.

- Pay extraordinary attention to detail.
- Take pride in their physical surroundings.
- Use creativity to find new ways to meet the needs of customers.
- Actively support the community.
- Encourage associate volunteerism through a variety of organizations.

Marriott employees have such a strong, caring nature that many donate their personal vacation time to be transferred to other employees in need of leave.

*Source: Marriot International, Inc.*

## ❖ DEMONSTRATE SERVICE STANDARDS

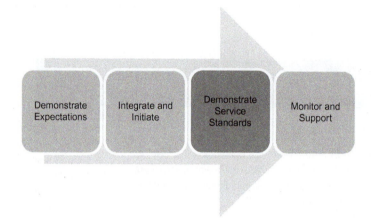

## EMPOWERMENT

A family is walking through an amusement park, enjoying the day. The children each have an ice cream cone in hand when suddenly the smaller child's ice cream cone falls on the ground. The child immediately begins to cry. The parents are consoling the child, and considering options. They look over and see a long line for ice cream.

A nearby employee sees this and walks behind the counter, serves up a replacement cone and brings it over to the crying child. The child is pleased and the parents are relieved.

Certainly controls are in place, and items must be accounted for, but customer satisfaction comes first. Actions like this are common at Walt Disney World. In fact, they share this story with employees at orientation, describing the idea of **empowerment**. This is enabling the employees with the authority, or power, to make decisions in the best interest of the guests. This is done with training and trust. It permits guest service issues to be handled more quickly. It gives the employees a feeling of accomplishment and trust. It frees time from management. To implement this:

**Empowerment**
Enabling employees with the authority to make decisions in the best interest of the guests.

- Establish a culture.
- Detail the guest service expectations.
- Give examples.
- Set limits.
- Have a reporting procedure.
- Management must support employee decisions.
- Recognize great decisions.
- Be constructive with lesser decisions.

Empowerment permits employees to make a difference. It reduces frustration by removing the need to involve managers and speeds up the resolution process.

An amazing example of empowerment: when the two-time Baldrige Award-winning Ritz-Carlton first applied for the Malcolm Baldrige Quality Award, they empowered employees to resolve customer situations as they saw fit up to $2,000.

# Ritz-Carlton Hotel Company Standards

## Motto

At The Ritz-Carlton Hotel Company, L.L.C., "We are Ladies and Gentlemen serving Ladies and Gentlemen." This motto exemplifies the anticipatory service provided by all staff members.

## The Credo

The Ritz-Carlton Hotel is a place where the genuine care and comfort of our guests is our highest mission. We pledge to provide the finest personal service and facilities for our guests who will always enjoy a warm, relaxed, yet refined ambience.

The Ritz-Carlton experience enlivens the senses, instills well-being, and fulfills even the unexpressed wishes and needs of our guests.

## Three Steps Of Service

1. A warm and sincere greeting. Use the guest's name.
2. Anticipation and fulfillment of each guest's needs.
3. Fond farewell. Give a warm good-bye and use the guest's name.

## Service Values: I Am Proud to Be Ritz-Carlton

1. I build strong relationships and create Ritz-Carlton guests for life.
2. I am always responsive to the expressed and unexpressed wishes and needs of our guests.
3. I am empowered to create unique, memorable, and personal experiences for our guests.
4. I understand my role in achieving the Key Success Factors, embracing Community Footprints and creating The Ritz-Carlton Mystique.
5. I continuously seek opportunities to innovate and improve The Ritz-Carlton experience.
6. I own and immediately resolve guest problems.
7. I create a work environment of teamwork and lateral service so that the needs of our guests and each other are met.
8. I have the opportunity to continuously learn and grow.
9. I am involved in the planning of the work that affects me.
10. I am proud of my professional appearance, language, and behavior.
11. I protect the privacy and security of our guests, my fellow employees, and the company's confidential information and assets.
12. I am responsible for uncompromising levels of cleanliness and creating a safe and accident-free environment.

## The Employee Promise

At The Ritz-Carlton, our Ladies and Gentlemen are the most important resource in our service commitment to our guests.

By applying the principles of trust, honesty, respect, integrity and commitment, we nurture and maximize talent to the benefit of each individual and the company.

The Ritz-Carlton fosters a work environment where diversity is valued, quality of life is enhanced, individual aspirations are fulfilled, and The Ritz-Carlton Mystique is strengthened.

*Source:* The Ritz-Carlton Hotel Company, L.L.C.

## ✭ MONITOR, ASSESS, SUPPORT, AND REWARD

| Demonstrate Expectations | Integrate and Initiate | Demonstrate Service Standards | Monitor and Support |
|---|---|---|---|

### Service Insight

#### *Explaining the Purpose*

There was once a chef who demanded that all of the warming boxes be wiped out every night. This seemed unreasonable to the employees because the warming boxes were never dirty. The food was wrapped and there was no need to clean the boxes. This task was left undone when the chef was away on vacation. After a few days, employees realized that food was being left in the warming boxes. What the chef was really getting at was that he didn't want food left in the boxes. If they were wiped out, they were emptied out, and extra food would not be wasted. Sometimes there is much wisdom behind rules that employees don't understand. People need to understand why things are done. It was a joke that "Generation Y" would be renamed "Generation Why?" because they needed to be told the purpose behind it. Surely other generations also wondered, but it is prevalent in new entrants to today's workforce. Explaining the "why" is yet another practical tip to gaining buy-in with employees.

### MONITOR

There is a belief that a manager should let little things go. They should not constantly police and monitor their employees. Instead, they should train their staff, trust them, empower them, and be more like a coach. Another belief is that a manager must begin strictly because once they let things slip it is very difficult to resume control and that employees will respect the strictness of the manager. While yet a third idea is that lenient (and coaching) is fine and strict is fine, but inconsistency is what causes frustration and dissention. Most agree with the third idea.

### ASSESS

Evaluations can be difficult to give and receive. Evaluations should be a formality with no surprises. Employees should receive continuous feedback and know how they are doing all along. Feedback should be treated as an opportunity to improve.

Meetings are another chance to let employees know how they are doing. Managers should also have day-to-day conversations with employees, and meetings should be for things that cannot be done through other methods. The following are tips for conducting successful meetings:

- Have an agenda and try your best to stick to it.
- Make meetings short, less than 30 minutes.
- Attention spans are short, and so should be the topics of meetings.

- Stick to the important things, making meetings meaningful, or don't hold meetings at all.
- Show respect for people at meetings and they will reciprocate.
- If the purpose of the meeting is dissemination of information, consider whether it could it be done in another way.
- Ensure that all participants can see and hear each other.
- Pre-shift meetings should be essential information only and last 5 minutes or less.

## SUPPORT

Frontline workers have various priorities. Some want to excel into management. Others are working for only a short time until they finish school or complete something else; they are using this as a stepping stone or buying time with it. Some have limited options for their future. Others are out of work and this job is something to do until they get a better job. It's important to know where employees come from, where they want to go, and what they want out of a job.

However, the business also has priorities, and everyone needs to realize this. When discussing this with employees, address the idea of their future in the industry and with your company. There is a relationship between the needs of the business and the needs of an employee. Those priorities must be balanced. Just like a traveler stops by a hotel for a short visit and then is on his or her way, so do employees. However, an employee must pay with hard work and dedication, just as the traveler must pay with money for the accommodations. It is a trade-off, and each party needs to know where the other stands.

Another point to mention is that of conflict. When conflict occurs, realize that some conflict is acceptable. People are different, and without conflict we would grow stagnant. Try to realize what is behind the emotions, and always be professional. As a manager, you should anticipate problems before they occur.

> ### Service Insight
>
> #### Checking In with Employees
>
> One manager would walk around every day and say good night before he left for the day and have a brief conversation with each and every employee. What was he really doing? Was he a really friendly guy? Perhaps. Did he really want to say good-bye? Probably not. He was monitoring the employees. He was checking on their status and their accomplishments, troubleshooting, and keeping a general view on what was happening within the ranks. He developed a relationship with each employee. Everyone knew him and felt comfortable speaking to him. This was his way of monitoring operations.

## REWARD

Incentives and reward are key motivators. **Why does a dog bark at the mailman? Because every time the dog sees the mailman, he barks and then the mailman goes away. So, why wouldn't the dog bark?**

How are your employees motivated? Employee reward systems should have clear goals and address appropriate behavior and actions. When done properly, it has a great impact.

- The rewards should be consistent.
- They don't have to be monetary. Rewards can be intangible.
- Rewarding specific actions and service works better than an overall reward.

Remember, providing good service should be more of a habit than a reward. The opposite of reward is punishment. If a company punishes based on complaints, the employees and managers will hide the actual number of complaints.

# Team Management

Implementing service rarely occurs with just one person. It is usually part of a team effort. Team management has been very popular in the literature and practice over the past 20 to 30 years, providing much insight on team practice. The original idea of teams was to form a cohesive group instead of passing problems and customers from department to department. A group effort was seen as a solution to the disjointed, *silo effect* that plagued organizations. The goals of the teams were to improve productivity, quality, and efficiency in an effort to best serve the customers. A team should provide **synergy**, which is an idea that groups can accomplish more as a team than their sum as individuals. Teams have offered many benefits such as:

**Synergy**
Worth more than the sum of its parts. The idea that members of teams are more productive than as individuals.

- Workload distribution
- Idea generation
- New perspectives
- Oversight for responsibility and objectivity

Despite these advantages, many teams have not been entirely successful. Teams must be run well so the benefits exceed the costs. If not, the demands of resources on a team could easily exceed the costs. At an early age, most people have already been exposed to a team environment that was unfavorable. As a result, some employees dread the idea of teamwork and prefer to work alone. Why then, do teams fail? Teams fail for a number of reasons. Communication and personality are commonly cited reasons, but there are more. The following lists the most common reasons why groups fail to become highly successful:

- Communication and awareness
  - Lack of communication leading to a lack of understanding
  - Unaware of expectations

- ○ Unreal expectations
- ○ Unaware of the pitfalls
- ○ Misjudgment of conditions
- ○ Lack of contribution to group communications
- ■ Personalities and traits
  - ○ Not realizing personalities differ
  - ○ Bad blending of personalities
  - ○ Insecurity within self
  - ○ Lack of flexibility
  - ○ Lack of concern
  - ○ No trust between members, in process
  - ○ Self-importance
  - ○ Not managing known weaknesses
  - ○ Lack of diversity
  - ○ Fear of conflict
  - ○ Lack of commitment
  - ○ Lack of ability
- ■ Planning and scheduling
  - ○ Lack of motivation, resulting in a lack of timeliness
  - ○ Poor time management of members
  - ○ Inappropriate allocation of assignments
  - ○ Failure to have a backup plan
  - ○ Lack of recognition of work
  - ○ Not given proper resources
  - ○ Lack of accountability
  - ○ Inappropriate management of strengths and weaknesses
  - ○ Loss of focus on objectives
- ■ Past team issues

## ❦  TYPES OF TEAMS

Teams can be classified in many ways. The most common classifications use characteristics of functionality, purpose, duration, supervision, and dependency.

### Functionality of Team

**Cross-Functional Teams**
Teams with members from different areas of the organization, but at about the same supervisory level. Teams typically problem-solve specific assignments.

Functional teams
- ○ Description: Within the same area, but with different levels of supervisory. Typically focused on specific issues.
- ○ Frequency: Several times/week or constant.
- ○ Size and duration: 4 to 20 people and relatively permanent.
- ○ Example goal: Quality customer service.

### Cross-functional teams
- ○ Description: From different areas of the organization, but at about the same supervisory level. Teams are for problem-solving, created for specific assignments.
- ○ Frequency: 1 to 3 times/week.

○ Size and duration: 4 to 12 people; a few weeks to 1 year or until problem is solved.
○ Example goals: Improved efficiency or communication.

## Purpose of the Team

Operational
○ Goal: Production-oriented
○ Example: A staff team at a box office
Problem solution
○ Goal: Solving specific issues; implement solutions
○ Example: Waste-reduction team
Product development
○ Goal: Developing new or improved products or systems
○ Example: Adding a new boutique line
Employee development
○ Goal: Staff development
○ Example: Group bonding at ropes or obstacle course

## Duration of Team

Terminal: Team disbands when project objectives are completed
Non-terminal or on-going: Team permanent until reassigned

## Supervision

Self-directed teams
○ Description: All responsible for objectives/goals; no formal supervisor; all vote, evaluate each other, and form group consensus
○ Frequency: 1 to 3 times/week
○ Size and duration: 4 to 15 people; until problem is solved, a few weeks to 1 year
○ Example goals: Efficiency, customer service
Directed teams
○ Supervisor directs efforts and monitors

## Dependency

Interdependent
○ Description: Rely on each other to reach objectives
○ Example: Security team at a concert
Independent teams
○ Description: Work mostly independently; one not supporting the role of the other
○ Example: Waitstaff team at an à la carte restaurant

## Virtual Teams

Description: Meet, communicate and work through problems from a distance through the use of electronic methods, such as telephone or video. Virtual teams have both advantages and disadvantages. Despite this, they have become very popular, particularly with larger organizations that have multiple properties. They

work especially well when the group members do not need to work together or continuously depend on each other, as in the case of independent teams. The following are some of the advantages and disadvantages of virtual teams:

Advantages
○ Not geographically specific, location does not matter
○ Easily allows members to join from outside the organization
○ Permits those who might never had been able to join otherwise because of logistical reasons
Disadvantages
○ Lack of nonverbal communication cues
○ Exchange of information difficult
○ Technology-dependent

A common type of team in the 1980s was known as a Quality Circle. This was a team of about 8 to 10 employees and supervisors. They met regularly to discuss quality problems, research the causes, and recommend solutions or corrective actions; they didn't actually implement the changes. Many were very successful. According to the above characteristics, these would have been described as nonterminal, directed, and interdependent.

## ❦ TEAM STAGES

The most commonly used framework for team development stages was devised by Bruce W. Tuckman in the 1960s: forming, storming, norming, and performing. Tuckman's model has been given alternative names, but the general idea has withstood the test of time and is still used to describe the progression of groups.

1. Forming: Familiarization, getting acquainted to leadership issues
2. Storming: Fighting, goal/objective issues
3. Norming: Beginning to trust and form a structure
4. Performing: Productive teamwork

Groups are yet another key to customer service. Recognition of these stages helps the team leader and members to realize what is occurring and what is to come. Realizing these stages, expecting these stages, and working with the stages helps the group to progress through them more efficiently and effectively. As a result, they can progress to the fourth and final stage of performing in a productive manner.

## ❦ TYPES OF TEAM MEMBERS

Everyone brings something to the team. Hopefully, it is a positive attribute. Recognizing and channeling the characteristics of others is the key to successfully working together. Diversity of characteristics often leads to conflict, but also produces some of the best results when overcome. There are many classifications of team members. Many combine a few variables and give descriptive names, such as, "Dominator," "Invisible Man," or "Diplomat." Most are categorized by the following headings:

### Approach to Problems

- Acceptance: Do they accept problems or question them?
- Solution style: Do they seek an immediate answer or wish to collect more information and suspend judgment?

### Interaction/Expression

- Communication: How do they prefer to communicate? How frequently? How involved are they? What is their preferred tone?
- Ability to negotiate: Do they seek a win–win, dominate, or give up?
- Conflict: Is it welcomed or avoided? Do they argue loudly or softly?
- Transitions: Can they move on from a topic or an argument?
- Empathy: How concerned are they for others?
- Introversion: Do they generally prefer interacting with others or alone?

### Work Style

- Stage: Do they prefer to begin, work on, or complete a task?
- Work pace: Are they fast or slow?
- Work quality: Is their work sloppy, average, or perfect?
- Balance: Are they most concerned with completion or perfection?
- Work focus: Are they detail-oriented, or are they focused on the big picture?

### Personal/ Emotional

- Motivation level: Are they naturally motivated?
- Honesty: Are they straightforward, or do they downplay or embellish?
- Ability to control: Can they control their emotions?
- Priority: What level of priority are the group objectives?
- Comfort: Are they comfortable with the group?
- Confidence: How confident are they in their abilities?

### Expertise/Intellectual

- Specialization: What is their specialization?
- Capacity: Are they below, at par, or above the average intelligence of the group?

## ✼ HOW TO MAKE TEAMS WORK

To make teams work is an ongoing refinement of many qualities. To begin, have knowledge of the team members and the issues. Then, assess and regulate the members, activities, and environment. Have the ability to stay focused and meet the objective, yet be flexible enough to accommodate changes. While seemingly contradictory, all of these things must be kept in mind. In order for teams to be successful, you must:

- Know the types of teams and assign members appropriately.
- Know the typical roles of the members.
- Keep the pitfalls in mind.
- Stay focused on the objective and monitor.

# Introduction to Service Marketing

##  MARKETING AND CUSTOMER SERVICE

Marketing and customer service work in tandem. The following are excerpts from marketing literature:

> "Place the customers first."
> "Without our customers we have nothing."
> "The purpose of a company is to serve the customer."
> "The purpose of a company is to create and maintain satisfied customers."
> "Reward the employees. They will take care of the customers."
> "Establish an organizational culture that cares for the customers."
> "Develop a service culture."
> "Customer service is in the hands of the frontline workers."

Most of these marketing quotes involve quality customer service. Marketing embraces customer service because neither can exist alone. Marketing and customer service go hand in hand. They are part of a larger system of business processes.

##  MARKETING DEFINED

**Marketing**
The coordination of the exchange of goods and service in an effort to fulfill the wants and needs of the customers. This involves deliberate control of advertising and brand management.

Before we go further, let's examine what marketing is. **Marketing** is the coordination of the exchange of goods and services in an effort to fulfill the wants and needs of the customers. This involves a deliberate control of advertising and brand management.

Now, let's take this definition apart to better understand it. Marketing is:

### the coordination

*Coordination* means that it does not just happen spontaneously. It is a deliberate process. It is analyzed and planned and executed with intention.

### of the exchange of goods and services

The exchange is open to include the many distribution channels such as in person, through a website, or through a distributor such as a travel agent. Goods and services embrace hospitality in that there is typically both a tangible and intangible component to what is provided.

### in an effort to fulfill the wants and needs of the customers.

This is a hallmark of customer service. Marketing aims to fulfill the wants and needs of its customers.

### This involves deliberate control of advertising and brand management.

The term *deliberate* means that it is by design and on purpose. It is something intentionally orchestrated, or controlled, by the business.

Advertising is the actual act of getting the message out to the customer. It may be passive (remember us) or active (buy now). It can involve many forms such as print, e-mail, direct mail, phone, website, or a third party.

Brand management is maintaining the brand image. It is the end product of marketing. **Brand image** is what your business stands for and what it means to others. It is what the customers think when the name of your business is mentioned. It is an ongoing process that involves every aspect of the business. It is represented in the uniforms, the signage, the greetings used, and so on. Brand management is key! It is important that your customers believe that you deliver quality service.

**Brand Image**
The end product of marketing. It is what your business stands for and is evident in every aspect of your business.

## ✦ CHANGES IN MARKETING

Much of what occurs in the hospitality industry occurs off-line. For example, you cannot dine online. What *is* changing is the way that we interact with our guests. The service provider can:

- determine guest expectations.
- sell the product, encouraging new and return guests.
- refer others, offer promotions with last-minute deals, or just soft sell.

And the customers can:

- receive services like concierge, reservations, and advance purchase.
- make complaints in the public sector.
- form initial ideas regarding quality.

In the past, customer care and personal service were closely related. Consumers had few choices because of a lack of communication, transportation, and technology. Customers were treated as regulars, and they appreciated the comfort of being known. The world was, in a sense, small.

More recently, there have been many changes in the way businesses market to the public. The world has become much larger and more knowledgeable. Smart phones are ubiquitous. Consumers can access information using numerous methods, purchase from anywhere, and drive or travel much farther than ever before. As a result, customers now have much more knowledge and freedom of choices than ever before. Newer technologies like voice-activated applications (e.g., Apple's Siri) and map-activated applications are also changing how hospitality markets provide guest service.

The number of online travel agencies (OTAs) has also dramatically increased. They are used in browsing, reservations, concierge, shopping, and travel planning. In the past ten years, the percentage of hotel rooms booked on these third-party, OTA sites has increased from 1 percent to about 9 percent. Trip Advisor and Booking.com receive millions of hits each month.

According to Smith Travel Research and Market Matrix, 89 percent of respondents claimed to be influenced by the online reviews, making these very important to hoteliers. Never before have the expectations of guests been so heavily influenced by other guests. In fact, they rated guest experience factors (past experience, recommendations, and online reviews) at 51 percent, making it the biggest predictor of purchase. Second was location, and third was price.

## ☙ EVERYONE HAS CUSTOMER SERVICE

These days, everyone is dedicated to customer service. They boast of personalized guest service, whether or not they actually deliver it. It is written in their mission statements, in their training manuals, on business cards, and on the walls behind the counter. Why then, isn't everyone actually delivering quality customer service? Why does service suffer miserably? Do customers or staff even believe the statements? Unfortunately, the answer is usually no. Customers don't typically believe quotes that boast quality service because they are overused and often don't deliver what is promised.

# The Four Steps of Marketing for Quality Guest Service

This section discusses the process of marketing as it relates to customer service. It is divided into four steps that flow from one to another as the concepts of marketing are applied to a service business. Each section is further divided, delving into details within each of the four steps. We begin with a presentation of the four steps because it is important to keep in mind the big picture (see Figure 13.1). This will help to better place the details into their proper context.

1. Analysis and Identification of Needs.
2. Establishment of a Marketing Plan.
3. Implementation of Controls to Position.
4. Follow-up—Service after the Sale.

**FIGURE 13.1   The Four Steps of Marketing for Quality Guest Service.**

## ☙ STEP 1: ANALYSIS AND IDENTIFICATION OF WANTS AND NEEDS

What defines a buyer's choice of brand, type, amount, timing, and expectations? By answering the questions in the following sections, you will begin to piece together a picture that will answer this question (see Figure 13.2).

### 1.1 DEFINE THE PROFILE

Establishing a profile requires answering questions to help define the market and competition. The following list of questions begins the classification and establishment of a profile.

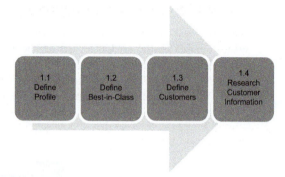

**FIGURE 13.2** **Four Sub-Steps within Step 1 of Marketing for Quality Service: Analysis and Identification of Wants and Needs.**

- What business are you in? This may seem obvious, but it establishes a foundation.
- What are you known for?
- Who is your competition?
- What is the competition known for?

Answering these questions will produce a profile and an initial list of competitors. The next section begins to rank the competition by providing a list of the best-in-class.

## 1.2 DEFINE BEST-IN-CLASS

The following list can be used as a ranking to strive for, and a benchmark for adapting best-practice methods. These questions begin the ranking of competitors for your industry.

- Who first comes to mind when your industry is mentioned?
- Who is the best at quality service?
- Who has the overall best product?
- Who has the nicest property?
- Who has the nicest options or amenities?
- Who leads in innovation?
- Who leads in market share?

Learn what the competition is doing. Go visit them. Talk to others. Read journals and reviews. Take note of what the best-in-class are doing to excel in areas and processes. Ask why they are successful.

## 1.3 DEFINE THE CUSTOMERS

After the best in-class has been established you must also define the customers. So, what defines a customer? Customers can be explained in, or divided into, groups. The information is referred to as customer intelligence and the divisions are called market segmentation. They could be internal or external. They could be potential, actual, or former. The following chart illustrates this point.

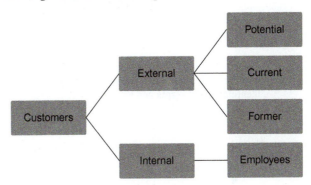

**Market Segmentation.**

**Customer Intelligence**
The process of gathering information regarding your customers—including history of use, demographics, and psychographics—in an effort to understand former, future, and current customers. Used in marketing, strategic planning, and training.

**Market Segmentation**
The process of dividing the market into groups. This is typically done demographically; however, numerous other ways exist.

**Expected Customer Turnover** When customers leave for reasons beyond the control of the business.

**Unexpected Customer Turnover**
When customers leave for reasons within the control of the business.

### Customer Intelligence

The process of gathering information regarding your customers. This includes a history of use, demographics, and psychographics in an effort to understand former, future, and current customers. Used in marketing, strategic planning, and training.

### Market Segmentation

The process of dividing the market into groups. This is typically done demo-graphically; however, numerous ways exist.

- ○ What do the customers want?
- ○ What do the customers expect?
- ○ How do customers define value?
- ○ Is there such a thing as an average customer? (Note: we are still assuming that all customers are unique and deserve respect and attention, but there can be certain averages.)
- ○ What is the average lifespan of a customer?
- ○ Is the customer relationship one-time or continued?
- ○ Where do new customers come from?
- ○ Why did former customers leave? Customers leave for a variety of reasons. Some relocate and others change lifestyles. These reasons are known as **expected customer turnover**, which is part of the nature of sales—when they leave for natural reasons beyond the control of the business. What a business can control is the **unexpected customer turnover**, or, loss of business due to a fault of the business. This could be from poor service, inferior products, or a number of other controllable aspects.

   ○ Why did potential customers choose to never patronize your business? Customers could be turned off by a telephone conversation without even patronizing your establishment. They can be turned off by something that they heard from someone else. They can be turned off by an advertisement that they saw—perhaps it was an image or what your establishment is perceived to be like.

   ○ Who accepts responsibility for your current and potential customers?

### Decision to Purchase

Have you ever wondered what makes a person buy something? What are the customer's other choices? Is the decision based on price? Is it based on the number of stars the product received? Is it based on the product? Is it based on location, convenience, or lack of alternative choices? Or, is it based on service? Service quality is one of the main reasons consumers purchase items, but it isn't the only reason. It is part of the overall message they receive. People are motivated to purchase for a variety of reasons. We must gauge customer interest in a product or service. We assess this with individuals and as a demographic segment. Every customer is slightly different, and some reasons overlap.

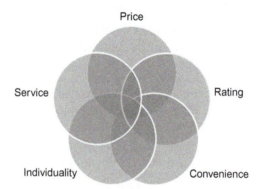

**Reasons That Motivate Customers to Purchase a Product or Service.**

### Generations

**Generations** are a common way to segment the U.S. market. People are divided according to the year they were born. Four of the most common and relevant generations are the Baby Boomers, Generation Xers, Generation Ys, and Generation Zs.

### Baby Boomers, 1946–1964, 77 million

The Baby Boomer generation was the biggest generation the United States had ever seen. Consequently, the shift in demand for goods and services has increased as their age demanded it. They are now nearing or at retirement age. They have grown up, raised children, and started careers and are now experiencing "empty-nest syndrome". They are now earning more money than they

have ever made in their lives. They are cautious, but also beginning to branch out to spend and experience technology in their empty nest age. Consequently, they present a new challenge. They are beginning to spend their money for new and different reasons. Providing service to them is a unique blend of appreciation, quality, and price. They know a quality product, great service, and a reasonable price and they are fully aware of how to find an alternative if they don't receive these.

### Generation X, 1965–1974, 45 million

Generation X was originally given the name X because it was deemed worthless. It turned out they, like every other generation, was just misunderstood. They have given us the X-Games and the 1980s. They are now in their family-formation years and steadily climbing in their careers. Consequently, they are now patronizing hospitality with a different set of values. Finally set free from the Baby Boomers, they are the core of the market. Providing quality service to them is a challenge. They have always been held to a high standard and they hold others to that same standard.

### Generation Y (also known as echo boomers), 1977–1994, 72 million

Generation Y is the first generation to grow up with good economic times and dual-income households. Consequently, they have eaten differently from any generation before them. They grew up consuming food from a box, from a can, from the freezer, or from a restaurant. There was little time for a home-cooked meal, as other generations have experienced. We now have the first generation that does not know how to cook.

Their lifestyle and eating habits will forever be different from those of the preceding generations as a result. Add in the proliferation of television shows dedicated to appreciating food, wine, travel, gambling, and events and you have a very different customer. Their lifestyle is conducive to eating, traveling, and enjoying hospitality as a leisure, a necessity, and a way of life. This has produced a very different, unique blend of customer characteristics. This new type of customer has a little bit of knowledge about many things that interest them. Their patronage is not as often a special celebration but a pastime and a way of life.

### Generation Z (also known as Millennials), 1995–Present

Generation Zs are our youngest segment. They fully embrace technology and have a heavy influence on their parents. They have less discretionary income because of their age, but they spend a higher percentage of it. They have grown up in an age of technology and communication. Marketing and providing services to them is much different from any generation before them. They have always been accustomed to technology and have much higher expectations of speed of service and communication responses. Like other generations, they really don't care about "how it used to be" because they only know how it is today. This, again, changes the landscape of expectations and service.

## 1.4 RESEARCH CUSTOMER INFORMATION

Now that you know the best-in-class and the profile of the customer, it is important to look at it from the customers' point of view. What do they see, hear, and experience? A secret shopper is a great way to monitor procedures, but there is much else to be researched. Begin by asking:

- What are the sources of customer information?
- How are you represented?
- Who is the face of your business?

The face of your business is often the frontline employees. It also may be suppliers, marketing intermediaries, websites, blogs, reviews, or advertisements. All of these need to be monitored and managed to be in line with your brand image.

- What does the customer see and experience?
- Analyze the service process. Try to see the organization through the customers' eyes.
- Are customers taken care of at each step? (In the bed and breakfast segment, the innkeeper spends nights sleeping in each of the different vacant rooms.)

### Management Information System (MIS)

An MIS is more than a computer. It is everything in a system of people, equipment, and procedures to collect and interpret information in an effort to make the best management decisions. This includes comment cards, surveys, focus groups, company records, property operation systems, and information.

### Property Operation Systems (POS)

All POSs are part of the MIS. They may also be referred to as property-management systems (PMSs). Nearly every business has a system. Several great brands are on the market to help manage information. PosiTouch, Micros, Fidelio, Squirrel, and Aloha are just a few of the most popular systems available. All serve as cash registers, schedule reservations, and keep track of inventory. Newer features permit staff scheduling and projections. All of this information can be used in the research-collection process.

## ✴ STEP 2: ESTABLISHMENT OF A MARKETING PLAN

Step 2 consists of the four steps of establishing a marketing plan. Realizing the possibilities, selecting a goal, segmenting a market, and selecting a strategy are standard steps within this process. This is illustrated in Figure 13.3.

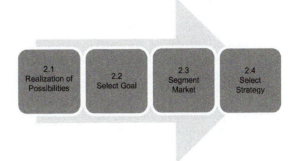

**FIGURE 13.3   Four Sub-Steps within Step 2 of Marketing for Quality Service: Establishment of a Marketing Plan.**

## 2.1 REALIZATION OF POSSIBILITIES

The first step is to open your mind and brainstorm. Be creative. Open up to unlimited possibilities. Enlist the help of others. Benchmark other businesses to see what is out there.

## 2.2 SELECT A GOAL OR OBJECTIVE

Then, begin to narrow it down. Tools could assist in narrowing the options. Think about your answers to these prior questions:

- What business are you in?
- What does your brand stand for?
- What is your selling point?

## 2.3 SEGMENT YOUR MARKET

You've began to profile your market. Now it is time to put these profiles into action, deciding which will be most appropriate. Consider the following questions in determining which you want to go after:

- Which market do you currently serve?
- Which market does the competitor serve?
- Which market is most profitable?
- Which market is emerging?

## 2.4 SELECT A STRATEGY

Next select a strategy that would fit your needs. It will be the vehicle to transport you to meet your objective.

## Options

- Are you changing the:
  - Product?
  - Service?
  - Reputation?
  - Overall package?
- Are you going to concentrate on just making sales?
- Are you to earn profits through:
  - Volume?
  - Price?
  - Increased sales per customer?

## After the Direction of the Strategy Is Determined You Must

- Establish a timeline.
- Dictate resources.
- Support your brand.

All of these decisions impact customer service.

---

**Corporate Responsibility**

The idea that a company upholds values and ethical standards to be a good steward to its community and environment.

### Service Insight

*Corporate Responsibility*

**Corporate responsibility** is the idea that a company upholds values and ethical standards to be a good steward to its community and environment. It is a form of self-policing that ensures proper conduct of actions and, therefore, benefits its stakeholders. Marriott International is a hotel company that is very committed to corporate responsibility. Their business values ensure that they are good stewards to their customers, employees, investors, communities, and environment. They are not in it just for the profits. They are in it for the benefit of all, and their words are backed up with actions.

They have created a Global Green Council that works on reducing emissions, water conservation, and pushing for environmental climate conservation policies. In the community, they are heavily involved in volunteerism. They mounted a major relief effort after 9-11 and Hurricane Katrina. They donated $34.6 million to charitable contributions in 2010.

This idea of social responsibility shines through in their brand image and makes a difference in how they serve the customers. Customers notice and investors appreciate the lengths to which Marriott goes to respect the communities and resources that have made them so successful. The employees feel good about being on a team that cares about the community in which they work and live.

## ❧ STEP 3: IMPLEMENTATION OF CONTROLS TO POSITION—THE 4 PS

**4 Ps of Marketing**
Categories common to any marketing plan: place, promotion, product, and price.

Now that you have selected a goal and a strategy, it is time to implement the controls. These were established in the previous section, but here is where the actual changes are made. Strategies come to life and begin to take hold as they are transferred from paper to practice. A great way to begin is by considering The **4 Ps of Marketing** (see Figure 13.4). These are common to any marketing plan—place, promotion, product, and price. Occasionally, there are one or two more Ps included (such as "people"), and on rare occasion, a P is omitted, but the four are the core as they relate to marketing and serving the customer. Each of these should be considered and controlled in the overall plan.

**Word-of-Mouth**
Opinions expressed by the general public regarding your business. This may have a very powerful influence on customers and is often difficult to control or quantify.

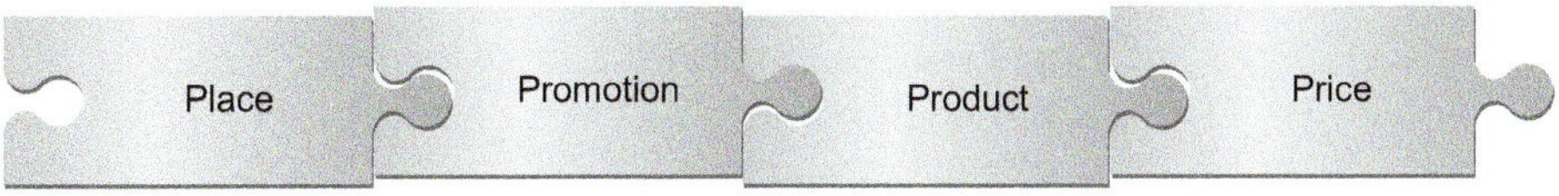

**FIGURE 13.4   Step 3 of Marketing for Quality Service: Implementation of Controls to Position—The 4 Ps.**

**Fam Trips**
Short for familiarization trips. Typically used by hotels. They are invited, all-expense paid trips given to people who will purchase or influence the purchase of future sales.

## PLACE

*Place* includes the atmosphere, the environment, and the all of the surroundings. It involves the capacity, the décor, the amenities, and the physical appearance. Place is like a headache or hiccups. Most people don't think about it until there is an issue. These are the physical attributes that make up the entire guest experience. Even smell has recently become a big consideration.

## PROMOTION

The promotional mix is a combination of advertising, public relations, and promotions. They include word of mouth, television, newspaper, familiarization (fam) trips, and online presence, including social media and publications. All need to be controlled. Monitoring and improving this is called "reputation management".

**Word-of-Mouth:**

> Opinions expressed by the general public regarding your business. This may have a very powerful influence on customers and is often difficult to control or quantify.

**Fam Trips**

> Short for familiarization trips. Typically used by hotels. Invited, all-expense paid trips given to people who will purchase or influence the purchase of future sales.

---

### Service Insight

**Service Capacity**

Is more really more? Does service suffer and do complaints rise significantly when a facility is at over 80 percent of capacity? Yes. You will ultimately only do as much as you can effectively manage. Meaning, you won't sustain a capacity higher than you can effectively deliver. Customers will become dissatisfied and will leave until your business level drops and you can reasonably service them.

**Reputation Management**
The science of monitoring and consistently improving or maintaining your assessment among the public and outside constituencies. This often involves surveys and entire brand management.

### Reputation Management

The science of monitoring and consistently improving or maintaining your assessment among the public and outside constituencies. This often involves surveys and entire brand management.

### Chipotle App

A great example of a channel, or method of service delivery, is an ordering app offered by Chipotle, making it quick and easy to order from them. It locates the nearest Chipotle, places your order, and pays without logging in to a computer or waiting in line. To continue with its presence, Chipotle also held a "build your own video" contest for its fans. The contest and videos went viral and helped to boast about its alternative way of doing business.

### Social Buying

Groupon, Living Social, Tippr, BuyWithMe all feature a new trend in social media referred to as *social shopping*. By offering group discounts, and asking for money up front, small companies are bringing new customers quickly to their door. Most deals last about a day. The business is cut a check after the deal has ended.

- Pros: Customers try your product and you gain exposure and generate quick cash. Also, buyers pre-pay and not all of them use their coupons.
- Cons: You are selling your product at a highly discounted rate (perhaps 50 percent), which could lead to brand erosion and loss of luxury brand status; also, it is difficult to achieve high profit margins on the products.

---

### Service Insight

**Community Involvement**

Does it matter if a company is involved in the community? The community believes so. Most respondents surveyed think it is a good idea, but would they patronize an establishment because it is involved in the community? Would they boycott a company because it doesn't help the community? Do companies do it for the employees, the core belief, the image, or the marketing? Sure, it is a good idea, and the most successful companies engage in community activities, but the opinions about the motives are mixed. Estimates also vary greatly between demographics, type of businesses, and communities.

---

## PRODUCT

Earlier we analyzed our product; now it is time to control it. Everything the customer experiences and consumes constitutes a product. This includes service. Draw on those findings and consider everything that goes into the product, both tangible and intangible.

### MLB.TV App

Major League Baseball (MLB) offers subscriptions to MLB.TV with an iPhone app. This allows smartphone users access to live video and local audio coverage. It also has video archives, game standings, and other statistics. MLB.TV was awarded Best Mobile Video and Best iPad Branded App at the 2010 MOBI Awards. MLB also makes versions of the app for Android and BlackBerry users.

## PRICE

Price is often an indicator of quality. Prices change and customers notice. Price must be in line with all of the other Ps. Numerous pricing strategies exist, such as the following:

- Comparative pricing
- Mark-up pricing
- Desired profit pricing
- What the market will tolerate pricing
- Market skimming pricing

The customer will always consider price as a factor. It must be determined *how* much they will consider it. Based on this assessment, pricing adjustments can be made.

The 4 Ps help to set the expected level of service. Below is a chart illustrating three hospitality companies as they adjust each of the Ps.

**The Four Ps and Expectations Related to Hospitality Organizations**

| Four Ps | Universal Studios | Carnival Cruise Lines | Holiday Inn Express |
| --- | --- | --- | --- |
| Product | Hotels, amusements, dining, shopping | Leisure cruise ship, accommodations destination, activities | Hotel, business center, amenities, meetings |
| Price | ~$120/person/day | ~$1,000/person/trip | ~$125/room/night |
| Place | Orlando, Florida Hollywood, California | Ports, ocean, destinations | National |
| Promotion | TV, radio, print, Internet, social media | TV, print, Internet, social media | TV, Print, Internet |
| Expectations | Entertainment | Fun cruise | Business stay, reasonable accommodations at price |

## PEOPLE

People are sometimes referred to as the fifth P, although purists maintain that people would fit in under another of the Ps. No matter where it falls, the human resource function is key. All should be considered in hiring, promoting teamwork, satisfaction,

training, and development. Your employees make the difference. Everything can be controlled, with the exception of the human element. Humans must be cultivated and managed because what they are capable of is often beyond belief. Your strategy should prepare and adjust for new customer situations and also take into account the physical and emotional labor involved.

### Additional Thoughts

- Do employees treat customers as if this is the last time they will ever see them?
- Are dissatisfied customers treated as problems or opportunities?
- Do your employees believe that yours is a great company?
- Every organization claims to strive for customer service. However, just saying the term without backing it up is insincere and will be noticed.
- Treat your frontline workers as well as you want them to treat customers.
- Give customers a reason for returning in the future.

### Internal Marketing

> **Internal Marketing**
> The idea of marketing to the employees by conveying information regarding the company to them, as well as publicizing their accomplishments. Allows employees to realize their important role as a team member.

**Internal marketing** is the idea of marketing to the employees—conveying information regarding the company to them. It is publicizing the accomplishments of the employees. It provides them with news regarding the company. It may be directed to their department and to the company as a whole. It allows them to feel part of a team and realize their important role as a member.

Remember that employees are either directly involved with the customer or serving someone else who is directly involved with the customer. They are the window to the company. Many intrinsic points are conveyed through your employees:

- Company image
- Corporate culture
- Hiring criteria
- Training
- Efficiency
- Concern for guests
- Concern for employees
- Empowerment

To convey these points, you might use an employee newsletter, preshift meetings, in-service meetings, or meetings with management. To orchestrate internal marketing to the employees, steps to follow involve motivating, involving, reminding, and maintaining the communication to the employees.

**The Four Steps to Orchestrating Internal Marketing to Employees.**

### Motivating

- Getting them interested
- Getting buy-in
- Showing value
- Providing incentives
- Presenting incentives

### Involving

- Letting them know their roles
- Showing them how to perform their roles

### Reminding

- This cannot be a one-time event.
- Be aware that over-reminding is just as bad as underdoing it.
- Remember that employees are intelligent individuals.

### Maintaining

- Follow-up is key.
- Check to ensure they are getting the true message.
- Maintain consistency.

---

**Service Insight**

#### Service Expectations

How else are expectations and services changing? With social media, also known as Web 2.0. The following is a list of the most popular sites that are changing the landscape:

- Facebook check-in and Four Square: Geolocation via mobile device
- Blogs (sharing experiences)
- Forums (seeking, sharing, and answering questions)
- Social networks (referrals, connecting)
- Twitter (discount and dialogue)
- Second Life (which partially designed the new Aloft Hotel concept by its virtual residents)
- YouTube (make your own video, add or comment, viral videos)
- Trip Advisor (online reviews)
- Urbanspoon, Orbitz, Expedia (online reservations and reviews)
- Yelp (restaurant reviews)
- AAA (travel ratings)
- Twitter (with the ability to hashtag an event or a concierge with questions)

##  STEP 4: FOLLOW-UP–SERVICE AFTER THE SALE

**Relationship Marketing**
The process of fostering and cultivating a long-lasting relationship with your current customers. Can be in person or through the use of electronic media.

Often, the relationship is begun well before the sale, but the after-sale period is crucial.

Service does not stop with the sale or transaction. A few will move on, but for many it should be the beginning of the relationship. You should make sure the customers feel good about their decisions and work on building a long-term relationship with them. This is commonly called **relationship marketing**.

### POSTPURCHASE BEHAVIOR OF THE CUSTOMERS

#### Transactional Customers

Transactional customers are one-time patrons. This isn't always bad. They could be traveling through, changing life segments, or be looking for other great experiences. Customers who are pleased may speak well of your establishment. The main thing is to make sure they aren't displeased. Surveys and tools can assist with this.

*Tourist Traps* are businesses that take advantage of transactional customers. The business knows that it will be a one-time purchase, and looks good on the outside. Prices are often high and service and quality is often greatly lacking.

#### Relationship Customers

Returning customers are the key to businesses. It is estimated that it costs three times more to attract a new customer than it does to retain a return customer. Relationship management is crucial. Loyal customers speak well of the business, require less customer training, and are more forgiving. Technology has facilitated the customer connection a great deal. Websites, e-mails, tweets, and fan pages all help to build and maintain a relationship.

> ### Service Insight
>
> #### High-Tech High-Touch Dilemma
>
> There is an issue in practice and literature referred to as the high-tech high-touch dilemma. As technology progresses, the need for service workers has been reduced by automated services such as online reservations and self-check-in. Customers and technology drive service automation to advance. Speed of service is increased and costs are reduced. As this is done, personalized service is being replaced by machines and technology. At what point is it too much? At what point are we losing the customer contact that is so desired in hospitality? There are many different points of view and the dilemma continues.

##  CHAPTER REVIEW QUESTIONS

1. What is the difference between expected and unexpected turnover?
2. What signals do managers give off that create an organizational culture?
3. List and briefly describe the four steps of the marketing process.
4. List and briefly describe the 4 Ps of marketing, relating them to customer service.
5. How has marketing changed in recent times?
6. Why is a return customer preferable to a transactional customer?
7. How do marketing and customer service relate to each other?
8. Predict the outcome of the high-tech high-touch dilemma in 15 years.
9. What is internal marketing and how can it help a business?
10. Which generation are you from? Outline five tips that you could give a business owner to best accommodate your generation.

# ◆ CASE STUDIES

### Profiling Burgers

Bobby's Burger Palace is yet another creation by the famous Bobby Flay. It features artisan-crafted burgers that are difficult to beat. Its no-frills layout and open design promote a bare-bones approach to consuming the ultimate burger. It features the best grade of beef and other ingredients in combinations that are sure to please. It also offers a full bar with plenty of cheer and competent service.

Red Robin is another chain that has also seen recent growth. A bit larger in volume, Red Robin has undergone a marketing blitz to promote its slogan "Red Robin—Yummmmm." Also offering full-service, it looks more like a typical casual restaurant, although it specializes almost exclusively in burgers. It also has a bar and offers drink specials.

Wendy's is a well-known burger restaurant. It features counter service and drive-through. It makes fresh burgers to order and boasts that it never freezes its meat. Wendy's offers a sit-down area and is priced much lower than the competition. On its menu it also features salads, wraps, and other dishes in addition to the typical burger.

1. Describe the profile and classify each of these restaurants.
2. Identify the brand image of each of these restaurants.
3. In your opinion, who is most successful at conveying their image?
4. Which concept is the most appealing to you? Explain.

### An Old Lodge

The Log Lodge is a huge, old log lodge located in the Catskill Mountains. It features a view of a private lake, mountains, and a vast array of wildlife. It is absolutely peaceful and is located less than 2 hours from New York City. The Log Lodge is also known for being a past host of such celebrities as Rodney Dangerfield and Frank Sinatra. It has enjoyed a loyal clientele from New Jersey, New York, and Connecticut for many years, but this is beginning to change. More recently, the progressing age of the clientele is making it difficult for them to travel and be comforted by the lodge because of their deteriorating health. Nowadays, it features lesser-known acts and is lesser attended in its Grand Ballroom and has become a sleepy, tired old lodge. The owners are considering attracting a newer, younger demographic to the Log Lodge, but do not have the capital to make major renovations or take out major newspaper advertisements. They aren't even sure what they could offer the younger demographic. They also fear that the area is becoming depressed and that crowds no longer want to travel to the Catskills. They aren't sure which direction to take.

1. Are the owners correct in wanting to attract a younger crowd?
2. What constraints are preventing the owners from targeting a new demographic?
3. List the positive aspects of the Log Lodge.
4. What options do the owners have with their limited budget and all the other constrictions?

### Benny's Restaurant

Benny graduated from a culinary program in high school and worked for several small restaurants for years. He had always dreamed of opening his own restaurant. Now was his chance. He didn't have much of a plan, but had much desire and passion and knew that he could make it work. He loved the art of cuisine. He recalled reading a quote in a food magazine that stated, "If you build a simple restaurant, and prepare a truly great dish, they will come in great numbers." Essentially, if you prepare it, they will come. Benny was rather idealistic and his personality and passion were quite appealing. He believed in the power of cuisine as a motivator for business. He watched several shows on television and was sure that he was as good as, if not better than, the chefs he saw.

Benny finally got his break when a local, old bakery went out of business. It was the first place that Benny found for which he could afford the rent. He immediately placed a security deposit on it and began to make his dream a reality. He couldn't sleep for over a week. He spent every spare moment at the restaurant. He loved it. He decided that he would open as soon as he possibly could. This meant that he would have to go without a few things, but he was sure that he could manage.

He couldn't think of a great name, so he called it Benny's. He wasn't sure of a precise cuisine so he decided that he would use a chalk board as he had seen at other establishments. He had two servers to start, his girlfriend and her brother. He would find the rest as needed. Then, he decided to open.

1. How successful do you think Benny will be with his initial opening?
2. Assess Benny's marketing from the standpoint of the 4 Ps.
3. From a marketing standpoint, what advice would you offer Benny?

# EXERCISES

### Exercise 1: Advertisement Review

**Directions:**

- Research hospitality-related journals and choose an advertisement.
- Attach the advertisement to the back of your assignment. Answer the following questions.

**Audience:** What generation were they targeting?
**Tactic:** Was it an impulse (purchase now) or passive (remember us) advertisement?
**Brand:** What image did the advertisement portray?
**Success:** Do you believe it is a successful advertisement? Explain.

## Exercise 2: The 4 Ps

**Directions:** Invent a hospitality business of your choice and relate it to the 4 Ps plus People in the chart below:

**Name of Establishment:** _____

**Type of Establishment:** _____

| Ps | Description |
|---|---|
| Place | |
| Promotion | |
| Product | |
| Price | |
| People | |

## Exercise 3: Analysis and Identification of Customers

**Directions:** Choose a hospitality company within the segment of your choice and answer the following questions relating to the analysis and identification of customer wants and needs.

**Define the Profile**

- What business is it in?
- What are they known for?
- Who is their competition?
- What is the competition known for?

**Define Best-in-Class**

- Who first comes to mind when your industry is mentioned?
- Who is the best at quality service?
- Who has the overall best product?
- Who has the nicest property?
- Who has the nicest options or amenities?
- Who leads in innovation?
- Who leads in market share?

**Define the Customers**

- What do the customers want?
- What do the customers expect?
- How do customers define value?
- Are customers one-time or continued?
- Where do new customers come from?
- Why do some potential customers choose never to patronize the business?

# Glossary

## A

**Accommodations**  Typically a room for bedding, but also food, services, or anything else needed during a trip.

**Affinity Diagram**  A process that sorts ideas into categories for further interpretation.

**Age of Communication**  A current period of time in the U.S. where the proliferation of technology has created instant communication through many channels. Regarding the service industry, information can be accessed cheaply, easily, and ratings can be readily found.

**Age of Manufacturing**  A time in which the U.S. was a thriving manufacturing nation. Originally, the U.S. was largely an agricultural nation. It evolved into a manufacturing nation in the past century but then quickly lost its dominance to other nations. A large portion of the management techniques used in the service industries have been adopted from manufacturing, which dominated the literature before the late 1900s.

**Age of Service**  The current age in the United States. As the United States lost its manufacturing jobs, they were replaced with service-related jobs.

**Age of Technology**  Another recent age in the United States is the increase and dominance of technology in U.S. culture and business operations.

**All-Inclusive Tour**  Tour package sold for a total price, including rooms, food, taxes, and most or all incidentals.

**American Plan (AP)**  A plan in a hotel in which all meals (breakfast, lunch, and dinner) are included in the rate.

**Aperitif**  Alcohol served before a meal.

**Authorization**  Permission from credit company to make a charge.

## B

**Back of the House (BOH)**  All areas that are not seen by the typical customer.

**Baseline Measurements**  "Before" measurements that describe a situation or condition prior to intervention.

**Benchmarking**  A comparison of best-practice methods.

**Block**  Rooms placed on a temporary hold for a group.

**Body Language**  Nonverbal communication that gives clues to one's underlying premise.

**Book**  To sell or reserve a room or space.

**Brainstorming**  Free-form thinking to generate ideas.

**Brand Image**  The end product of marketing. It is what your business stands for and is evident in every aspect of your business.

**Brand Management**  The idea of organizing and controlling a theme that is consistent throughout the entirety of a company.

**Bucket**  A file-holder for guest folios and other reserved material kept behind front desk.

## C

**Call**  A high-quality alcohol referred to by its specific brand name instead of type.

**Carbon Footprint**  A person's effect on the amount of carbon dioxide released into the atmosphere. Also used in more general terms as being environmentally conscious.

**Centralized Reservation System (CRS)**  A central system for multiple properties. Often accessed internally and externally.

**Champion**  A person commissioned with the task of achieving a desired goal. This individual would be responsible for organizing all staff, systems, and procedures to align the organization in its efforts to achieve the assigned goal.

**Change Theory**  A science behind helping businesses transition through changes.

**Charge Record**  A list of all transactions specific to a department or account.

**Charter**  Bulk purchase of a boat, plane, auto, or bus carrier. Sold by time, distance, head count, or a combination of these and other variables.

**Check-in**  A procedure of receiving guests and completing the guest registration process.

**Check-out**  A procedure of closing a guest folio upon the guest's departure.

**Check Sheets**  Tabulation list of frequency for repeated data.

**Chit**  Slang for order ticket. Often printed for line-cooks to prepare food. Sometimes referred to as a dupe (short for duplicate from the old carbon-copy checks).

**City Account**  An account for nonguests.

**Classical Kitchen Brigade**  A system of stations in the kitchen where everyone has a specific purpose.

**Cocktail**  Any combination of alcohols; also known as a mixed drink.

**Code Sharing**  Agreement between two or more airlines that permits the use of viewing and booking on the system of another.

**Comps**  Free compensation for food, beverage, rooms, or other gratuities to reward guests.

**Conservation**  Reasonable and responsible use of natural resources to ensure optimal current and future appreciation.

**Continental Plan (CP)**  A room plan that includes only continental breakfast—a very light breakfast offering.

**Continuous Improvement**  A premise of instituting quality through a cycle of planning, monitoring, interpreting, and revising.

**Control Chart**  Graph that measures deviations of processes over a period of time. Other name: statistical process control (SPC).

**Coproduction**  The extent to which the customer should be involved in the process of service, which gives the customers a sense of control and tailors their service, contributing to the success of the encounter. Customers must be trained, and the instructions obvious and clear and support given.

**Cordial**  Any flavored, sweetened alcohol. Also known as "liqueur."

**Corkage Fee**  A fee charged to open or uncork and serve bottles brought in by the customers. Note that this is legal in only a few states.

**Corporate Responsibility**  The idea that a company upholds values and ethical standards to be a good steward to its community and environment.

**Cost–Benefit Analysis**  Used to decide whether an idea or project is worthy of spending money on it.

**Cost of Error**  The total amount of costs associated with a customer service mistake or losing the customer.

**Cover**  A dinner or meal for one person. Taken from the classical style of covering each dish when leaving the kitchen.

**Credo**  Originally used for professing religious beliefs, was adopted by companies as a passionate label to describe what the organization stood for.

**Crisis Management Plan (CMP)**  A detailed outline of procedures that a Crisis Management Team enacts. A specialized plan to respond to a crisis or catastrophe.

**Cross-Functional Teams**  Teams with members from different areas of organization, but at about the same supervisory level. These teams typically problem-solve specific assignments.

**Crumbing**  Use of a tool to scrape bread crumbs from the table between courses in fine-dining restaurants.

**Customer-centric**  The premise of placing the customer first in all a company does. Focusing on pleasing the customer and organizing the company with customer service as a primary goal.

**Customer Intelligence**  The process of gathering information regarding your customers—including history of use, demographics, and psychographics—in an effort to understand former, future, and current customers. Used in marketing, strategic planning. and training.

**CVBs (Convention and Visitor Bureau)**  Organization that provides destination information regarding an area. It is financed through a bed tax at lodgings.

# D

**Day Rate**  A lower rate charged to guests who do not occupy the room overnight. Typically between 10 A.M. and 4 P.M.

**Decanting**  Separating sediments from the wine.

**Delphi Method**  A method of gaining group consensus.

**Destination Management Organization (DMO)** A company that leads and promotes the marketing of a destination.

**Diamond Rating** AAA rating system of 1 to 5 diamonds scoring hotels, restaurants and campgrounds. The largest guide of its kind.

**Digestif** Alcohol served after a meal.

**Direct Competition** Other businesses who compete for the same clientele, in the same industry, delivering similar goods and services.

**DNS** Did not stay; guest who checks in and quickly returns to the desk without having occupied the room.

**DRIFT** Do it right the first time. A quest to reduce errors and inefficiencies so that you won't have to fix as many things and pay the price for producing a poor product.

**Duty of Loyalty** Regarding employees, it implies they have a responsibility to act in the best interest of the business in all of their actions. This means that they should want to help, be empathetic, give their full and personalized attention, and have a sense of pride regarding their work.

# E

**Eco-tourism** Travel to, or promotion of, environmentally conscious actions, typically based around awe-inspiring natural resources.

**Emotional Intelligence (EI)** A view of personalities, personal encounters, and success. It consists of four dimensions. Self-awareness—knowing your emotions; Self-management—controlling your emotions; Social awareness—knowing others' emotions; Relationship management—the ability to manage interactions with others.

**Emotional Labor** Psychological demands of customer service.

**Empathy** Understanding and compassion for someone else's emotion. When expressed, it often creates a connection between the staff member and the customer.

**Employee Turnover** A measure of the rate of employee losses and gains during a given period.

**Empowerment** Enabling employees with the authority to make decisions in the best interest of the guests.

**Eurailpass** A ticket for unlimited train travel through 15 European countries. Sold by day units.

**European Plan (EP)** A room rate with no meals included.

**Excursion** A small trip, typically less than a day.

**Expected Turnover** When customers leave for reasons beyond the control of the business.

**Explicit Expectations** Expectations of service that are clearly provided or given by the business.

# F

**Fam Trips** Short for familiarization trips. Typically used by hotels. They are invited, all-expense paid trips given to people who will purchase or influence the purchase of future sales.

**Fishbone Diagram** Identifies potential causes for a problem in categories. Other names: Ishikawa diagram, cause-and-effect diagram.

**Flow Chart Diagram** A graphic account of sequential steps in a process.

**Focus Group** Qualitative (verbal) research in which a group (usually 4 to 10 people) is surveyed about their ideas and opinion about a certain product, company, or field.

**Folio** Guest account.

**4 Ps of Marketing** Categories common to any marketing plan: place, promotion, product, and price.

**Force-Field Analysis** A technique for analyzing the forces that help and hurt a decision.

**Front of House (FOH)** The service area in view of the customers.

**Frontline Workers** The employees who directly serve the customers.

**Full House** Hotel in which all rooms are occupied. (Also a theater or venue in which every seat is filled.)

# G

**Gantt Chart** A project-planning tool that clarifies who does what and by when.

**General Competition** Businesses that compete for the same clientele's time and/or dollar.

**Generations** Common divisions of the U.S. market: Baby Boomers, Generation Xers, Generation Ys, and Generation Zs.

**Gratuity** (also known as tip) Typically money given or charged for service.

**Gueridon** A cart for tableside service.

**G.U.E.S.T.** Greet–Understand–Empathize–Suggest/Solve–Track. A system of resolving guest conflicts using an acronym to remember how to handle customer complaints or issues. An easily adaptable problem-solving model.

**Guest History File** Record of guest's previous transactions.

## H

**House Count** Record of the total number of hotel guests at any one time.

**Hub and spoke** A configuration of air travel resembling a wheel with a center hub being the main airport with spokes leading out of it connecting to smaller cities or other hubs.

## I

**Implicit Expectations** Expectations of service not fully expressed or stated, but certainly implied by a business.

**Incentive Travel** A reward tour, typically given to an employee by the organization for outstanding achievement. Usually in a festive environment. Spouses typically accompany employee.

**Indirect Competition** Other businesses who compete for the same clientele, delivering related, but not identical, products and services.

**Intent to Return** The belief that a customer will patronize the establishment or services in the future.

**Internal Customers** Staff who are served by other employees. This mindset helps employees to recognize that they are serving those who serve the customer and the importance of assisting them in their roles.

**Internal Marketing** The idea of marketing to the employees by conveying information regarding the company to them, as well as publicizing their accomplishments. Allows employees to realize their important role as a team member.

## J

**Job Description** Details what the position does: duties and responsibilities.

**Job Specification** Details what the position requires: knowledge, skills, and abilities.

## K

**Keirsey Temperament Sorter** Tool used to outline personality types into four primary categories: Artisan, Guardian, Idealist, and Rational.

**K.I.S.S.** *Keep Important Stuff Simple (K.I.S.S.),* also known as "Keep it simple, stupid." This is the idea that processes don't always need to be complicated. There is great merit to sticking to the basics. This term is widely used among many industries. It refers to keeping processes as simple as possible, thus reducing the chance for error.

## L

**Lateral Service Principle** The idea that employees are to stop what they are doing and help to solve customer problems even if it is not in their department.

**Lifetime Customer Value** All potential future sales from the customer.

**Low Rollers** Guests who spend very little on gambling.

## M

**Market Segmentation** The process of dividing the market into groups. This is typically done demographically; however, numerous other ways exist.

**Marketing** The coordination of the exchange of goods and service in an effort to fulfill the wants and needs of the customers. This involves deliberate control of advertising and brand management.

**MBWA** Management by walking around. The idea that managers should "get in touch" with the employees and customers to learn what is really occurring.

**Meyers–Briggs Type Indicator (MBTI)** Tool used to outline personality and temperament types.

**Mise en Place** Loosely translates to "everything in its place." Having all materials assembled prior

to starting a task. For example, a waiter obtains his mise en place prior to beginning his shift. He would ensure that he has his uniform in order, checks his reservations, checks the specials, and makes sure he has his notepad, corkscrew, crumber, pens, and so on.

**Mission**    A statement that explains the purpose of your business. It is usually a paragraph and states the core purpose of the organization. It should be the origin and foundation of all other decisions for the business.

**Modified American Plan (MAP)**    Also known as Demi-pension. A room pricing package that includes breakfast and one other meal, typically dinner.

**Moment of Truth**    Popularized by Jan Carlzon of SAS Airlines, a phrase and best-selling book, *Moments of Truth* explains how a guest experience is made up of many individual moments of truth—points at which quality guest service can be made or lost. This concept helps businesses to break down the service experience, understand its importance, and be able to monitor and improve upon it.

**Multivoting**    Technique that prioritizes and narrows a large numbers of decisions to reflect the general favor of a group. Other name: nominal prioritization.

# N

**Neat**    Alcohol at room temperature, without ice.

**New Customer Cost**    All of the costs associated with obtaining a potential customer.

**Niche Travel**    Travel to a small, unique area of specialty or special interest.

**Night Audit**    Daily reconciliation of all accounts receivables, performed at night.

# O

**On the Rocks**    A drink with ice.

**Open Jaw**    A flight in which a passenger arrives at one point and departs from another, making the outline of an open jaw on the map.

**Organizational Culture**    The personality of a business—its style, pace, and attitude. It can be managed while also having a life of its own.

# P

**Pareto Chart**    A bar graph that displays frequency of time, errors, or money.

**PDCA**    Plan–do–check–act cycle. A four-step process for instituting continuous improvement.

**Pension**    French term meaning guesthouse or boarding house or the payment for such. It is essentially a lesser lodging establishment with or without meals.

**Player-Tracking System**    A system that monitors the frequency and usage of gamblers. Used to give rewards or comps.

**Poka-Yoke**    A system that helps to self-correct itself. Poka-Yokes are everywhere that you look. We take most of them for granted. They are engineered fail-safe systems.

**Post**    To make an entry on an account.

**Premium**    The highest and most expensive brands of alcohol, above "call." Also known as "top shelf."

**Primary Expectations**    Essential expectations, crucial to the quality guest service experience.

**Problem Statement**    The root problem or fundamental cause of why something is happening. Often the results of both internal and external analysis.

**Process Reengineering**    A dramatic redesign of a system, process, or business.

**Proof**    The amount of alcohol in a beverage. Twice the percentage of alcohol.

**Property Management System (PMS)**    A computer system that records and integrates many systems throughout the hotel. Useful in tabulating, reporting, and predicting.

**Pros–Cons Sheet**    A technique that compares the benefits and drawbacks of a given idea or solution.

# Q

**Quality Assessment Tools and Techniques**    A research instrument used target, analyze, develop, or evaluate a service system.

**Quality Customer/Guest Service**    Meeting and exceeding the individual expectations of the customer.

## R

**Rate**   Price charged for a room night. Also combined within best available rate (BAR) and lowest available rate (LAR).

**Rate of Dissatisfaction**   Amount or percentage of errors in a system. If calculated through a survey, the amount of low-scoring results.

**Red Flags**   Indicators that go off in customers' minds when they do not receive what they need and expect. Not easily detected by employees. The red flags have a cumulative effect and result in a poor service experience.

**Relationship Marketing**   The process of fostering and cultivating a long-lasting relationship with your current customers. Can be in person or through the use of electronic media.

**Reputation Management**   The science of monitoring and consistently improving or maintaining your assessment among the public and outside constituencies. This often involves surveys and entire brand management.

**Resource Viewpoint**   The idea that every business has three resources (human, financial, physical) with which to work and to use to their benefit.

**Root-Cause Analysis**   Determining the underlying reasons why something happens.

## S

**Scatter Diagram**   A graphing of pairs of numerical data. Other names: scatter plot; X–Y graph.

**Secondary Expectations**   Expectations of lesser importance to the guest service experience. Somewhat tolerable when omitted, but appreciated when present.

**Secret Shoppers**   Evaluators who pose as customers and report findings to the management and owners.

**Service Guarantee**   A promise of satisfaction for your products and services.

**Service Mission and Service Vision**   Similar to a traditional mission and vision statement, but targeted toward service.

**Service Process Implementation**   The overall mechanics of implementing actual standards in the guest service process.

**Service Promise**   Often stated internally and externally, a guarantee of goods or services that the customer will be satisfied. In the event that this is not achieved, the business promises to correct the error. Common in organizations.

**Service Recovery**   Popularized by Ron Zemke, a system for acknowledging, apologizing for, and fixing customer complaints. Other authors have devised their own variations of rectifying mistakes, each version being slightly different.

**Service Strategy**   Formula for delivering a service that defines the practical interpretation.

**SERVQUAL**   Measures five dimensions and assesses five different types of gaps in service organizations: reliability, assurance, tangibles, empathy, and responsiveness (RATER).

**Silo**   A metaphor used to describe the separate departments of an organization that work independently and fail to communicate with each other, thus replicating processes, working inefficiently, and causing frustration.

**Six Sigma**   Quality program aimed at reducing defects to less than 3.4 in 1 million. Define, measure, analyze, improve, control (DMAIC).

**Social, Military, Educational, Religious, Fraternal (SMERF):**   A type of meeting category that groups together the "others" that are not business or association-related: social, military, educational, religious, and fraternal organizations.

**Speed Rack**   An assortment of the bottles of alcohol most commonly poured. The rack is strategically placed in the most accessible area within easy reach of the bartender. Typically in a certain order, or light to dark, but varies: vodka, gin, rum, tequila, triple sec, whiskey.

**Stakeholder**   Any person or group that would be affected if the event, company, or situation were to cease to exist.

**Standard Operating Procedure (SOP)**   A formalized method. Crucial in training to achieve consistency.

**Star Rating**   Forbes Mobil Guide rating system of 1 to 5 stars. Unannounced inspectors rate hotels, restaurants, and spas, assessing over 550 standard aspects for its 4- and 5-star applicants.

**Straight Up**   An alcoholic beverage that is chilled, then strained to remove the ice. Also known as "up."

**Strategic Service System**   A four-part system that involves purpose, product, plan, and people.

**Strategy** A calculated plan to achieve a common, chosen objective.

**Survey** A poll of a group. Can be formal or informal. Works well with small to large groups.

**SWOT Analysis** An analysis of the strengths, weaknesses, opportunities, and threats of an organization, containing internal and external examination.

**Synergy** Worth more than the sum of its parts. The idea that members of teams are more productive than they are as individuals.

# T

**Tall** Served in a highball or Collins glass, usually with a larger amount of mixer.

**Touch Points** Each time that a guest has an experience with your organization, a representative of it, or an aspect the organization planned.

**Tourism** Everything associated with traveling more than 50 miles from home, typically for leisure.

**Transactional Analysis** System for understanding and controlling behaviors. Coined by Dr. Eric Berne, it was the first to popularize the premise that every time two people come together, they are constantly evaluating each other.

**Turnover** Also known as seat turnover, customer turnover, dining room turnover, and churn in a full-service restaurant. Typically expressed for a shift, meal period, or day. The number of times that a seat or table has been seated with a new customer.

**Twist** Served with a twist of a lemon or lime peel and rind.

# U

**Unexpected Customer Turnover** When customers leave for reasons not within the control of the business.

# V

**Varietal** A wine referred to by the type or variety of grape used to make it.

**VIPs (very important people)** Celebrities, high-profile people, or high rollers who receive special attention and services from the casino or other venue.

**Vision** A statement, usually a sentence or two, that explains where a business is striving to go or be in the future. Typically inspirational and sometimes a bit lofty, it is used in strategic planning.

# W

**Walking a Guest** When the guest has a reservation that the hotel cannot honor because they are over capacity. Usually due to overbooking. The guest is transferred to another hotel.

**Well** The lowest-quality alcohol of a type on the premises. Usually in the speed rack. Also known as a "pour."

**Whales** Gamblers who spend very large amounts gambling. They are accustomed to receiving very high levels of service.

**Word-of-Mouth** Opinions expressed by the general public regarding your business. This may have a very powerful influence on customers and is often difficult to control or quantify.

# Y

**Yield Management** Pricing structure common to air and hotel companies. The goal is to optimize profit while balancing supply and demand.

# Index